PRAISE FOR *MEMENTO MORI*

"Joanna Ebenstein has studied—and, more importantly, lived—this practice of death engagement for decades. This makes her one of the people I most trust to guide us through the pain, joy, fear, and ultimate euphoria of facing our own mortality."

—Caitlin Doughty, *New York Times* bestselling author and
founder of the Order of the Good Death

"There could be no better guide than Joanna Ebenstein to the enriching and startlingly uplifting benefits of confronting our mortality. This wonderfully readable, witty, practical, and philosophically profound book has the power to shift your perspective and lead you into a more intense experience of life."

—Oliver Burkeman, *New York Times* bestselling author of
Four Thousand Weeks: Time Management for Mortals

"A thoughtful, erudite survey through history and across cultures for all of us who wonder about death in order to lead more meaningful lives."

—Steve Leder, *New York Times* bestselling author of *The Beauty
of What Remains* and *For You When I Am Gone*

"Can contemplating and even befriending death allow us to live more fully? Joanna Ebenstein uses a multicultural and historical lens to make a compelling case for just that. A thought-provoking and fascinating guide to trading fear for curiosity in pursuit of joy and meaning in our finite time here."

—Suzy Hopkins, coauthor of *What to Do When I'm Gone*

"There is no better person than Joanna Ebenstein to help someone come to terms with death and dying. *Memento Mori* is a crucially important read for anyone who is going to eventually die, which is all of us. This incredible book spells out the steps everyone should take to make those inevitable death experiences more manageable. Not since Elisabeth Kübler-Ross has an author done more to help readers of all ages and backgrounds plan for their final days."

—Dr. John Troyer, Death Studies Scholar-at-Large,
Centre for Death & Society (UK)

"For well over fifteen years, Joanna Ebenstein has been at the forefront of conversations around how we think about death and the cultural rituals that surround it. Throughout it all, her approach has always been simultaneously serious and curious, sensitive to all the difficult and complex emotions involved while still maintaining a sense of wonder and excitement. *Memento Mori* shows her at her absolute best: open, engaging, and full of wisdom—an excellent and thought-provoking book."

—Colin Dickey, author of *Ghostland: An American
History in Haunted Places*

"What if regularly contemplating the thing we most fear could have incredible benefits, not just for us but for all of society? This book offers a chance to transform your life in profound, deeply courageous ways, and it also serves as a fascinating tour through the history and culture of death acceptance."

—Bess Lovejoy, author of *Rest in Pieces: The Curious Fates of Famous Corpses*

"Joanna Ebenstein has succeeded in making death fascinating, transformative, and even friendly in this poetic and engaging book. This book made me laugh, brought me to tears, intrigued me, instructed me, and delivered on its promise to make me reflect on what mattered most—it enhanced my life. It initiates an appreciation of what is most important amid the busyness of our daily lives. Ebenstein has written the modern book of the dead: a guidebook about death, but significantly, about life and how to achieve a life well lived."

—Diana Walsh Pasulka, professor of religious studies at the University of North Carolina, Wilmington, and author of *American Cosmic: UFOs, Religion, Technology*

MEMENTO
MORI

The Art of Contemplating Death to Live a Better Life

JOANNA EBENSTEIN

A TarcherPerigee Book

an imprint of Penguin Random House LLC
penguinrandomhouse.com

Library of Congress Cataloging-in-Publication Data

Names: Ebenstein, Joanna, 1971– author.
Title: Memento mori : the art of contemplating death to live a better life / Joanna Ebenstein.
Description: [New York] : TarcherPerigee, [2024]
Identifiers: LCCN 2024003484 (print) | LCCN 2024003485 (ebook) |
ISBN 9780593713440 (hardcover) | ISBN 9780593713457 (epub)
Subjects: LCSH: Death—Psychological aspects. | Life—Psychological aspects. | Self-realization.
Classification: LCC BF789.D4 E23 2024 (print) |
LCC BF789.D4 (ebook) | DDC 155.9/37—dc23/eng/20240603
LC record available at https://lccn.loc.gov/2024003484
LC ebook record available at https://lccn.loc.gov/2024003485

Printed in the United States of America
1st Printing

Book design by Angie Boutin

To my beloved ancestor Dina Ebenstein, and my chosen kin, Bryan Melillo.
And, also, to Mexico.

CONTENTS

INTRODUCTION

For as long as I can remember, people called me morbid for being interested in death, and for many years I simply accepted their opinion as fact. But as I grew older, I began to think about it more deeply. If everyone who has ever lived has died; if I—barring some medical miracle—will also die; if we still don't know what happens after we die—if it is, in essence, still the great human mystery; then how could one *not* be interested in death? Isn't more morbid *not* to think about it? And what does it say about a culture that seeks to avoid any serious engagement with this unavoidable fact of life?

Many of us in the contemporary Western world view death as purely negative—something to be pushed out of our minds, shunned, and avoided. Thinking about death, particularly *one's own*, is seen as morbid, if not downright pathological. But, not long ago, contemplating death was widely used as a powerful tool that helped us fear mortality less, put the difficulties of our lives in perspective, and live according to our higher values. (It still is, in some places.) By coming to terms with our own death, we were understood to become wise.

Today in the United States, we are taught that if we focus on the positive, avoid (or eliminate) sadness and negativity, and achieve success, wealth, and fame, we will find happiness. This approach, however, does not appear to be successful. As reported by *Newsday* in 2017, even as their income had increased, Americans reported lower levels of happiness; at the time of writing, the US ranked fifteenth in the *World Happiness Report*.[1] If the rising incidences of mass shootings, as well as record levels of addiction, anxiety, and depression, are any indication, then it seems that a culture of positivity that encourages personal prosperity does not, in fact, lead to general happiness.

In a culture determined to avoid bad or sad thoughts, and when scientific medicine regards death chiefly as a failure of intervention, the unavoidable fact of death becomes a serious issue. Death was once a part of everyday life; dead bodies were seen on a regular basis, and our encounters with death were contained by rituals, traditions, or belief systems that enlivened it with meaning. Today, in a largely secular world, death has simply become the enemy, the antithesis of that we hold dear: light, pleasure, and life. We regard death as a great evil, a problem to be solved, and an idea to be avoided.

Those who learned to know death, rather than to fear and fight it, become our teachers about life.

—DR. ELISABETH KÜBLER-ROSS, SWISS AMERICAN PSYCHIATRIST

It might come as a surprise to know that, for millennia, people all over the world have actively cultivated a relationship with death, as an important part of both living and dying well. Shamans and priests acted as psychopomps—literally, "soul guides"—to help people move through the death process. People consulted "books of the dead," guides to preparing for a good death and afterlife experience. And our ancestors utilized *memento mori* (Latin for "remember you must die"), which were objects, works, or practices meant to remind them of their death in order to encourage them to live the life they truly wished, before it was too late. Paradoxically—or so it might seem to us—by forging a relationship with death, our ancestors mitigated their fear of it, and were able to live fuller and more meaningful lives.

I, too, have found that contemplating death is a powerful tool that, regardless of beliefs about a god or an afterlife, can transform our lives. It is the best practice I have found for discovering and clarifying one's truest values. I have also found that it provides one with the necessary courage to *live* one's values, even when they might run contrary to the ideals of one's family or community.

I am far from alone in this conviction, and throughout this book I will draw on the wisdom of like-minded contemporaries as well as the many who came before me. Our ancestors understood the power that an encounter with mortality had to catalyze greater wisdom and personal growth. Buddha called death the greatest teacher. Socrates, the founding father of Western philosophy, asserted that the aim of philosophy itself was "practice for dying and death."[2] In some Indigenous cultures, people were taught to regularly ask themselves if today would be a good day to die—if they knew they would die tomorrow, what might they change today? Striking a similar note in more recent times, Steve Jobs, the founder of Apple, told an audience of college graduates in 2005, "Remembering that I'll be dead soon is the most important tool I've ever encountered to help me make the big choices in life."[3]

Science also affirms the benefits of contemplating death. Psychologist George Bonanno, head of the Loss, Trauma, and Emotion Lab at Teachers College, Columbia University, has demonstrated that sustained reflection on death—bringing our own mortality to our full, conscious attention for an extended period of time—can mitigate our fear of it and deepen our connections with others. There are also studies that suggest that learning about what frightens us, or safely exposing ourselves to those things, can help us overcome our fear. Researchers have also found that those who possess what they term "morbid curiosity"—a motivation to learn about death and other threatening phenomena—enjoy greater positive resilience, a characteristic that allows them to thrive during uncertain or difficult times. All of these findings point to a compelling truism: although we cannot change the fact that we will die, we can, with the right tools, change how we *feel* about it.

Death is like a mirror in which the true meaning of life is reflected.

—SOGYAL RINPOCHE, TIBETAN BUDDHIST TEACHER

Sociological research tells us that befriending death is good not only for ourselves but for society. Terror management theory—a field of study based on Ernest Becker's Pulitzer Prize–winning book, *The Denial of Death*—demonstrates that if one has not come to conscious relationship with one's own death, reminders of mortality can lead to anxiety, aggression, xenophobia, and even violence against others, genocide, and dictatorships. Interestingly, these findings reaffirm one of the most important Buddhist tenets—that acceptance of the impermanence of life is the only way to true happiness.

The pioneering Swiss psychiatrist Carl Jung (1875–1961)—founder of analytical psychology and onetime protégé of Sigmund Freud (1856–1939)—also believed that contemplating our own death was profoundly important. In fact, it was his conviction that one of the most important tasks of the second half of life—in other words, from middle age on—was to prepare for death. To his mind, it was important to develop our own conscious myth about death, our own set of meaningful beliefs, to counteract our era's purely reasonable approach, which shows an individual "nothing but the dark pit into which he is descending."[4]

But how can one fulfill Jung's exhortation to find meaning in death? And how can we go about preparing for our own death, as well as the deaths of the many others we are likely to encounter over the course of our lives? There are many paths we can follow; some lie in the past, others lie in the distance, but all can be brought into our present consciousness. This book aims to act as a bridge between our own time and place and those who have so much to teach us about living and dying well. It is intended to act as a guide to a good death, much like the books of the dead utilized by our ancestors. It hopes to help chip away at the taboo of talking about death, and for this to act as a memento mori, using a direct and playful confrontation with death to help you ascertain your own truths and start to live by them.

A civilization that denies death ends by denying life.

—OCTAVIO PAZ, MEXICAN POET, ESSAYIST, AND DIPLOMAT

It is my hope that this book helps you face death—and come to fear it less—within a contained, transformative, and even *fun* process of personal discovery. Doing so will empower you with an appreciation of time that can only come from accepting the very transience that gives life its value. It will, through a combination of anecdotes, historical examples, meditations, exercises, journal prompts, and reflections, help you get to know death, clarify your true values, and learn to live more fully.

The material is organized into twelve chapters that focus on different ways of looking at death, dying, and loss. Each chapter is designed to be completed over the course of a week (or longer, if you wish) and includes activities, exercises, and journal prompts designed to help you incorporate what you learn into your daily life. By taking a week to immerse yourself in each chapter, you will be able to achieve a deeper and more subtle understanding of the material.

I use the ideas of Carl Jung as a framework for the organization of this book. I also draw heavily on his model of the journey of individuation, or becoming more completely oneself through the unification of one's opposites. This entails descending into the unknown of our deepest selves, facing the darkness within, and returning with a treasure that can revitalize both ourselves and the culture we inhabit.

Much of the material that follows is also drawn from my work with Morbid Anatomy, a project I founded in 2007 to explore death, life, and the in-between. This project began in response to my first trip to Europe as a young intellectual history graduate. Traveling through the museums and churches of Germany, Poland, Austria, and Hungary, I encountered hundreds of artworks and artifacts that combined beauty and death in ways I had never seen before. It was clear that such imagery had once been a common part of everyday life. How, I wanted to know, had we changed in such a way that so much of this historical record now seemed *morbid*? How had images such as these—and perhaps the event of death itself—become strange to us? Why had we changed, and what might we have lost in the process? These are questions I have been investigating via Morbid Anatomy since its inception.

Death twitches my ear.
"Live," he says.
"I am coming."

—VIRGIL,
CLASSICAL ROMAN POET

Over the years, Morbid Anatomy has taken many forms. It began as a blog and has since evolved to include exhibitions, films, and even—for a few heady years!—a three-floor museum in Brooklyn, New York. Today, Morbid Anatomy produces books, runs a research library and gift shop, and organizes international field trips and pop-ups. We also host a rich program of online and in-person classes, workshops, and events exploring death, life, and the in-between. Most importantly, we are a *community*—a safe space that attracts people around the world who wish to talk about, or develop a positive relationship with, death and mortality.

In the early months of the COVID-19 lockdown, I began teaching an online class for Morbid Anatomy called Make Your Own Memento Mori: Befriending Death with Art, History and the Imagination. It seemed to me that we in the industrialized, affluent West had reached a cultural moment when our awareness of death was keener than it had been for over a century. I developed this class as an attempt to use this frightening moment as an opportunity to help us look death in the eye, to create a closer, less fearful relationship with it. Even to *make friends with it.*

In the class, we look at the ways in which death has been understood and represented in different times and places. Students are invited, as a final project, to create their own memento mori—something that will remind them of their own death, as a goad toward helping them live their lives more fully. At the time of writing, I have taught this class to hundreds of individuals around the world, and each time it has been transformative. The content of this book draws heavily on my experience with this class.

A few years ago, one of my best friends was diagnosed with stage 4 metastatic cancer and given a prognosis of two years to live. She immediately quit her job as a corporate lawyer—an occupation that had gone against her values, but helped her pay off her student loans. She enrolled in a graduate program in mythological studies. Soon after, her prognosis changed. Now, as a result of experimental drugs (or perhaps my impassioned offerings at shrines to appropriate saints in Mexico?), the cancer is no longer visible in scans, and it's likely that she will live a long, full life. When I asked her if she would ever have quit her job to do what she really wanted without the cancer diagnosis, she said absolutely not.

For my friend, cancer was a painful wake-up call that led her to manifest the life she really wanted to live. For me, it was a regular contemplation of death that led me to do what I wanted in the here and now—to live a rich, rewarding life and career that is uniquely my own, and that (I hope!) will leave me with few deathbed regrets, rather than waiting for a future that might or might not come. It is my sincere hope that this book, through a combination of informative text and useful exercises, will cultivate an effect similar to that of my friend's near-death experience; that it will bring you a vivid and profound appreciation of your limited time on earth, and help you clarify your values and live a richer, fuller, and more authentic life.

For those who live neither with religious consolations about death nor with a sense of death (or of anything else) as natural, death is the obscene mystery, the ultimate affront, the thing that cannot be controlled. It can only be denied.

— SUSAN SONTAG, AMERICAN WRITER AND CULTURAL CRITIC

It seems like we are now truly cursed to live in interesting times. As this book goes to press, the news is filled with reports of wars, mass shootings, painful political divides, deepening global intolerance, desperate refugees, a cost-of-living crisis, and the unfolding effects of climate change. It feels like we are living through the breakdown of old systems that no longer serve us as they once did, and that the future has become inscrutable. In this time of change and uncertainty, an uncomfortable truth is laid bare: despite our illusions to the contrary, we cannot control our surroundings, we cannot predict our future, and we cannot know when we will die.

These truths, of course, have always been with us, but today, they are present in our conscious awareness in a way that they haven't been for decades. And unfortunately, our culture has given us very little to assist us in learning to tolerate this sense of vulnerability, mystery, and the unknown. By learning to live with our fear of death, we also learn to live with our fear of that which we cannot control, to sit with the mystery at the heart of life and still appreciate, and with great joy, the life we have been given.

My goal with this book is to help us find beauty and value in something that, culturally, we have been told in so many ways has no value whatsoever. I hope it can help bring us to a place where we can acknowledge the tragic elements of death, while at the same time recognizing its possibilities for beauty and profound emotion, for wisdom and gratitude. I also hope it will empower you to uncover your own truths and values, and inspire you to live them out in the world.

> *Perhaps this knowledge of death, as a force that impinges on the individual, the community, and the cosmos, is what marks our species as, potentially, wise.*
>
> —DR. CAROL ZALESKI, SCHOLAR OF RELIGIONS

I

STARTING THE PROCESS

THE DESCENT

HOW TO USE THIS BOOK

The book is made up of twelve chapters, meant to be completed over twelve weeks, a format I have found useful in books such as *The Artist's Way*. This extended period of time is aimed toward creating an immersive and safely contained experience with this material, leading to the possibility of real and lasting change. The number twelve is also significant, as it is, in many cultures, associated with wholeness and completion—there are twelve months in a year, Christ had twelve apostles, and Chinese and Western astrology both consist of twelve signs.

This book is meant to take you on a journey of exploration, learning, growth, and even transformation. More than a book, what you will find here is a *process*, and I hope you will continue to work with this material even when your time with the book is done. You will find suggestions and resources for continuing to cultivate growth in the appendix at the back of the book.

Each chapter ends with a number of exercises and writing

prompts. Consider these *invitations*; it is not necessary to complete them all. I recommend that you begin with the ones that really appeal to you, and return to the others if you wish to take a deeper dive. It is my aim to provide a variety of entry points designed to engage different kinds of thinkers and learners, and to include a sufficient number of prompts so that the book will continue to be rewarding if you wish to return to it at a future date (as I hope you will!).

You will notice that many of these prompts revolve around learning about—and connecting with—ancestral traditions. The way we look at death today, as a scientific and psychological issue, is, historically speaking, quite new. If any of us scratches the surface of our own familial heritage, we will find religiously or mythologically informed beliefs that might have something to offer—even if only symbolically or metaphorically—as we undergo our own journey. Delving into our history also roots us more deeply in our ancestral line, provides an entry point for developing a relationship with those that came before us, and begins the groundwork to facilitate change in the future.

> *In the attempt to defeat death man has been inevitably obliged to defeat life, for the two are inextricably related. Life moves on to death, and to deny one is to deny the other.*
>
> —HENRY MILLER, AMERICAN WRITER

Many of the prompts that I provide are designed to elude the rational mind and tap into the unconscious. Sigmund Freud, founder of psychoanalysis, popularized the notion of the unconscious, which refers to the part of our mind to which we have no direct access, but which nevertheless influences our lives and actions. As Carl Jung put it, "The psychological rule says that when an inner situation is not made conscious, it happens outside as fate."[1]

When dealing with something as ultimately unknowable and emotionally powerful as death, the rational mind can only go so far. To that end, I include frequent free-writing prompts. Try, when working with these, to write as quickly as possible, without allowing your analytical faculties to get in the way. By simply jotting down things that come into our mind, we can begin to know and befriend our unconscious, and access material that might not be available to our conscious awareness. You might also make use of the meditation and relaxation techniques in addendum three, page 243, before beginning any such exercises to maximize your ability to connect to the nonrational and the unexpected.

I also encourage you to pay attention to the images and ideas that bubble up spontaneously from the unconscious over the course of the week. For me, a short daily walk—or activities such as yoga, cooking, meditation, and writing in a journal—give hidden ideas space to emerge. Others report that, for them, showering, driving, dancing, painting, or writing poetry serves the same purpose. Whatever works for you, give yourself the time to enjoy an activity that allows your mind to wander, and pay attention to what emerges from mysterious sources. Try to make a record of whatever appears in words and/or images.

A related practice is to keep a dream journal and work with the themes or images that emerge for you by writing, drawing, or honoring them in some other way. Jung asserted that the face we turn toward the unconscious is the one it turns back to us. The more we welcome it into our lives, the more it will give back. Taking your unconscious seriously will help you develop a relationship with it, allowing you to get to know yourself in a much deeper way than your conscious point of view allows, enriching your life and inviting in an ally for a life well lived. For more on working with dreams, see addendum four, page 246, in the appendix.

To get the most out of this book, I would suggest choosing a particular day to read the chapter each week. I personally like to do this kind of work on Sundays, a quiet day that seems perfect for setting an intention for the following week. You might choose a time of day you find particularly relaxing—for me, it would be first thing in the morning or right before going to sleep. You could begin by taking a bath or shower, lighting a candle, making a cup of your favorite tea, or some other simple ritual that sets this experience apart from everyday life and moves you into a different kind of psychological space. If moved to do so, you might enrich your experience by bringing yourself into a relaxed state beforehand via a simple, centering breathing exercise (see addendum three, page 243).

For the rest of the week, allow yourself to process the content—on both a conscious and unconscious level—by working through the exercises and journal prompts that are the most compelling to you, and by paying attention to what bubbles up in dreams, thoughts, and feelings. Studies show that learning is more effective when we take the time to reflect on our discoveries. For this reason, each chapter will end with a check-in, encouraging you to reflect on what you have learned. What was the biggest surprise this week? What did you learn about yourself? You will also be invited to consider—and note—anything that particularly resonated with you.

The meaning of life is that it stops.

—FRANZ KAFKA,
CZECH
WRITER

OUR OWN MYTH OF DEATH

Jung believed it was important for individuals to develop a personal myth about death. This myth was not meant to be a literal story, but rather a psychological framework to help us grapple with the inevitability of death and to find meaning in it. Jung believed that death was an archetype, a universal symbol that combines with our individual lives to make them whole. From his perspective, death was not an end, but a *goal*, and he understood life's inclination toward death to begin as soon as we passed life's meridian.

In his autobiography, *Memories, Dreams, Reflections*, he advised:

A man should be able to say he has done his best to form a
conception of life after death, or to create some image of
it—even if he must confess his failure. Not to have done so is
a vital loss. For the question that is posed to him is the age-old
heritage of humanity: an archetype, rich in secret life, which
seeks to add itself to our own individual life in order to make
it whole. . . . The more the critical reason dominates, the more
impoverished life becomes; but the more of the unconscious
and the more of myth we are capable of making conscious, the
more of life we integrate.[2]

Throughout this book, we will look at a wide variety of ways people
have thought about, imagined, befriended, embraced, and approached
death, in many times and places. Hopefully some of these will resonate
for you. We will also work on excavating—and clarifying—our own
personal understanding of death. At the end of this book, I will invite
you to reflect on your journey and to formulate your own myth of death,
informed by the inner and outer work you've done.

At journey's end, I will also invite you to create your own personal memento mori. This could take the form of an object, practice,
artwork, piece of writing, or anything else that feels right. Regardless
of the form it takes, your memento mori is meant to remind you—in a
useful, life-enhancing way—of your own death. It is meant to help you
keep an awareness of death, as you understand it, close at hand, to encourage you to live the life you want now, before it's too late. It will also
serve as a tangible souvenir of the psychological, emotional, creative,
and/or spiritual journey you've undertaken. Each chapter will include
prompts to help guide you there.

MAIN PRINCIPLES

I live in Mexico, which has been a very special place for me. What first drew me here was the culture's attitude toward death, life, and the relationship between the two. I find it extremely different—and much more life-affirming—than the one I grew up with in the United States.

I first visited Mexico on a Morbid Anatomy field trip. Led by Mexican scholar and writer Salvador Olguín, it was organized around Día de Muertos, or Day of the Dead. This festival, celebrated each November, is the product of the *syncretization*—or the combination of two traditions that creates something new—of Catholic All Saints' and All Souls' Days and pre-Hispanic ancestral practices. It is celebrated by families in Mexico and throughout the Mexican diaspora, and is understood to be a special time of year when the veil between the land of the living and the land of the dead is uniquely permeable, allowing the souls of the ancestors to return to enjoy some time with their families.

As part of the festivities, people build shrines where they leave offerings for their dead loved ones, including favorite foods, drinks, and even vices (such as tequila or cigarettes). They also visit the cemetery, where they clean and decorate the family graves. Children laugh and play, and elegantly dressed mariachi bands rove from grave to grave, playing requests. All is flickering candles and orange marigolds, and the overwhelming feeling is that of a very moving beauty, a sort of transportive, magical, solemn joy.

My friend Edson lives in Puebla. He is a bit younger than I am, and spent his whole life in Mexico. He trained to be an engineer, but is now a museum director. One day, I asked him how he celebrated Day of the Dead. He said, "Well, I go to the cemetery to visit my grandmother."

"And what do you do there?" I asked.

"I talk to her," he replied. After a pause, he added, "Well, I don't know if I am really *talking* to her, but you know, *that's what we do.*"

This was a sentiment I heard echoed again and again in my conversations with friends who grew up in Mexico. There were rituals and practices related to the dead that people engaged in. Many were not sure whether they *believed*, but they did these things because this is what they had done growing up, what their families had always done. It was *tradition*.

I have found this distinction between practice and belief to be a very useful one when seeking to learn from the wisdom of other cultures. Many of the traditions I discuss in this book rely on beliefs many contemporary Westerners might find challenging, such as the existence of an immortal soul, an inspirited world, or a deity of some sort.

When grappling with the material that follows, I would like to respectfully offer that asking yourself whether these things are literally true or false might not be the most valuable question. Rather, you might ask, are they *useful*? Do they have some sort of symbolic or metaphorical truth? Do they seem to make people happy? Might my life be enriched if I tried them out?

A related idea is the concept of *sincere pretending*, outlined by psychology professor Oakley Gordon in his book *The Andean Cosmovision* (2014). Presenting a collection of meditations and energetic exercises that he learned from Peruvian shamans, he advises Western readers how to engage with these practices, many of which presuppose an animistic cosmovision. His suggestion is to enter into them with a particular "spirit of intent," which he describes as "sincere pretending." I invite you, then, as you undertake the activities that fill this book, to try to bring sincere pretending to bear and to concentrate on your

*Dying is a wild night
and a new road.*

—EMILY DICKINSON,
AMERICAN POET

intentions. Do this with the most passion you can muster, and be as present as you can throughout the activity. You do not have to believe anything, but try to maintain an attitude of sincerity and humility. As Gordon puts it, "Through this process of 'sincere pretending' subjectively real experiences emerge."[3]

There is no need, then, to *believe* anything for this book to be effective. Simply *do*, and then pay attention to what happens. The proof, as they say, is in the pudding. *Practice rather than belief is the key.*

As you work your way through this book, I would also like to invite you to consider the difference between authentic and good. I have found in my own experience that focusing on trying to make things *good*—and by "good" I mean as close to perfect as possible,

THE PARADOX: OR, MANY LENSES ON REALITY

I have been blessed, over the course of my life, to have traveled extensively, and to have lived for extended periods of time in other countries. This has led me to the conviction that a worldview is like a lens; each lens is true, as far as it goes, but each provides a limited view of the world. The more lenses we have access to, the more expansive our understanding of the world might be.

In a recent talk for Morbid Anatomy, anthropologist and author Jeremy Narby framed this idea in terms of bilingualism. He explained that he speaks several languages, including French and English. Each, he pointed out, allows him to see and express different aspects of reality. Rather than finding the different realities contradictory, he sees them as *complementary*.

Narby's way of looking at the world was deeply impacted by the time he spent with Amazonian shamans while researching their relationship with tobacco and ayahuasca. The communities he was studying understood the plants as personified, inspirited beings. They were also regarded as valuable teachers, each of which offered its own specific gifts, visionary environment, and lessons.

Rather than simply discounting this way of looking at the plants, Narby tried to hold both ideas in his head at once: his Western scientific view on the one hand, and the native animistic view—in which everything in the world is inspirited—on the other. This way of approaching the material allowed for a sort of cosmological bilingualism, requiring a measure of humility to recognize that no one worldview can tell us everything; that the more lenses we have, the fuller and more complete version of reality we might be able to access. Striking a similar note, Marion Woodman, a Jungian analyst and author, advocates for cultivating a "both/and" rather than "either/or" approach to life, which depends upon acknowledging and embracing the contradictory elements of our existence. When we do so, we gain a more comprehensive understanding of our lived experience and remain open to the complexity of reality, which cannot be fully contained or understood by any single theory or worldview.

Holding seemingly contradictory ideas in your head at one time is what we call a paradox. A *paradox* (literally, "against the way one thinks") is defined as a seemingly absurd or self-contradictory statement or proposition that, when investigated or explained, may prove to be true. A paradox demonstrates the limitations of a system of thinking imposed on the complex, ultimately unknowable world around us. In Carl Jung's opinion, "Only the paradox comes anywhere near to comprehending the fullness of life."[4]

Paradox is commonly used to express religious truths, or to aid in religious realization. Perhaps the best-known example would be the Zen koan, which is a paradoxical statement or question used by Zen Buddhists as a meditation discipline. Some familiar examples include "What is the sound of one hand clapping?" and "If a tree falls in a forest with no one to hear it, does it make a sound?" Such paradoxical questions are presented to students to help them break free of the tyrannical hold of the rational mind (which cannot make sense of such statements) and to get beyond habitual, conditioned ways of thinking. Interestingly, the science of quantum physics affirms paradox. When looking at whether light is a wave or a particle, for example, the answer it presents is, paradoxically, both!

professional, or social media– or marketplace-ready—chills the possibility of creating something *authentic*. This book is committed to helping you uncover a larger sense of self—which can be messy, paradoxical, and nebulous—not just the self that you present to the world. Finding this larger self necessitates ambiguity, ambivalence, imperfection, confusion, messiness, inconsistency, and even ugliness. So if you notice that you are judging your work, I encourage you to thank your rational mind for its contribution, which is crucial in so many situations, but tell it that this is not the best approach for this particular activity. Your goal here is self-

> *The closer we come to the negative, to death, the more we blossom.*
>
> —MONTGOMERY CLIFT,
> AMERICAN ACTOR

discovery; excellence and perfection—as well as comparison of your work to that of others—are enemies of curious exploration.

Speaking of messiness, I have found in my own life that what feel like mistakes are never a waste of time; they are, rather, part of the process of discovery that leads to new things. Every true exploration will lead you down paths that do not pan out in a direct way. If you pay attention, you will find that they lead somewhere, usually somewhere new that was unimaginable when you began. So try not to feel discouraged if you make mistakes. They are very much a part of the process, and can lead to new and unexpected growth.

It's also important to remain curious, even if that may lead you in difficult directions. If dark or uncomfortable ideas or emotions emerge for you, rather than avoiding them, I encourage you to approach them with a spirit of curiosity. Curiosity implies a certain detachment, a standing outside oneself that allows for the distance necessary to sit with something but not identify with it or be brought down by it. I have found that curiosity trumps judgment; when in doubt, come back to curiosity.

Finally, as you work with this book, I encourage you to be alert to your intuition. The way I experience my intuition is as a nagging, tugging idea that will not go away, no matter how many times I dismiss it. If something keeps demanding your attention, consider giving it some time and energy and see where it might lead.

I would also like to acknowledge the fact that for some people, dealing with death can be challenging or anxiety-producing. This is not easy material for us. We are not given a language or a useful framework for looking at or talking about death in our culture, and it takes courage to engage in these sorts of inquiries. Luckily, there are many simple, accessible techniques for working responsibly with darker emotions. These include mindfulness techniques for calming, gratitude, and perspective, which you will find in addendum three, page 243. If this material still feels like it's too much for you after trying out these techniques, perhaps this is not the best time to embark on this journey; you might consider setting the book aside for now. You might also reach out to a professional (see addendum ten, page 258) or friends and family for help. You know your own limits, so trust yourself, pay attention to how you feel, and never do anything that feels like too much for you.

The world is a playground, and death is the night.

—RUMI, PERSIAN POET AND SUFI MYSTIC

A RECAP OF THE MAIN PRINCIPLES

- Practice versus belief
  You don't need to believe anything to make the most of this book. Simply do and observe.
- Authentic versus good
  When engaging in the exercises, aim for results that are authentic rather than "good."
- There are no mistakes
  Mistakes are part of the path, and often lead to new and unexpected places.

* Be curious
  Curiosity trumps judgment. Try to be curious about anything that comes up for you.
* Be alert to your intuition
  If an idea or image keeps tugging at you, give it some time and energy, and see where it might lead, no matter how odd it seems!
* Check in with yourself
  This material can be challenging. If you need to, take a break, talk to a friend or professional, or work with the relaxation tools in addendum three, page 243.

SUGGESTIONS FOR GETTING THE MOST OUT OF THIS BOOK

Note: These are suggestions based on what I have found useful in my own journey. Utilize only what works for you!

* **Keep a daily journal.** I suggest that you use a journal reserved specially for your work with this book. Choose one that really appeals to you, with paper that you enjoy writing on, and write with a pen or pencil that feels good to use. You might want to decorate the journal as well. Use your journal to respond to the prompts and exercises that end each chapter. I also encourage you to write in it daily, making note of any thoughts the book brings up, and checking in with how you feel each day. You might even draw how you feel, or paste in images that are resonating for you. Your journal can also be a great place for unexpected ideas to emerge. Research has also shown that journaling can reduce depression and anxiety, boost our immune system, and improve our physical health.[5]

* **Create a special space.** Use a ritual to set apart your time when working with this book, to designate this as a special process outside of everyday reality. This could be as simple as lighting a candle, taking some deep conscious breaths, or working in a space that is special to you.

* **Take time to breathe.** If time allows, I strongly suggest a regular yoga or meditation practice. Not only is it good for our mental and physical health, it's a great way to calm our minds and empty them, creating space for new images and ideas to emerge. There are lots of great yoga classes available free online. If yoga is not your thing, there are plenty of other ways to ground yourself in your body, such as dancing, swimming, running, going to the gym, or tai chi. For guidance on meditation practices, see addendum eight, page 256.

* **Walk to process.** For me, walking is an indispensable processing tool. I encourage you to walk outside four to five times a week for at least twenty minutes; added bonus if the walk is in nature! Walking is a great way to bypass the rational mind. Pay attention to thoughts, ideas, tunes, or images that bubble up, and write them down, or record them on your phone.

* **Keep a daily gratitude list.** In your journal, or in your mind when you're falling asleep at night, list five things that you are grateful for each day. This is a useful daily practice that helps us appreciate our life exactly as it is, right here and now, and helps reframe difficult moments and thoughts into a larger perspective.

* **Get to know your unconscious.** Write down (or draw) your dreams, and/or doodle or free-write and note any images or ideas that spontaneously bubble up. What images do you find reoccurring? What new ideas are emerging? For suggestions on how to work with dreams, see addendum four, page 246. You might also work with any interesting dream material via active imagi-

nation, a Jungian technique for working with unconscious material. See addendum twelve, page 260, for more.

- **Practice self-care.** This is not easy material for us, culturally. It takes courage to look at death. I encourage you to be gentle, patient, and compassionate with yourself for the duration of your time working with this book. Pay attention to your body and its needs and responses. Give yourself treats, and celebrate progress and milestones, no matter how modest.

EXERCISES

JOURNAL PROMPTS
Please answer these in your own journal

1. **As We Begin . . .** How do you feel starting this book and this exploration? Excited, anxious, or something else entirely? What are your hopes? Fears? Free-write—in other words, write quickly, thinking as little as possible—about your feelings. Perhaps draw yourself as you are now, and as you hope to feel at the end of this journey.

2. **No Fear of Death.** How might your life be different if you had been raised in a culture that did not fear death? How might it change your life, in both small and large ways? What might you have done differently? How might you think about your future differently?

ACTIVITIES

1. **Make a Commitment to the Process.** Daruma dolls are used in Japan to help focus one's energy in order to achieve a goal. These adorable, colorfully painted dolls have big white spaces where the eyes should be. One is meant to draw in the first eye when you set

your intention, and the other when the goal is completed. You might consider using a Daruma doll—easily available online and in Japanese specialty stores—as a ritual way to commit to the completion of this book. If this does not appeal to you, consider finding another way to signify your commitment and focusing intent; this might take the form of a self-designed ritual (see addendum six, page 248), writing a promissory note to yourself and sealing it with intent, or making an offering at a place of worship or in nature.

2. **Make a Mandala.** Try out the mandala technique from addendeum three, page 243, in your journal or a sketchbook. Make sure to date it as well.

3. **Meditate.** Try out one of the mindfulness meditations from addendum eight, page 256. How did it make you feel?

4. **Personify an Emotion.** Try out the exercise of personifying your emotional states from addendum three, page 243. Draw or write about what you discover.

5. **Dance an Emotion.** Try dancing an emotion to a song that evokes those feelings for you.

6. **Create and Work with an Altar.** An altar is a great way to engage with the unconscious and intuitively work with symbols, images, and ideas that have energy for you at a particular time. Tend the altar regularly and add, remove, or move around the objects based on what feels intuitively right. You might light a candle on your altar when you are engaged in an activity that you want to distinguish from everyday life, such as working with this book, doing meditation or yoga, or writing in your journal. You might also place something on your altar symbolic of your intent to complete the process of this book. See addendum five, page 247, for guidelines on constructing an altar of your own.

2

WHAT IS DEATH?

A s a descendant of Jewish Holocaust survivors, death was part of my awareness from an early age. I spent my summers with my oma and opa, my paternal grandparents, who had been forced to flee Vienna for the United States when Hitler annexed their native Austria. They were very lucky to get out, but many of their family members were not so fortunate and perished in concentration camps. As children, we knew we were not allowed to ask about this time in their lives, but it hung heavily over everything.

Jewish people probably have a more intimate relationship with death than many. But for the vast majority of those in the industrialized, affluent West, death was—until the recent COVID epidemic—something exotic, foreign, and outside of everyday experience. This distancing from death—and our expectation that we will enjoy a long, healthy, happy, and pain-free life—is, so far as I can tell, an anomaly in all of human history. The luxury of viewing death as remote and "other" seems to be unique to our particular time and place.

As recently as the nineteenth century, death and dead bodies were frequently encountered in everyday life. The average life expectancy in the US in 1860 was around forty years of age,[1] and in the first decades of the 1800s, as many as 50 percent of children died before they reached adulthood.[2] Death was closely experienced and familiar: it was common to butcher one's own animals, deadly epidemics were rampant, and it was not out of the ordinary to die from a surgery or during childbirth.

For our ancestors in the nineteenth century, a good death was considered one in which you died at home, in bed, surrounded by your friends and family, including the children. This was an era before old-age homes and hospices, when people tended to live in extended families and die in the home. After death, the body would be cleaned, prepared, and dressed by (usually female) family members. It would then be laid out in a coffin in the home parlor for viewing, and possibly a wake. The body would be surrounded by flowers, which not only created a feeling of beauty and sanctity, but also helped keep unpleasant smells at bay.

After the death of a loved one, it was common to observe a period of formal mourning, which would be clearly signaled to others by your clothing and jewelry. You might also have marked your home with black ribbons or other ornaments to make it clear to the community that a death had taken place. There were cultural guidelines for what ways—and for how long—to mourn, depending on your relationship with the deceased. Arts and crafts, usually made by women, were part of the mourning process to keep the memory of the dead loved one close at hand.

These traditions began to erode from the late nineteenth to the early twentieth century, a time marked by many social changes. People were living longer—and with a better quality of life—due to medical and hygienic advances. More and more people were dying in hospitals rather than at home. And after death, the body was increasingly tended to by professional (usually male-run) funeral homes, which were employing the new technology of embalming fluid to keep bodies looking fresh for a longer period of time. Personal mourning began to disappear from view, and people saw it as problematic, or even pathological, if it went on too long. In response to these cultural changes, in the early twentieth century, a writer for the *Ladies' Home Journal* made a case for renaming the home parlor "the Living Room." The parlor, once a place to mourn and honor the dead, could now become a place for the living to enjoy their lives.[3]

At the same time that death was moving further from the daily lives of many, it simultaneously, perhaps for the first time in human history, became largely unexplained by the traditional methods by which humans have created a sense of meaning—that is, religion, ritual, and mythology. The subject of death moved from those realms to that of science and medicine, and while the scientific worldview offers a great many *facts* about death, it provides us with little sense of *meaning*. From the perspective of science, not only has death meant simply an end, but it has also commonly been seen as a failure of medical intervention rather than a meaningful rite of passage.

DEATH, MYTH, AND RELIGION

Part of what it means to be human—part of the human condition, if you like—is to be aware that we will, one day, die. To be human is to be aware of, *and concerned with*, our mortality. The mystery of death has, for millennia, led us to ask the big, existential questions: Why are we here? What is the meaning of life? Why do we die? What happens after we die? What is the point of existence?

It is worth reminding ourselves that the vast majority of our ancestors saw the world in a very different way than we do today. They understood their universe to be ensouled or inspirited, with invisible deities intricately entwined with all aspects of life and death. For most of human history, the questions and answers of life and death were sought not in the causal relationships of a historical worldview or the scientific method, but rather through mythology and religion.

In ancient Rome, for example, it was not one's genetic inheritance or socioeconomic class that was understood to determine the length and quality of a life, but rather the Fates, a trio of goddesses who spun, wove, and cut the threads of life. In Christian medieval Europe, the black plague was understood not as a bacterial illness but, to many, as a sign that the culture—or sufferer—had committed a sin deserving of divine punishment. Similarly, in the Maya world, disease was understood as a result of physical and spiritual imbalance, with illness resulting from the transgression of the laws of nature and society or the captivity of the soul by supernatural beings.

That it will never come again is what makes life so sweet.

—EMILY DICKINSON, AMERICAN POET

Many people today dismiss myths as simple stories from the past, but psychoanalysts Sigmund Freud and Carl Jung and mythologist Joseph Campbell, among many other important thinkers, understood them as narratives that express profound truths about what it is to be human, albeit in a symbolic form. As Jungian psychoanalyst Marion Woodman points out, myths also, crucially, provide us with a sense of meaning around the trials and tribulations that are an inherent part of the human experience. In her own words, "Without an understanding of myth or religion, without an understanding of the relationship between destruction and creation, death and rebirth, the individual suffers the mysteries of life as meaningless mayhem alone."[4]

Myths also help us understand a culture's deepest values and beliefs. They reveal how a culture conceptualizes the relationship between humankind and nature. They tell us what is prized or disdained. They tell us why we are here, and what our lives mean. They also tell us how death relates to life, why we die, and what happens to us after we die.

Looking at death-related myths around the world, we find a nearly unanimous agreement that death is not an end, but a doorway to a new stage of life. We find, in many cultures, richly imagined afterlife journeys, gods of the dead, and lands of the dead. Many myths also avow that humans were once immortal, but for some reason—often having to do with overpopulation, hubris, or disobedience—death was introduced to the world.

The best-known such story in the Western world is the story of Adam and Eve, found in the book of Genesis in the Old Testament. Adam and Eve, the first humans, were originally created by God as immortal. A serpent persuaded Eve to eat a fruit from the tree of the knowledge of good and evil, which God had expressly forbidden. Eve took a bite of the apple, and encouraged Adam to do the same. As punishment, God banished Adam and Eve from their paradise—a peaceable kingdom where nothing died and all lived in harmony—and introduced toiling, suffering, and death to the world. The Christian tradition offers a redemptive addendum: by sacrificing his only son, Jesus Christ, God absolved the curse of death by enabling good Christians to be resurrected, body and soul, and live forever at the end of time.

> *Life and death are one thread, the same line viewed from different sides.*
>
> —LAO-TZU, CHINESE PHILOSOPHER CREDITED AS THE FOUNDER OF TAOISM

The ancient Greek myth of Pandora likewise traces the origins of death in the world to disobedience, and similarly places the blame on woman's weakness and curiosity. According to Hesiod, Pandora, the first woman, was created to punish humanity for the gift of fire, which Prometheus stole from the gods. Zeus sent Pandora, a beautiful and alluring creature, to earth with a box she was instructed not to open. She was unable to contain her curiosity and opened the box, which released death and numerous other human ills into the world.

Death is just infinity closing in.

—JORGE LUIS BORGES, ARGENTINIAN POET AND WRITER

In the ancient world, many cultures believed that after death one's soul—or one of one's many souls—would travel to an afterworld, or land of the dead, which often required special knowledge and skills to navigate. In ancient Egypt, after you died, it was believed that one of your souls would undergo a treacherous and complicated journey to the Hall of Truth. There, your heart—thought to contain a record of your actions in life—would be weighed against the feather of truth. If your heart weighed no more than this feather, you would be ushered to the Field of Reeds, where your soul would live happily for all eternity. If you failed the test, your heart would be swallowed by a goddess called Ammut—who had the head of a crocodile, the body of a lioness, and the rear of a hippopotamus—and this would be the end of your afterlife experience.

Many myths assert that the souls of the dead returned to new life via reincarnation, also referred to as transmigration of the soul. The Mosuo of southern China believed that after you died, your soul would return to the realm of the ancestors in the northern sky. Soon after, you would be reincarnated back into your original clan. When a child in the clan was old enough to be initiated into adulthood, their resemblance to a deceased ancestor would be clear, upon which they would receive the name of that ancestor.[5] Today, many Hindus understand that the soul undergoes repeating cycles of birth, death, and rebirth until it achieves spiritual liberation and breaks free from the cycle. The future incarnations of your soul are reliant on your karma, which is created by the actions and choices you make in life.

CONTEMPORARY UNDERSTANDING OF MYTH

Today, many of us no longer believe in the reality of myths, nor can we fully accept religious explanations for why things happen in the world. But that does not mean we are not influenced by myth. As Carl Jung put it, many of us think ourselves wiser than our ancestors, having left their "phantasmal gods far behind." But:

> What we have left behind are only verbal spectres, not the psychic facts that were responsible for the birth of the gods. We are still as much possessed by autonomous psychic contents as if they were Olympians. Today they are called phobias, obsessions, and so forth; in a word, neurotic symptoms. The gods have become diseases; Zeus no longer rules Olympus but rather the solar plexus, and produces curious specimens for the doctor's consulting room.[6]

That said, might there be a myth that we in the industrialized, affluent, secularized West live by today, either consciously or unconsciously? Are there ideas that delineate our worldview about life and death, why we die, and what happens after we die, and undergird our beliefs about the world and the cosmos and our place in it? I am not alone in positing that this myth would be science, or more specifically, the branch of science called scientific materialism.

Scientific materialism, also known as materialistic reductionism or scientism, presupposes that only matter and the concrete world around us—that which can be studied by the natural sciences—exists. In this worldview, human consciousness is understood as brain activity, so it naturally follows that our consciousness ends with bodily death. As far as this cosmology goes, we are only the body; there is no such thing as the soul or a part of us that lives on after bodily death. And when we die? That's it. The end. Game over.

I want to be very clear here that when I propose science as our guiding myth, I do not in any way mean to suggest that I do not believe in science, or that I do not think it is real or true. Instead, I am offering that the lens provided by science might be seen as serving a similar role to that of myth. As Nobel Prize–winning biologist François Jacob pointed out, "Myths and science . . . both provide human beings with a representation of the world and of the forces that are supposed to govern it. They both fix the limits of what is considered as possible."[7]

Science, like other myths, then, answers the questions humanity has always been asking, such as the origin of the world (the Big Bang), how we got here (natural selection), and what happens after we die (nothing but the decomposition of the body). It tells us what we need to do to live a good and long life. And, as with myth, we take much of it on faith, with our modern experts—scientists and doctors—taking the place formerly held by priests and shamans.

Although there are numerous challenges to scientific materialism within the scientific community (more on this in chapter five), many people accept its tenets as fact. But it is worth remembering that the idea that death is the end is *very, very new*, and runs counter to the beliefs held by nearly all people for nearly all of human history all over the world.

MYTHOLOGY AND RELIGION IN OUR LIVES

I once had a boyfriend whose mother was an extremely devout Catholic. She attended church every Sunday, tithed regularly with the crispest bills she could find, and made many personal sacrifices to live what she had been taught was a good Catholic life. When she was ill and it was clear she was approaching death, I said to him, "Well, at least she has her faith, so she is not afraid to die!" No, he replied sadly. His mother had confided in him that she had serious doubts, and was very afraid of her death.

Death shows up to remind us to live more fully.

—OPRAH WINFREY, AMERICAN ACTRESS, PRODUCER, AND PHILANTHROPIST

Maybe you are lucky enough to have a belief that addresses, in a satisfying way, the mystery of death. But many of us, in this particular historical moment, do not. And, in contrast to the vast majority of our ancestors, we have not been provided with a myth or belief about what happens when we die beyond the scientific model, which posits death as an end. This means that many of us are, whether we like it or not, under an obligation to develop our own belief and understanding or, as Carl Jung would say, our own personal myth. As he said in his autobiography, *Memories, Dreams, Reflections*:

Death is an important interest, especially to an aging person. A categorical question is being put to him, and he is under an obligation to answer it. To this end he ought to have a myth about death, for reason shows him nothing but the dark pit into which he is descending. Myth, however, can conjure up other images for him, helpful and enriching pictures of life in the land of the dead. If he believes in them, or greets them with some measure of credence, he is being just as right or just as wrong as someone who does not believe in them. But while the man who despairs marches toward nothingness, the one who has placed his faith in the archetype follows the tracks of life and lives right into his death. Both, to be sure, remain in uncertainty, but the one lives against his instincts, the other with them.[8]

As we have explored in chapter one, what Jung means by "myth" here is a *personal* myth, your own particular story for understanding the world and making sense of your life. These symbolic stories embody deep, profound truths that come from the unconscious. Jung deemed it "the task of tasks" to get to know one's own myth and believed that, until you do, you can only live in "an uncertain cloud of theoretical possibilities."[9]

Over the course of this book, we will work on discovering or developing a more *conscious* myth about death. In the exercises that follow, we will excavate what ideas we may hold about death without even knowing it, and where they might come from. This is an essential first step to making more discriminating, considered choices about what we believe, knowing that the beliefs of our cultures and families are not in any way inevitable or provably true; they are just the traditions we happened to be born into. This knowledge empowers us to release ideas that are not our own—that may be damaging, toxic, or simply not useful—and replace them with something that feels true to us. What is unknown is often scary. By familiarizing yourself with death and cultivating your own myth and image of death, you can become more curious and less afraid.

Life is a great surprise. I do not see why death should not be an even greater one.

—VLADIMIR NABOKOV, RUSSIAN AMERICAN NOVELIST, POET, AND CRITIC

EXERCISES

JOURNAL PROMPTS

1. **Death Memories.** What is your earliest experience of death? How old were you? How did you feel? Was it a pet? A person? How was it talked about by your family? What was your grieving like? How about that of your family?

2. **Death in Your Family.** Was death talked about in your family? Were you invited to attend funerals? What were you told when a pet or loved one died? What did you think about what you were told?

3. **Associations with Death.** What are your associations with the idea of death? Without thinking, write down every word that comes to your mind. They might include: *fear, decay, end, sadness, grief, rebirth, corpse, horror films, release, surrender* . . . Added bonus: Divide these words into two columns, one for positive associations, one for negative associations. Is there an imbalance between the two?

4. **Death as a Pen Pal.** One of my Make Your Own Memento Mori students found herself wondering: How might a child try to get to know death? Her answer: as a pen pal! To that end, she wrote a series of letters to death, asking it the kinds of questions a child might ask: What do you like to do? What is your favorite food?

What colors do you like? What did you do today? By writing these letters—as well as death's responses to her—she was able to forge a relationship with this mysterious other and become less afraid of it. I invite you to follow this student's lead and write your own series of letters between you and death. Ask death anything you are curious about, as you would a new childhood friend!

5. **A Good Death.** In the nineteenth century, a good death was considered one at home, surrounded by family. What is your idea of a good death? Do you hope to die painlessly in your sleep? Would you like to die in a special place? Alone or with someone (or many) you love? Write, in detail, about what an ideal death would look like to you.

6. **Thought Experiment: Death Is Not the End.** The death of the body also meaning the end of our existence is, historically speaking, very new, and it runs counter to the beliefs of people for nearly all of human history in all parts of the world. One fun thought experiment I have enjoyed: What are the odds that all of human history is wrong, and our particular historical moment has it right? Further, what have been the fruits of the past 150 years that we have lived with these beliefs? Has it made a better, kinder society? If it were as simple as choosing, what would you believe? Write down your thoughts.

7. **Learning from Myths.** We can learn a great deal about a culture through its myths. If our dominant myth is that death is the end, how can we see that playing out in our culture, in its cultural products such as films and books? In our deep-seated, seemingly intractable societal problems? How might our culture be different if we believed in the continuation of life after death?

8. **Myths and Death.** Were you brought up with a mythic or reli-

gious understanding of death? What did these stories tell you about your life, your relationship to the natural world, and punishment? What did they tell you about death and what happens after? How did they impact the way your life unfolded? What are your thoughts about it now?

9. **What Is Death?** Neil Gaiman, in his comic series *The Sandman* (1989–96), imagines death as taking the form of a lovable goth girl. If you were to personify the concept of death, what might it be like? Male or female? Young or old? Friendly or not? Describe this figure as fully as possible, and/or draw what you envision. You might also try your hand at these statements: If death were a god, it would be . . . If death were an animal, it would be . . . If death were a color, it would be . . . If death were a place, it would be . . . You might also try working with this idea via the practice of Jungian active imagination (see addendum twelve, page 260) or the shamanic journey (see addendum thirteen, page 261).

10. **How I Feel about Death.** Complete these sentences.
    - The worst thing I can imagine about death is . . .
    - The best thing I can imagine about death is . . .
    - The thing that most frightens me about death is . . .
    - The thing that most frightens me about being dead is . . .

11. **Death as a Fairy Tale.** Write a fairy tale or short story in which death is the protagonist. Added bonus: To bypass the rational mind, engage in one of the meditations or relaxations found in addendum three, page 243, before beginning.

12. **Your Own Death.** Write a short story about your own death, in as much detail as possible. What was dying like? Who, if anyone, was with you? How did it feel? Was there any sort of post-death existence? What was it like?

ACTIVITIES

1. **Books for Kids.** A surprisingly large number of popular children's books and films revolve around death; a few examples from my own youth: *Charlotte's Web, Bambi, Where the Red Fern Grows, Old Yeller, Bridge to Terabithia, The Black Stallion.* What books or movies do you remember as a young person that dealt with death? Were any of them important to you? Revisit a book or film that made a big impact on you. How did it make you feel? What do you think attracted you to it as a child? What questions do you think it might have raised or answered for you? What might it have taught you about death?

2. **The Body.** Were you fascinated by mummies as a child? Have you spent time with or seen a dead human body? Are you familiar with what happens when a body decays? Are you curious? If so, do some research on whatever pulls you. Collect images in a folder—virtual or otherwise—if that appeals to you.

3. **Familial Death Traditions.** Research a death belief that comes from your family heritage (even if it's no longer observed) or, failing that, one that interests you. What speaks to you about it? How does it open up your ideas about what death might be?

4. **Death Deities in Your Familial Past.** Some of us might consider ourselves secular, but the vast majority of our ancestors had a religious understanding of the world. What were the religious beliefs of your ancestors? Research death gods, stories, or mythologies from that tradition, or another that appeals to you.

5. **Death Film Fest.** Watch a film or television show that explores mortality in a thought-provoking way, and expands our ideas of what death might be. See the list on page 269 for a full list of suggested titles, but you might consider: *All That Jazz* (1979), *Blade Runner* (1982), *Donnie Darko* (2001), *Jacob's Ladder* (1990),

Solaris (1972), *The Leftovers* (2014–17), *American Gods* (2017–21), *The Sandman* (2022–), and/or *Undone* (2019–22). Added bonus: Watch with friends and discuss afterward.

6. **The Beauty in Death.** Collect and arrange (clean) found animal bones, or add them to your altar.

7. **What Happens to the Body after Death?** Curious about what happens to the body after death? Take a deep dive by reading *Will My Cat Eat My Eyeballs? Big Questions from Tiny Mortals about Death* (2019) by Caitlin Doughty or *Stiff: The Curious Lives of Human Cadavers* (2003) by Mary Roach.

8. **Getting to Know Your Body.** Antique anatomical images are beautiful artworks that explicate—and celebrate—the human body, inside and out. Look at antique anatomical images on the internet or in my book *Anatomica: The Exquisite and Unsettling Art of Human Anatomy* (2020), a treasury of such images. Collect your favorites.

9. **Resonance Check.** Did any material in this chapter particularly resonate for you? Is there something that piqued your interest? I invite you to keep track of the things that spoke to you in a special place in your journal. I also encourage you to go further, to do more research on anything that you felt excited about, and if you are a visual person, to collect images related to things that interested you. Start a folder of these images or create a Pinterest board.

10. **Check In.** What were the biggest surprises this week? Did you learn something new about yourself? Make notes in your journal.

3

LIFE, DEATH, AND REBIRTH

Many of us think of death as simply the end. But for most of human history and all over the world, death was seen not as an end, but rather as just one part of eternal, repeating cycles of life, death, and rebirth. Death was seen as a transition to a new stage of life: a *transformation*.

Cycles of life, death, and rebirth are a ubiquitous part of the natural world. Before we lived in cities with electric lights and insulation from the elements, before we shopped at grocery stores for our sustenance, people lived deeply embedded in nature and its cycles. Our ancestors would observe each day the rising and setting of the sun. They would see the moon grow full each month only to disappear, and then return as a sliver that began to grow again. They would witness the green of new life emerging from the apparent death of the fallow season, and they would see seeds buried in the earth, like the corpses of their dead, be reborn into crops that nourished the community.

Many scholars believe that, before the rise of patriarchal civilizations, around 4000 to 3000 BCE,[1] human cultures were matriarchal. These mother-centered cultures were peace loving and egalitarian, and understood everything in nature to be inspirited and sacred. They venerated great goddesses, who represented, in one unifying figure, life, death, and rebirth. These goddesses were *immanent*, meaning they were understood to be divine, and at the same time were present in everything in the natural world, not only the earth itself, but also the plants, animals, and people that inhabited it. Death of the body was seen not as the *end* but as a step toward the soul's next incarnation. Many of these core ideas still live on today in Indigenous cultures around the globe.

The earliest patriarchal cultures also venerated deities that embodied ideas of death, fertility, and rebirth. In ancient Egypt, Osiris was ruler of the dead and the underworld; he was also a god of agriculture, the afterlife, fertility, and rebirth. The ancient Germanic goddess Freyja was ruler of a land of the dead *and* a goddess of love, beauty, fertility, and abundance. These ideas still live on today. In Hindu cosmology, Shiva is—with Brahma and Vishnu—part of a triumvirate of gods responsible for the creation, preservation, and destruction of the world. Shiva's role is to destroy the universe so that it can be re-created. He is a god of death, time, destruction, and the arts; the destroyer of evil; and patron of yoga and meditation.

Some cultures believe that history itself goes through cycles of life, death, and rebirth. The Maya believed that the world went through a series of cyclical apocalypses and rebirths that occurred every 5,200 years or so. The end of each of these cycles was marked by times of great greed and cruelty. When each iteration of the world was destroyed, a few humans managed to escape and repopulate the planet, not unlike the biblical story of Noah's ark. Similarly, in Hindu mythology, the world was understood to go through eternally repeating cycles of decay, redemption, and rebirth. The end of each cycle would be marked by the descent of the demon Kalki—the final incarnation of Vishnu—who would bring an end to the Kali Yuga. The Kali Yuga is believed to be a time full of strife, discord, and conflict that takes place near the end of each cosmic cycle. Some assert that this is the era we currently find ourselves in.

In a largely secular, scientifically minded, rationalistic society, many of us find it difficult to believe, literally, in the idea of life after death. But if we look at it symbolically, meta-phorically, and *psychologically*, we can find it is a useful model, and a prevalent one. It is so ubiquitous, in fact, that Carl Jung considered "death and rebirth" a prime example of what he called an archetype, by which he meant a universal, recurring symbol, motif, or theme, found in all human cultures throughout time. It is for this reason, he suggests, that we see cycles of life, death, and rebirth in mythology, religion, art, and the personal and cultural imagination throughout time in places all around the world.

Birth is the death of the life we have known. Death is the birth of the life we have yet to live.

—MARION WOODMAN, JUNGIAN ANALYST AND AUTHOR

Jung also tells us that from the perspective of the Self—which he defined as our entire psyche, including the conscious, unconscious, and ego, as well as a self-regulating center—death is understood not as an *end*, but rather as a transformation. From the broader, more ho-listic point of view of the Self, death is seen as an initiation into a new life, one we cannot yet imagine. Marie-Louise von Franz, a student of Jung who went on to be an important author and analyst, observed that when close to dying, her clients commonly shared dreams in which they were embarking on a journey. This is corroborated by hospice workers and other deathcare professionals, who say that, soon before their death, patients commonly report visions or dreams in which they are leaving for a journey. Marion Woodman noted that her clients nearing death also often described dreams of a wedding, representing the union of opposites, which is the same imagery that accompanies the completed individuation process.[2]

This way of understanding death—as a transformation rather than an *end*—can also be found in the sciences. Albert Einstein's first law of thermodynamics asserts that energy cannot be created or destroyed; it can only be changed from one form to another. Following this model, the elements that once made our body are recomposed, after our death, into other structures or organisms. As astronomer Carl Sagan poetically noted, we ourselves are "made of star stuff," which is to say that the matter that makes up our physical bodies was "forged in the bellies of distant, long-extinguished stars."[3]

Psychologically or metaphorically speaking, we might also have noticed repeating cycles of life, death, and rebirth in our own lives. For many years, whenever my energy felt low and I was unmotivated, if my inspiration dwindled, I worried that that was it; my creative life was over! But by this point in my life, I have spent enough time observing my own rhythms to know that this is just part of my own cyclical nature. There will be times when I am full of creative energy and others when I just want to watch movies in bed. There will be times I want to travel around the world, and others when I want to sit at home and not talk to anyone for a week. When I am in one of these lower-energy times (which experience has taught me to see as necessary gestation periods), I accept them and allow my energy to go where it wishes, knowing that, when the time is right, my more active, creative self will be reborn, as it always is.

DESCENT AND RETURN

A frequently used metaphor when looking at cycles of life, death, and rebirth is that of a descent followed by a return. This model draws on a rich body of mythology revolving around individuals who have made their own descents into the land of the dead. When they return, they bring a literal or psychological treasure that enriches not only their own lives but the lives of those who have not made the journey. Often the individual finds some healing in the process, and emerges from their journey with the capacity to heal others, or returns with a treasure that rejuvenates their culture.

Psychologically speaking, we might see this idea of a descent followed by a return as a poetic, metaphorical description of the temporary sojourn we take into our own psychological underworld—the unconscious—during dark, transitional times. Paradoxically, these times—though they might seem unendurable in the moment—often engender not just growth but transformation. Although they're not necessarily pleasant, I and many others have found such descents essential to growth and real change.

Such descents and returns are an integral part of the life and work of the shaman. In Indigenous cultures around the world, shamans are healers of body and soul who are understood to have a special capacity to mediate between the worlds of humanity, the spirits, and the ancestors. Their presence stretches back millennia, and many scholars believe that we can trace all religions to shamanistic roots. Many believe that the transformative figure of the shaman is a precursor of today's priests, doctors, psychologists—and even artists and performers. Shamanic cultures are animistic, meaning that they understand everything—from rocks to plants to mountains to animals—to be inspirited, possessing agency and consciousness. In their cosmovision, or overarching worldview, everything on earth and in the cosmos is intimately connected in a web of life.

Shamans are often called to their profession through a sickness that can be healed only by a descent into the underworld. They make this descent in an altered state of consciousness, such as a trance induced by drums, fasting, or plant medicines. In the underworld, they report being killed, dismembered, and then put back together again, piece by piece. This ordeal of death, dismemberment, and re-memberment is understood to give them the skills necessary to heal their community. Often they return with a special ability to heal the very diseases represented by the spirits that dismembered them.

We see the same motif at work in many myths, most iconically the ancient Greek story of Persephone. Persephone—who began life as the maiden Kore—was the daughter of Zeus, king of the gods and lord of sky and thunder, and Demeter, goddess of grain and agriculture. One beautiful day, the young maiden was innocently picking flowers in a meadow when the ground suddenly opened up and her uncle Hades—god of the underworld and ruler of the land of the dead—emerged. He seized the young woman and forcibly dragged her to his underworld lair.

Kore's mother, Demeter, was despondent and roamed the earth searching for her missing daughter. Overcome by her grief and rage, she stopped tending to the fertility of the plants. People began to starve and, more crucially, stopped making the sacrificial offerings so treasured by the gods. To remedy the situation, Zeus demanded that Hades return the girl to her mother on earth, but because Kore

The call of death is a call of love. Death can be sweet if we answer it in the affirmative, if we accept it as one of the great eternal forms of life and transformation.

—HERMANN HESSE, GERMAN SWISS NOVELIST AND POET

had eaten some pomegranate seeds in the underworld, this could not be done. A compromise was reached. The former maiden Kore—now transformed into Persephone, queen of the dead—would be allowed to return to earth and reunite with her mother for part of each year; the rest of the year she would spend in the underworld as queen of the dead. While Persephone was on earth, the lands would be green and fertile. When she returned to the land of the dead, winter would fall, and the natural world would lie fallow and dormant for the winter.

Carl Jung saw this motif of a descent to the underworld followed by a return as a model of a psychological reality, a metaphor for a descent into the unconscious. During such a descent, which is a part of the process of Jungian analysis, one must face, acknowledge, and integrate what is called "the shadow," which is made up of elements of ourselves that we have disowned and pushed into the unconscious because they were undesirable to our families or cultures. One emerges from such a descent with increased self-knowledge, a more inclusive sense of self, greater maturity, and a psychological treasure.

FIGURES WHO TRAVELED TO—AND RETURNED FROM—THE LAND OF THE DEAD

THE SUMERIAN INANNA

One of the earliest known literary works in recorded history narrates the story of the Sumerian goddess Inanna and her descent into the underworld. Inanna was queen of the heavens and the goddess of love, sexuality, beauty, divine law, fertility, and war. One day she decided to visit her sister, Ereshkigal, queen of the land of the dead, in her underworld realm. Here, Inanna was killed and dismembered, but through divine intervention, she was re-membered and brought back to life. She then returned to earth imbued with a new wisdom and power.

THE GREEK ORPHEUS

Orpheus, known for his ability to charm even the gods with his music, was married to his beloved Eurydice, who died of a serpent bite. Heartbroken, Orpheus resolved to journey to the land of the dead, in hopes of bringing her back. Hades, the king of the dead, was so entranced by Orpheus's music that he agreed to let him bring Eurydice back to the world of the living—on one condition: Orpheus must walk in front of his wife and not look at her until they had both crossed back into the human realm. Unfortunately, Orpheus could not resist the urge to look back, and his beloved wife, who had not yet crossed, was immediately pulled back into the realm of the dead, lost to him forever.

THE GREEK ODYSSEUS

In Homer's epic poem the *Odyssey*, the hero, Odysseus, undertakes a journey to Hades. There, he meets loved ones from his past and seeks guidance and information from the deceased, particularly the blind seer Tiresias, to aid him in his long and perilous journey back home to Ithaca.

THE MESOPOTAMIAN GILGAMESH

Gilgamesh goes on a quest for immortality after the death of his best friend. He makes a trip to the underworld, the so-called House of Dust, in search of Utnapishtim, a man who has managed to cheat death. Though he fails to achieve a literal immortality, Gilgamesh returns from the underworld with new, hard-won wisdom about the nature of life and death, and the knowledge that one must content oneself with the *symbolic* immortality that comes from being remembered after your death.

JESUS CHRIST

In what is called the Harrowing of Hell, Jesus Christ is believed by some to have descended to hell or limbo to free the souls of virtuous or sinless individuals who died before they had been baptized or had access to the true faith. This descent is believed to have taken place in the liminal time between his death by crucifixion and his bodily ascension to heaven.

CREATION AND DESTRUCTION: DESTRUCTION IN THE SERVICE OF LIFE

Another place we see the cyclical relationship of life, death, and rebirth is in the common notion that something must die to create room for something new to emerge. In nature, we see this most dramatically in the life cycle of the butterfly. This creature begins life as an earthbound, wormlike caterpillar. One day, under the impetus of a mysterious internal clock, it encloses itself in a chrysalis, within which its body dissolves and is reconstructed. Finally, a magnificent butterfly emerges. Metaphorically, we see the death of something outworn destroyed only to be reborn as something more expansive, beautiful, and transcendent.

The mystery of the caterpillar's metamorphosis into a butterfly suggested to our ancestors that there might be two aspects to a single life-form, and that one might emerge from the destruction of the other. The butterfly, not surprisingly, became one of the most universal images of the regeneration of life, suggestive to our ancestors of the survival of the soul after the death of the body. It is also a common symbol for the soul itself.

Many cultures around the world understood the human life cycle as echoing that of the butterfly. Many believed—and some still do!—that the time we spend embodied on earth is only a small part of our overall experience. After dropping the body at death, the soul (or a part of the soul, or one of several souls) might transform into a wise ancestor, linger as a ghost, journey to a new home in an afterworld, or be reborn in a new body.

The idea of destruction and rebirth is also embodied by the phoenix, an immortal, mythical bird tracing back to ancient Egypt that was thought to burn itself to death only to be reborn from its own ashes. Similarly, in the Hindu cosmology, Kali is a goddess of life and death. She is a creator of worlds *and* a destroyer of worlds, and is often depicted wearing a necklace of human skulls and carrying a bloody sword, attributes that signify her ruthless ability to separate the wheat from the chaff, knowing what needs to die in order for life to thrive.

This idea of the descent and return might also be seen as living psychologically through what is called "the dark night of the soul," a term drawn from the writings of the sixteenth-century Spanish Catholic mystic Saint John of the Cross. He used it to describe a painful but necessary stage in the process of enlightenment or spiritual awakening. Today the term is sometimes used to describe a crisis in one's life—such as the death of a loved one, the loss of a relationship, or the diagnosis of a terminal illness—and the subsequent feeling of being in a dark and unknown place of confusion and despair. This dark night of the soul is often regarded as a state of development that, although painful, is necessary for growth and transformation. In the words of mythologist Joseph Campbell, "The dark night of the soul comes just before revelation. When everything is lost, and all seems darkness, then comes the new life and all that is needed."[4] Or, as Jung put it, "There is no coming to consciousness without pain."[5]

Life is not separate from death. It only looks that way.

—BLACKFOOT PROVERB, QUOTED BY SYLVIA BROWNE

We see a similar dance between creation and destruction in alchemy. Alchemy, a prescientific precursor to chemistry, combined approaches we would label as magical, spiritual, and scientific in an effort to transform base metals into gold. To transform, the substance had to undergo states of mortification (literally, killing) and putrefaction (decomposing) in order to be resurrected in a new, perfected form.

Carl Jung saw alchemy as a reflection of a psychological process, recognizing in its techniques an analogue to the principles of his own path of psychological transformation, which he called individuation. Individuation, the goal of Jungian analysis, is meant not to make a person *perfect*, but rather to make them *whole*, to integrate all the elements of the psyche. As in alchemy, this involves a necessary death of the old identity before the fully realized individual can be born.

Individuation also necessitates a descent into the realm of the unconscious. For Jung, this realm includes not only the *personal* unconscious—that which we have experienced but no longer have conscious access to—but also what he called the *collective*

Let children walk with Nature, let them see the beautiful blendings and communions of death and life, their joyous inseparable unity, as taught in woods and meadows, plains and mountains and streams of our blessed star, and they will learn that death is stingless indeed, and as beautiful as life.

—JOHN MUIR, SCOTTISH AMERICAN NATURALIST

unconscious, which he saw as a deeper layer of the psyche, in which we have access to the shared and inherited psychological elements common to all human beings. We might look at the collective unconscious as a sort of symbolic, psychological, or metaphorical land of the dead, a place where the souls of our ancestors live on and can—at least sometimes—be communicated with and learned from.

For Jung, individuation necessitates a bringing together and unifying of the opposites: chief among them, life and death. He saw these not as warring elements, but rather as polarities—opposite ends of a single spectrum—with neither to be understood as better or worse. It is only through learning to embrace our polarities and holding them together simultaneously that we can experience wholeness and participate in the totality of human experience.

DEATHS AND REBIRTHS IN OUR OWN LIVES

The death card of the tarot—with its grinning skeletal reaper, scythe in hand—often provokes alarm when drawn. It does not, however—as any tarot reader will tell you—generally signify a *literal* death, but rather a *symbolic* one; it represents the death necessary to make space for something new. It indicates change, the need to let go, *transformation*.

An old adage says, "A door must close for another door to open." We have all had experiences in our lives that demonstrate this painful truth. No doubt you have had to, at one time or another, *sacrifice* (literally, to render sacred) something you loved that you knew was no longer good for you, to open the door to something new and unknown. Sacrifices are an important element in initiations and mystical traditions around the world, in which a symbolic death of the old is ritualized so that one can be born anew, transformed. As Marion Woodman points out, these sacrifices or deaths of an old way delineate the entrance to a more profound understanding, a symbolic rebirth.[6]

And indeed, each life can be looked at as a series of small deaths. The child metaphorically dies, often via a painful loss of innocence, and becomes an adult. We leave our homes, we endure breakups, we give up on old, once-vital dreams. We graduate and move into new careers. All of these transitions involve symbolic deaths and rebirths as we move from one stage of life to another.

In many cultures, such transitions are contained by rites of passage, which are rituals that help one navigate smoothly from one realm to the other. These rites usher the participant through what is called a liminal space. The liminal, from the Latin for "threshold," is a space we inhabit when we have already left one space but not yet entered another. This concept of liminality was developed in the twentieth century by French folklorist Arnold van Gennep and anthropologist Victor Turner as part of their studies of tribal initiation ceremonies.

In traditional societies, rites of passage—especially those marking the transformation of child to adult—were crucially important to the community. These rites would usher a youth into their new role in society, with its respective mysteries and responsibilities. They would also guide the initiate to ritualistically and psychologically sever their ties to their family of birth and transfer their allegiance to the larger community. This was done via a symbolic death of the old identity and birth of the new through rites that often involved very real pain and danger.

Rites of passage live on, if in reduced form, in our culture today. We see them in school graduations, in weddings, in Judaism's bar and bat mitzvahs, in the baptisms and confirmations of Catholicism, and in Mexico's quinceañeras. Funerals or memorial services are also important rites of passage, ushering the dead loved one into a new status, and helping those left behind acknowledge and mourn their loss in a safe, contained space.

TRANSITIONS: THE SPACES IN BETWEEN

Transitions from life to death and back again are not easy. They can be frightening and discombobulating, especially if one lives in a culture that does not offer adequate cultural containers—that is, if our culture does not provide shared language for, or rituals around, death and loss. To endure, without fear, the inevitable deaths that constitute a healthy life requires the trust that there will be something waiting on the other side. In a sense, this is always a leap of faith, because that something can only be known to us once we have crossed over.

Jungian analyst and author Jean Shinoda Bolen points out that people usually seek the assistance of a psychoanalyst only when they are in crisis.[7] This crisis might be precipitated by the death of a loved one, a dire medical prognosis, a divorce or breakup, or a job loss. Whatever the crisis may be, this situation thrusts the person into a liminal space—an uncomfortable, uncanny place suspended between two identities, when the old is no longer possible, but the new not yet clear.

Bolen also points out that the Chinese pictograph for *crisis* is made up of two symbols: one represents danger; the other, opportunity. These liminal times of crisis, she believes, can be a major turning point in life. They force one to slow down and assess one's life. Thus, they offer the opportunity to get back in touch with abandoned hopes, dreams, and talents, allowing us to reconnect with a more authentic sense of self and begin to work, as she puts it, from the inside out rather than the outside in.

When I look back on my life, I realize that my biggest crises—all of which I experienced as devastating deaths at the time—were essential to making me the person I am now, and were instrumental in helping me live the life I now cherish. The fact that I have witnessed these cycles of life, death, and rebirth in my own life again and again helps me access the fortitude necessary to endure difficult transitional times. I know—not from faith, but from a close, empirical observation of my life—that there *will* be something on the other side, and that this death might just be what I need to grow, whether I like it or not. This does not mean it's without fear and pain, only that I trust it is for the best, which creates meaning and adds ease to the process.

For thirteen years, I lived in a wonderful, affordable apartment in a safe and beautiful neighborhood in New York City. Anyone who has spent time in this expensive and overcrowded city will recognize that this was a small miracle—I certainly did at the time! I truly loved my home, the neighborhood, and my life there.

At a certain point, I broke up with the boyfriend with whom I shared the apartment. It was a very difficult breakup, and one that truly saddened me, but I knew it was necessary. When he moved out, my landlord informed me that she would be raising the rent significantly, to an amount I simply could not afford.

In less than a month, and with little money, I was forced to move

The surface of our mother is largely comprised of the transformed bodies
of our relatives who have been dying for millions of years. "Soil fertility"
is, in large part, nothing but a measure of the extent to which a particular
bit of ground is saturated with our dead ancestors and relatives.
Death, then, is a necessary part of life.

—JACK D. FORBES, FIRST NATIONS HISTORIAN

out of the home I had lived in for thirteen years. I went through a painful purging of my belongings and put all that remained in storage. I moved, as a temporary stopgap, into a tiny vacant room in a good friend's apartment.

For months, I was in a deep depression. It felt to me like the difficult choice I had made to end my relationship—a necessary death—had set in motion a series of events that destroyed everything that made me feel stable and grounded. I felt like a ghost—like I did not exist, like I could see the world but not touch it. Every aspect of my regular daily life had disappeared. I had been thrust out of everything I knew and loved and had no idea what I was going to do next.

The next step presented itself in the form of an artists' residency in London. During my time there, I began to have a profound feeling that London was the place I should be. I mentioned this to the friend I was staying with, and he offered me his guest room for as long as I liked. It was only because I was in a painful state of homelessness, with all my things in storage, that I had the freedom to accept this very generous offer. I ended up living in London for six life-changing months, where I had the opportunity to work for a favorite museum, met the people who published my first books, and made lifelong friends. As horrible as the experience was at the time, I cannot imagine what my life would have been like had I never been kicked out of my beloved home!

Regardless of whether you view cycles of life, death, and rebirth as metaphor, natural science, psychology, or in a literal sense, they can be a useful lens for finding meaning in the many endings and mini-deaths we will experience throughout our lives. Reflecting on these cycles can help us face these inevitable losses with less dread and more faith that rebirth will come to assuage the pain of death.

EXERCISES

JOURNAL PROMPTS

1. **Lives, Deaths, and Rebirths.** Where have you seen the cycles of life, death, and rebirth in your own life? Did you grow up with any familial beliefs around these ideas? How do you experience these transitions? With excitement? Fear? Note that, physiologically, these two emotional states are nearly identical.

2. **A Lives-and-Deaths Biography.** Write your own lives-and-deaths biography. What stages of life can you identify that you have passed through? What deaths and rebirths can you identify? Some examples may be places you have lived, important relationships that are no longer central, or hobbies or possessions you once loved that no longer hold importance for you. They might also be schools, jobs, organizations, churches, or mentors that were once central to your life. Were there any rites of passage that helped you transition from one self to another? Did your family of

origin or culture provide useful rites? What rites of passage might
have been missing? The rite that ushers many into adulthood today is having children. Do you feel there was a rite that helped you
enter the realm of adulthood?

3. **Sacrifice.** It is a familiar notion that nothing new can be born
without a sacrifice of something old. Was there something you
loved but knew you had to give up, perhaps a dream, a relationship, or a job? Did you find anything positive on the other side of
that sacrifice? Write about that experience.

4. **Transformative Events.** Was there anything in your life that
seemed terrible at the time but ended up leading you somewhere
new and transformative? Make a list of as many examples as you
can think of. Now choose one, and write about it in depth.

5. **The Descent.** Is there a time in your life when you experienced a
descent that led to a rebirth? Write about the experience. Perhaps
write it in the metaphorical, symbolic style of a fairy tale or a myth,
such as that of Persephone. What was the experience like? What
did you encounter there? What parts of your shadow might you
have confronted and integrated? What, if anything, did you gain?
Added bonus: Use a meditation or relaxation exercise before be-
inning to help you bypass the rational mind; see addendum three,
page 243.

6. **Lost Relationships or Jobs.** Write about a relationship or job that
was once important to you but ended. How did you deal with that
loss? How did you get to the other side? What new birth followed
that death? Reflect on what might have happened if you had not
allowed the death to take place. Where might you be now? What
would be different?

7. **Things I Loved.** Make a list of topics, books, places, or objects
that you were once passionate about but no longer hold energy

for you. For me, this might include: horses, Duran Duran, *Beverly Hills, 90210*, and drawing. How—if at all—do those things live on in your life today?

8. **Things I Loved to Do.** What did you love to do as a child that made time disappear? Was there a talent that you did not, for whatever reason, pursue? Can you revisit one of these, and see if it still holds the pleasure it once did?

9. **Destruction in the Service of Life.** In her book *Women Who Run with the Wolves: Myths and Stories of the Wild Woman Archetype* (1992), Jungian analyst Clarissa Pinkola Estés asks, "What must I give more death to today, in order to generate more life? What do I know should die, but am hesitant to allow to do so? . . . What should die today? What should live? What life am I afraid to give birth to? If not now, when?"[8] Ask yourself these questions as prompts, and see if anything useful or surprising emerges for you.

10. **Thought Experiment: Matriarchal Cultures.** If you didn't already, how might life be different for you if you grew up in a matriarchal or Indigenous culture—an egalitarian, freedom-focused culture that prized each community member for their unique individuality, viewed the world as inspirited and sacred, saw time as cyclical rather than linear, and believed in a happy afterlife leading to reincarnation into your extended family? What different ideas might you have for what you wanted to do with your time on earth? How might you feel about death?

11. **Get to Know and Honor Your Personal Cycles.** Have you noticed cycles in your own life in which you are more or less creative, more or less energetic, more or less outgoing? Are you hard on yourself in certain parts of your cycle, for whatever reason? Familiarize yourself with your cycles, and practice working with

them, allowing their natural ebb and flow and honoring wherever you are. Note these times in your journal and reflect on how a cyclical view of time allows you to understand yourself differently. You might also note where the moon is in its cycle—and if you are menstruating, your menstrual cycle—and track it over time to see if you can find any recognizable patterns.

12. **Thought Experiment: Historical Cycles.** Maya and Hindu teachings tell us that the world goes through cyclical apocalypses and rebirths. Some Hindu perspectives say we are now in these end-times. What if this were literally true—that the world we are now inhabiting will end, and a new one will take its place? How does this idea make you feel? Does it bring comfort? Why or why not?

13. **Darkness and Fertility: The Mystery of the Dark.** When something is dark, it is something we cannot see very clearly, something mysterious and unknown. The dark can be frightening, but it is also a place of growth and regeneration, as with seeds beneath the soil. Reflect on anything that our culture designates as dark that might have played a beneficial role in your life.

ACTIVITIES

1. **Dead Self Family Album.** Make a family album honoring your former selves. Use old photos, draw portraits, or write about yourself at a few pivotal ages in your life; for me, it would be 5, 12, 16, and 22. What were you like at each point? What were your main fascinations and concerns? What from this time lives on in your current self? What has been lost?

2. **Requiem for a Dream.** Create a memorial to one of your lost selves or an abandoned dream, and mourn it. Create a painting, an altar, a drawing, a collage, a poem, a short story, or anything

else that feels right and use that media to depict-that which was lost, and perhaps the act that precipitated it. Put it in a place where you'll see it every day and spend time with it.

3. **Create a Rite of Passage Ritual.** Create a ritual to aid in a rite of passage of your own. This could apply to something new or something from your past. See addendum six, page 248, for guidelines.

4. **The Richness of the Soil.** The soil is fertile precisely because of the death of other organisms and their decomposition into elements that can sustain new life. We tend to denigrate animal decomposers, seeing them as gross or unclean. Do some research on decomposition and its animal agents, such as maggots, vultures, and worms. Draw a picture or write about the one you find most interesting. Try to find the beauty in this creature.

5. **Death Tarot.** In the tarot, pulling the death card does not indicate a literal death in your life, but rather the necessary destruction of something old to make way for the new. Spend time looking at and/or meditating upon the death card in a tarot deck of your choice, or an image of one found online. If you wish to go further, free-write (see page 15) about what is going on in the image from the perspective of the figure of death. Added bonus: Try a meditation or relaxation technique in addendum three, page 243, before you begin.

6. **Shavasana.** If you practice yoga, try to really be present and curious when you are in the Shavasana, or "corpse pose," which ends each class. In the yogic tradition, death is seen as a passage to another state of existence, and some see shavasana as representative of the death of the ego being necessary before it can be reborn into a higher state of consciousness.

7. **Resonance Check.** Did any material in this chapter particularly resonate for you? Is there something that piqued your interest?

I invite you to keep track of the things that spoke to you in a special place in your journal. I also encourage you to go further, to do more research on anything that you felt excited about. If you are a visual person, collect images related to things that interested you. Start a folder of these images or create a Pinterest board.

8. **Check In.** What were the biggest surprises this week? Did you learn something new about yourself? Make notes in your journal.

4

❦

DEATH WITH VALUE

OTHER WAYS OF LOOKING AT DEATH

As a child, I was a voracious reader. My mother loved books, and she kept the house filled with them. I would read anything I could get my hands on, from *Garfield* comics to Stephen King to Simone de Beauvoir. But the first special book in my life was E. B. White's *Charlotte's Web* (1952). My mother read it to me when I was a young child; she later gifted me with a specially inscribed copy in celebration of my first school reading tests. Winner of many awards and one of the bestselling children's books of all time, this story is a clear-eyed and poignant introduction to the facts of life, death, love, and loss as experienced in rural, mid-twentieth-century America.

The book begins with a moving brush with death. Fern, a young farm girl, sees her father leave home with an ax. When she asks her mother why, she discovers that he is on his way to the barn to kill a

*Joy at the smallest things comes to you only when you have accepted death. . . .
To be, and to enjoy your being, you need death, and limitation enables you to
fulfill your being.*

—CARL JUNG, SWISS PSYCHIATRIST AND PSYCHOANALYST

recently born runt pig. Filled with compassion for the tiny creature, she tearfully begs her father to spare the pig's life. The father begrudgingly agrees, and allows Fern to keep it as a pet. When the pig—whom she names Wilbur—becomes too large to be kept as a pet any longer, Fern's father insists that they sell him to a farmer down the road. There, Wilbur is plunged into despair when he learns from the other animals in the barnyard that his destiny is to end up on the farmer's plate as Christmas dinner.

Heartsick and alone, Wilbur is befriended by a spider named Charlotte. Of all the characters in the book, Charlotte's life cycle is by far the shortest. She is also the one who possesses the greatest appreciation for life, along with a no-nonsense wisdom, compassion, and kindness.

Over the course of the book, Charlotte creates words in her web in an attempt to save Wilbur from his fate. By the end of the book, it is clear that her work has been successful and Wilbur will live a long and happy life. Soon after this revelation, Charlotte feels her end coming on. She spends her last hours focusing on what she calls her final work: an egg sac filled with 514 eggs. When Charlotte's children hatch, most of them fly off into the world on their spider silk, but a few choose to stay with Wilbur in the barnyard, becoming his friends.

In a classic 1973 animated film based on the book, Charlotte—voiced by actress Debbie Reynolds—sings a beautiful and poignant song to her friend Wilbur as she nears her death. This song constitutes her last words, and in it, she meditates on the dance of "mother earth and father time," and expresses profound gratitude for the privilege of having been, if for just a brief moment, "part of life's eternal rhyme."

Watching the film now, I continue to be deeply touched by Charlotte's deathbed sentiment. As she dies, she is acknowledging that death is an end, and expressing the sorrow she feels to leave the world behind. She is also reaffirming her view that life, no matter how brief, is a precious gift. In fact, acknowledging the brevity of her time on earth intensifies her appreciation of life and the prosaic farmyard world around her. Instead of lamenting how short was her allotted time, she expresses gratitude for having had the good fortune to live at all. I feel very lucky to have been introduced to death through this gentle narrative, which encourages an appreciation of the mystery of life, love, and death without the overarching framework of god or faith.

A more recent pop-culture offering exploring the relationship between wisdom and death can be found in Greta Gerwig's *Barbie* (2023). In this film, the titular protagonist, Barbie, is a doll who wakes up every day in her own Garden of Eden—a perfect, plastic world in which every day is the best day ever: a place where no one grows old and no one dies. One night, in the midst of a jubilant dance party, she finds herself, out of the blue—and to her own surprise—asking her friends if they ever think about dying. Immediately, all the music, dancing, and fun screech to a halt. Death has crashed—and shut down!—the party.

Barbie's unwelcome awareness leads her on a journey of discovery to the human world, which ultimately leads her to choose to incarnate as a real, flesh-and-blood woman. She makes this choice with the full understanding that it means she will someday, inevitably, die. Her encounter with the awareness of death gifts her humanity, compassion, and wisdom, and helps her understand—and act on—who she is and what she truly values. For Barbie, death is a small price to pay for the gift of truly living.

In this chapter, we will turn our attention to ways in which individuals in different times and places—like Charlotte in her barnyard and Barbie in her plastic paradise—utilized the idea of death as a means to achieve greater wisdom and to appreciate life. By accepting and contemplating death, we can access life's deeper meanings, form better relationships, and remind ourselves to make the most of however long we might exist in our current form, whatever lies beyond it.

MEMENTO MORI: REMEMBER YOU WILL DIE

A *memento mori*—Latin for "remember you will die"—is a practice, object, or artwork created to remind us that we will die, and that our death could come at any moment. By evoking a visceral awareness of the brevity of our lives, it was meant to help us remember to make choices in line with our true values. This use of memento mori, which seems so counterintuitive today, is a practice that was found in cultures all around the world and for many millennia; it even lives on today.

Memento mori were a part of life in ancient Egypt, where dried skeletons were sometimes paraded into a feast at its height to remind the revelers of the brevity of life. They were also frequently encountered in ancient Rome, where it was common to see skeleton mosaics on the floors of dining rooms and drinking halls. And, if you attended a feast, you might be gifted with a tiny bronze skeleton called a *larva convivialis,* or

Nothing can happen more beautiful than death.

—WALT WHITMAN, AMERICAN POET, JOURNALIST, AND ESSAYIST

Death. The certain prospect of death could sweeten every life with a precious and fragrant drop of levity—and now you strange apothecary souls have turned it into an ill-tasting drop of poison that makes the whole of life repulsive.

—FRIEDRICH NIETZSCHE, GERMAN PHILOSOPHER, CULTURAL CRITIC, AND PHILOLOGIST

banquet ghost. In both cases, these memento mori were meant to express the well-known Latin adage *carpe diem*—meaning "seize the day"—reminding viewers to eat, drink, and be merry, for tomorrow they might be gone.

Socrates, the ancient Greek founder of the Western philosophical tradition, asserted that a memento mori–like contemplation of death was at the core of the practice of philosophy. "The one aim of those who practice philosophy in the proper manner," Plato records him as saying, "is to practice for dying and death."[1] Similarly, the Stoics, a philosophical school in ancient Greece and Rome, believed that one must contemplate one's own death as a means toward living more fully and authentically. Seneca, a prominent Stoic philosopher, urged his readers to rehearse and prepare for death as a means of diminishing their fear.

Memento mori also play an important part in Buddhist practice. In the Buddha's own time, there was a practice called the Nine Cemetery Contemplations, in which practitioners were encouraged to visit the charnel grounds—where bodies were left, aboveground, to be eaten by vultures or to decompose—in order to meditate on corpses in different states of decomposition. This was meant to help people overcome fear of death and release attachment to the body. This tradition even extends to artwork, in the Japanese tradition of *kusōzu*, which are paintings that artfully depict these nine stages of a decaying corpse. Even today, it is not uncommon to find a human skeleton in places devoted to Buddhist meditation.

Christianity also makes use of the memento mori. In this tradition, it is meant to remind one to live a pious life, to resist earthly pleasures and temptations so that one will be ready to meet—and be judged by—God. Much as in the Buddhist tradition, Christians were, at one time, encouraged to meditate upon the dying and decomposing human body. Death was also, in the medieval era, brought to mind by the daily recitation of prayers called the Office of the Dead, which were supposed to prepare one's soul for death and the Last Judgment. And, of course, every year on Ash Wednesday, devotees go to church, where the priest renders a cross in ash on their foreheads, a visceral reminder that from dust we are formed, and to dust we shall return.

In the Christian tradition, memento mori could also take the form of jewelry, including skull rings—often distributed as funeral souvenirs—and intricately carved rosary beads. Memento mori imagery was also commonly used in watches and clocks, playing on the close association between the ideas of time and death. Gravestone art regularly featured winged skulls or skulls and crossbones, and some grave markers—such as the lavishly carved tomb sculptures known as *transi*—even depicted the deceased in the form of a decaying cadaver.

There were also a number of fine art genres that brought memento mori imagery into everyday life. One of these was the *vanitas* (literally "vanity") oil paintings, which featured imagery such as skulls and snuffed-out candles, symbolizing a life cut short. These were hung in

> *Death is our friend precisely because it brings us into absolute and passionate presence with all that is here, that is natural, that is love. Death stands before eternity and says YES.*
>
> ——RAINER MARIA RILKE, AUSTRO-HUNGARIAN WRITER AND POET

Death is so genuine a fact that it excludes falsehoods, or betrays its emptiness; it is a touchstone that proves the gold, and dishonors the baser metal.

——NATHANIEL HAWTHORNE, AMERICAN WRITER

---

the home to encourage the viewer to focus on the eternal, rather than the momentary pleasures of life on earth. Another popular genre was the triumph of death, in which an anthropomorphized figure of death plows down everything in its path, giving vision to the idea of death as an arbitrary and unstoppable destructive force. There is also the *danse macabre*, or "dance of death." Popular at a time when the black plague was decimating Europe, these works also feature an anthropomorphized figure of death, this time merrily leading people of every age and social station—from queen to pauper to child—in a dance to the grave. This allegory points to the fact that death makes no distinctions; to death, we are all equal.

Memento mori could even take the form of actual human remains. To this end, wealthy gentlemen often displayed a human skull in their library or cabinet of curiosities as a poignant reminder of the brevity of life. And cemeteries—in a time before permanent interment— would dig up defleshed skeletons and exhibit the bones, frequently in artistic arrangements, to remind the visitor of their own death.

A contemporary manifestation of memento mori can be found to- day in New Orleans's Mardi Gras, as part of the festivities of the Black Masking Indian krewe. Their annual procession begins at dawn when the so-called Skull and Bones Gang—dressed as skeletons—knock on the doors of neighborhood homes to remind them of the tran- sience of life and invite them to join the festivities. In a similar vein, Tibetan Buddhist festivals often incorporate so-called cham dances.

These are devotional performances that often feature costumed skeletons intended to remind revelers of the presence of death.

A fun and surprising modern manifestation of memento mori is a smartphone app called WeCroak. The app— inspired by a Bhutanese proverb asserting that the key to happiness is contemplating death five times daily—sends you several thoughtful quotations related to mortality throughout the day. In the words of the app's official text: "Contemplating mortality helps spur needed change, accept what we must, let go of things that don't matter and honor things that do."

For what is it to die but to stand naked in the wind and to melt into the sun? And when the earth shall claim your limbs, then shall you truly dance.

—KHALIL GIBRAN, LEBANESE AMERICAN ARTIST, POET, AND WRITER

Far from morbid, contemplating death in this way is the best method I've found for revealing, with clarity, what it is we really value. I have also found no better tool for inspiring us with the will and courage to make the changes necessary to live a life that is true to ourselves and in accord with our real values; one that will, or so we can hope, leave us with the fewest deathbed regrets.

EXERCISES

JOURNAL PROMPTS

1. **Death with Value.** In the 1973 version of the film *Charlotte's Web*, directed by Charles A. Nichols and Iwao Takamoto, the titular spider, as she dies, expresses her profound and heartfelt appreciation for the time she was gifted, for having been allowed to be a part of the beauty of life if only for a brief moment. What

do you think of this sentiment? If you found out that your death was imminent, is there any possibility you might feel the same? Or would you feel something completely different? Write your thoughts on this. Added bonus: Watch *Charlotte's Web* before engaging in this prompt.

2. **Choosing Death.** In the movie *Barbie* (2023), the children's doll chooses to become human, knowing that this means she is giving up her immortality; that she will, like all living creatures, one day die. Would you choose the same? Why or why not? Added bonus: Watch *Barbie* before engaging with this prompt.

3. **Death and Wisdom.** A confrontation with our own death has been seen by many cultures as a key to wisdom. What are your thoughts on this idea? Do you agree? Why or why not? Have you found it to be true in your own life?

4. **Your Own Memento Mori.** Is there something in your life that functions as a memento mori, whether you call it that or not? What is it, and how do you engage with it? How does it help you in your life? If there is not a memento mori in your life, can you see the benefits of having one? What might those benefits be?

5. **Your Family Tradition.** Does your family have any practice focused on reminding themselves, in a life-affirming way, of the inevitability of death? If not, how might your life have been different if they had?

6. **Ode to Death.** Write a love letter, poem, or song devoted to death.

ACTIVITIES

1. **The Stoics.** The Stoics of ancient Rome practiced a particularly positive death-oriented philosophy, believing that we must actively acknowledge our own death as a means of motivating us to live more fully and authentically. Marcus Aurelius, an emperor

of Rome who was also a Stoic, wrote, "Perfection of character is this: to live each day as if it were your last, without frenzy, without apathy, without pretense." If this approach resonates with you, read more of Aurelius's work, or that of other Stoics, such as Seneca and Epictetus.

2. **Learn More about Death.** For a change in perspective, read Phillipe Ariès's *The Hour of Our Death: The Classic History of Western Attitudes toward Death* (1982), an intellectual history of our changing relationship to death in the Western world. The author beautifully situates our own attitudes about death in a much greater historical context, demonstrating how varied approaches to death have been, even in the West.

3. **Image Work.** Look up some memento mori images on the internet. Choose one that really resonates for you. Spend a few minutes looking it over, left to right, taking in all its details. Meditate with this image, using these instructions: Close your eyes. Breathe and center yourself for five deep, conscious breaths. Bring the image to mind. See it in all its details. Start by visualizing it as a flat image, but then see if you can imagine it as a three-dimensional reality, and really explore it. When you open your eyes, free-write about the image, trying not to let your rational mind interfere. You might also try going deeper with the image using the Jungian technique of active imagination; for instructions, see addendum twelve, page 260.

4. **Death Meditations.** Catholic and Buddhist traditions both offer meditations that focus on death and the dead body. Some of these can be found as videos on YouTube. Find and try one that looks interesting, and write about your experience. I advise using search terms such as "Buddhist death meditation" or "Christian death meditation."

5. **Make Your Own Half-Living, Half-Dead Self Portrait.** In the seventeenth century, there was a genre of artworks where a person was depicted as if split down the middle. One side was young and beautiful, and the other was a skeleton or decomposing corpse. I invite you to make your own half-living, half-dead self portrait! You can begin by downloading a half-skull image from my website (joannaebenstein.com/half-skull); you could also draw or otherwise render your own. Either way, one half of the portrait should take the form of a skull, the other a portrait of yourself as you look today. I encourage you to decorate it with traditional and/or personal symbols of life, death, and immortality. Added bonus: Hang up the finished piece or put it on your refrigerator to serve as a fun and personally meaningful memento mori!

6. **Carry a Memento Mori.** Wear a small skull as jewelry or carry one in your pocket and try to touch it and think about it—and its meaning—throughout the day.

7. **WeCroak.** Download the WeCroak app, a memento mori–themed smartphone app that reminds you several times a day of your own death.

8. **Resonance Check.** Did any material in this chapter particularly resonate for you? Is there something that piqued your interest? I invite you to keep track of the things that spoke to you in a special place in your journal. I also encourage you to go further, to do more research on anything that you felt excited about, and if you are a visual person, to collect images related to things that interested you. Start a folder of these images or create a Pinterest board.

9. **Check In.** What were the biggest surprises this week? Did you learn something new about yourself? Make notes in your journal.

5

WHAT HAPPENS AFTER YOU DIE?

M any people believe that it is a scientific fact that when we die, that's it; the end. But the stranger, more fascinating truth is that *no one knows for certain what happens after we die.* Death continues to be *a*—if not *the*—great mystery of human life. In this chapter, we will look at some of the ways different cultures understood what happens to us after we die. We will also turn our eye toward scientific discoveries that are showing us glimpses of a world that seems far stranger— and less intuitive—than the one we thought we knew, and in which many things once derided as woo-woo now seem less easy to dismiss.

WHAT HAPPENS WHEN YOU DIE?

Until the past few centuries, it was a near-universal human belief that the body contained a life force—popularly known as a soul—that continued to live on after the death of the body. In many belief systems, the body and soul were understood to be two distinct entities, created individually. In the Old Testament's book of Genesis, for example, God crafts the body of Adam out of clay, and then animates him with the breath of life. Often, the body is understood to return to its origin, as in the Christian notion of "dust to dust," while the soul, no longer attached to the body, moves on to the next stage of existence.

Many cultures understood that we possess two or more souls (at some periods in ancient Egypt, as many as nine!) and that each represented a different part of ourselves. Some cultures conceived of what we might today refer to as a higher and a lower soul. The higher soul, often associated with the heart or breath, was the home of one's moral and intellectual nature and was the soul that would ultimately travel to the afterworld. In ancient Egypt, this soul was called *ba*, the ancient Greeks called it *pneuma*, and in Jewish lore it is referred to as the *ru'ach*.

The lower soul was the locus of the individual's passions and physical nature, and some cultures understood it to stay with the body after death. In ancient Egypt, this soul was called the *ka*, among the ancient Greeks, *psyche*, and the Jews called it *nephesh*. Some believed that this soul remained restless until the flesh had completely disintegrated; it might take the form of a phantasmal image of the deceased or the guise of animals such as bees, birds, or butterflies.

It is a very common belief, found throughout history and all over the world, that after the death of the body, the soul will journey to an afterworld of some sort, or a land of the dead. In many cultures, it was important to have a psychopomp—literally "soul guide" in ancient Greek—who would ensure that the deceased successfully made their way to their next destination. This role could be performed by a shaman, a priest or priestess, or even a divinity. In ancient Greece, Hermes, a trickster god, led the souls of the deceased to Hades, the land of the

The boundaries which divide Life from Death are at best shadowy and vague.
Who shall say where the one ends, and where the other begins?

—EDGAR ALLAN POE, AMERICAN WRITER, POET, AND LITERARY CRITIC

dead. In some Christian traditions, this role was played by the archangel Saint Michael. And in some Filipino cultures, ancestral spirits were believed to function as psychopomps. They would wait at the foot of the deathbed and escort the soul into the afterlife, not unlike the stories we hear of near-death experiences today (more on that in a moment).

In most of the earliest myths, all souls—no matter how important or virtuous the person had been in life—traveled to the same place after death. In matriarchal cultures, this afterworld was often seen as a fertile place of abundance, where one lingered until ready to reincarnate. In early patriarchal cultures, the afterlife was typically viewed as a dimmed continuation of life on earth, with the souls of the dead envisioned as anonymous and aimless shades living a sort of half-life, experiencing neither pleasure nor pain. In ancient Mesopotamia, for example, the underworld was conceived of as a desolate underground cave, where the dead ate dust and offerings left by their families. In the first Greek myths, Hades, the land of the dead, was a place of flittering, immaterial shades. And for the earliest Israelites, when someone died, their shade was understood to pass from the world of the living to Sheol, the afterworld.

In later cultures, we see the development of a variety of afterlife possibilities, some more desirable than others, each having its own guidelines for admission. In later Greek mythology, your afterdeath destination was reliant on the judgment of Hades and Persephone, king and queen of the dead. If you were a special favorite of the gods, or if you had lived a particularly heroic life, you might be sent to Elysium, or the Elysian fields, to live in eternal bliss with those you loved. If you had been wicked, or offended the gods, you might be sent to Tartarus, where you would be punished with tortures designed to suit your crime.

Perhaps they are not stars in the sky, but rather openings where our loved ones shine down to let us know they are happy.

—INUIT PROVERB

Similarly, the Christian worldview purports that after we die, our soul undergoes a judgment that determines its fate. The soul is then consigned to either heaven, a place of eternal reward, or hell, a place of eternal punishment. In some Christian traditions, there is also an intermediate place called purgatory, where all but the most holy must go temporarily to purge their sins before they are fit to enter heaven. This idea of an intermediary location where one must go to purify oneself for one's next afterlife destination is not uncommon in cultures around the world.

A great number of cultures believe that after death, the soul, or one of the souls, will be reincarnated. This was a characteristic of matriarchal cultures, many of which believed that after death, one's soul would be reincarnated back into their own clan. The idea of reincarnation is also central to many contemporary Eastern religions, including Hinduism, Jainism, and Buddhism.

In some sects of Buddhism, death is seen as part of the repeating cycles of life, death, and rebirth—called samsaras—that animate the cosmos. Your karma, which is the sum of your life choices and actions in this and previous states of existence, determines how you will be reborn in future lives. The ultimate goal is to step out of this cycle altogether, to end the relentless rounds of life, death, and rebirth that are always accompanied by the suffering that is part and parcel of impermanence. This is called *nirvana*—literally "blowing out."

WHAT HAPPENS AFTER YOU DIE?

PSYCHOPOMPS

Hermes: In the ancient Greek tradition, Hermes was a deeply liminal god. In addition to leading the souls of the dead to the river that separated the land of the living from that of the dead, he was also messenger of the gods, and a crosser of boundaries. He was a beloved trickster and the patron of travelers, thieves, and merchants.

Xolotl: Xolotl was an Aztec god who guided and protected the souls of the dead on their journey to Mictlan, the land of the dead. Often depicted as a combination of dog and man, he was also the god of fire and lightning. He was thought to play a role in the sun's movement through the underworld at night, and was associated with transformation and renewal, representing the idea of life emerging from death. He was said to be able to transform into different animals, emphasizing the cyclical nature of life and death.

The archangels: In some Jewish folklore, the archangel Raphael is associated with healing, and is also a psychopomp who guided the dead to Sheol, the land of the dead. In the Christian tradition, the archangel Saint Michael, best known as the leader of the heavenly army against Satan in the Bible's book of Revelation, is also seen by some as a psychopomp. He is thought to not only help souls make their way to heaven, but also, some say, to hold the scales that designate whether or not you will be allowed to enter.

Azrael: In some branches of Islam, Judaism, and Christian mysticism, Azrael is seen as the angel of death. In some Islamic traditions, he is thought to take the souls of the dead from the body at the time God has designated. In certain Jewish and Christian mystic beliefs, he is understood to guide souls to the afterlife.

Vanth: In Etruscan mythology, Vanth is a winged female messenger of death and a psychopomp who lives in the underworld. She is said to have large arching wings full of eyes, representing all-seeing death, from whose sight no one can hide. If you saw her, it would herald your own impending death.

The Valkyries: In pre-Christian Nordic mythology, the Valkyries are divine warrior maidens who choose brave men from the battlefield and bring them to Valhalla, one of the possible afterlife destinations. Freyja, a goddess associated with love, fertility, death, and war, also selected warriors whom she would bring with her to Fólkvangr, the afterlife realm that she ruled over.

Siwarkinte: In the Andean tradition, Siwarkinte is a divine hummingbird who acts as a psychopomp. He has the special ability to travel with ease through the three worlds (the underworld, the heavens, and the middle world that humans inhabit) and cross-pollinate them. He is also the mediator of the shamanic awakening process.

Animals: In ancient Mexico, people would often be buried with real or ceramic dogs, which were believed to help guide souls safely to their afterlife destination. Other animals commonly identified with this ability include horses, deer, and birds.

SCIENCE AND THE QUESTION
OF LIFE AFTER DEATH

Many of us might think the possibility that our consciousness continues on after bodily death could only be wishful thinking, a quaint belief of our ancestors. But, in recent years, a number of compelling peer-reviewed studies have been emerging from the scientific community that explore this possibility in a serious way. Unless one wants to suggest that a large number of medical professionals and respected scientific professionals are lying, or have been expertly duped, I, at least, find it impossible to dismiss their reports as pure nonsense.

Perhaps the most persuasive challenge to the idea that death is the end is the near-death experience, or NDE. In the words of one of its foremost researchers, Dr. Bruce Greyson of the University of Virginia, near-death experiences are "vivid, realistic, and profoundly life-changing experiences occurring to people who have been physiologically close to death, as in cardiac arrest, or psychologically close to death, as in accidents in which they feared they would die."[1]

NDEs are not a new phenomenon; they have been reported for millennia. Some scholars cite the first mention of an NDE as Plato's vision of Er, reported in his *Republic* around 375 BCE.[2] Reports of NDEs have become much more common in the past fifty years or so, thanks to medical advances allowing us to revive people who have technically died.

In 1975, American psychiatrist and physician Raymond Moody

It is not more surprising to be born twice than once;
everything in nature is resurrection.

—VOLTAIRE (AKA FRANÇOIS-MARIE AROUET),
FRENCH ENLIGHTENMENT WRITER, HISTORIAN, AND PHILOSOPHER

published the bestselling *Life after Life*. In it, he coins the term *near-death experience* and explores the phenomenon's characteristics. Over the course of the book, he shares stories of many people who, while technically dead, experienced unexplainable and often mystical oc-curences. He notes that the phenomena experiencers report having witnessed in their post-death journeys share a great deal of similari-ties. Many report leaving their body and hovering above it or flying be-yond it; encountering loved ones (including family members, beloved religious figures, and even pets) who appear as psychopomps to guide them to the next stage of existence; seeing a bright light or a being of light; moving through a dark tunnel; the sense of being outside of space and time; and hearing a loud ringing sound. Many also experienced a sort of life-flashing-before-their-eyes overview of important moments in their lives, a sense of unconditional love and peace, and a profound sense of the oneness of everything. Numerous experiencers assert the impossibility of truly describing what they had encountered; it was, they report, *ineffable*—that is, beyond the powers of language.

Many experiencers revealed that this other realm was so beau-tiful and peaceful that they were reluctant to return to their earthly existence when they were called back. In 1944, Carl Jung, in the af-termath of a heart attack, had a near-death experience of his own, in which he was given what he described as a "glimpse behind the veil."[3] He later reported that "what happens after death is so unspeakably glorious that our imagination and our feelings do not suffice to form even an approximate conception of it. . . . The dissolution of our time-bound form in eternity brings no loss of meaning."[4] He too confessed that when he was called back, he was very reticent to return, and it took weeks before he could fully reconcile himself to earthly existence again.

Near-death experiences are often transformative, profoundly changing many people's lives for the better, and in lasting ways. Experiencers often report that, after the event, they found that they had a more spiritual attitude, increased compassion for others, a greater sense of purpose or meaning in life, a reduced desire for material possessions or fame, a more robust enjoyment of life, a more intense appreciation for relationships and nature, and the ability to live more fully in the moment. And, almost without exception, people who have had NDEs report that they are no longer afraid of death; they have had a preview of it, in a sense, and are now viscerally and experientially certain that death is not the end.[5]*

Provocatively, some near-death experiencers report, upon awakening, having observed things that can later be verified by reliable witnesses. This is baffling, as these observations are made by people who are either clinically dead (with no measurable brain activity) or under anesthesia, both of which are conditions understood to make observations of any sort impossible. These NDEs—called *veridical* NDEs—are often corroborated by doctors and nurses. Not only are these individuals our contemporary experts on death, life, and the in-between, but also the people one might expect to be most skeptical about these sorts of accounts.

---

* It should be noted that in this way, NDEs have much in common with mystical experiences more generally. Such altered states are cultivated in all cultures and all around the world through activities such as drumming, dancing, meditation, prayer, fasting, and the use of psychoactive substances or plants. Shared attributes include feelings of joy and calm, perception of a presence greater than oneself, ineffability, experiences of transformative healing, and loss of the fear of death.

In one case, a patient had been induced into a state of clinical death for medical purposes. Upon awakening, she reported that during the procedure she had felt herself drawn out of the top of her head, after which she was able to view the operating room from above. She accurately described the doctors, nurses, and technicians she had seen in the room, most of whom she had never met, as well as peculiar details of the procedure.[6] In another report, a heart attack patient said that during his operation he had risen above his body and watched what was going on below. He saw his doctor making strange arm-flapping motions, and expressed his surprise that the medical team was operating on a different part of his body than he had expected. All of what he witnessed was later corroborated by the doctor and medical team.[7]

Dr. Elisabeth Kübler-Ross, compassionate end-of-life care pioneer and author of the bestselling book *On Death and Dying* (1969), became interested in NDEs late in her career due to a number of strange things she experienced while sitting at the deathbeds of her patients. Children approaching death, she said, would regularly report that a loved one was waiting for them. In one instance, a young girl who had been injured in a car accident recounted to Dr. Kübler-Ross that her mother and brother had come to guide her to her next destination. This struck Dr. Kübler-Ross as peculiar, as she was under the impression that the girl's family had survived the accident. It was only later that she discovered that they had actually passed away before appearing to the girl.

There is no death. Only a change of worlds.

—CHIEF SEATTLE (SEALTH),
SUQUAMISH CHIEF

For those of us who would like to reap the benefits of a near-death experience without actually imperiling ourselves, a 2018 study by a group of psychologists at the University of Barcelona demonstrated that a virtual reality simulation could provide the same results as the real thing. Participants moved through a virtual reality life cycle that ended with the experience of a simulation of their own death, complete with classic features of an NDE. Many of those who experienced the virtual environment reported lasting positive changes in their attitudes toward life, including a greater concern for others, an increased interest in global rather than material issues, an enhanced appreciation for life, and a reduction in their fear of death.[8]

Research suggests that our ancient Greek and Roman ancestors might have been well aware of the power of a simulated near-death experience, and practiced them regularly in what were called the Eleusinian Mysteries.[9] The Eleusinian Mysteries were just one example of a number of mystery religions, which were secretive religious rites based around mythical journeys to—and returns from—the land of the dead. Initiates included luminaries such as the Roman emperor Marcus Aurelius, Roman statesman and philosopher Cicero, and, many believe, the ancient Greek philosopher Plato.

The Eleusinian Mysteries ritualized the myth of Demeter and Persephone (discussed in chapter three, page 37), in which the maiden Kore is abducted to the underworld and transformed into Persephone, the queen of the dead. Because initiates were sworn to secrecy—on pain of death!—there is much we do not know about what went on there. But many scholars assert that these rites took the candidate through the gates of death through a transformative immersive experience. It is believed that, through ritual and performance, initiates would experience a symbolic descent into the underworld, where the secrets of life and death would be revealed experientially, possibly with the assistance of a psychedelic beverage. Many initiates emerged in an enlightened state, reporting that they were now certain of a continued spiritual existence after death, and no longer afraid of their own demise.

We see a similar principle at work in the (highly successful) therapies that use psychedelic medicines as the basis for guided journeys designed to help terminally ill patients come to terms with their condition. Many who participate in these studies report a reduction in anxiety, improved mood, and a greater acceptance of their condition after only a single session. These experiences often facilitate a sense of connectedness and spiritual insight, and lead to profound shifts in participants' perspectives about life and death, as well as a reduced fear of death.

Another challenge to the notion of death as "the end" comes from studies of children who claim to remember a previous life. Much of the scientific research in this area has been conducted by Dr. Jim B. Tucker, a child psychiatrist and professor of psychiatry and neurobehavioral sciences at the University of Virginia School of Medicine's Division of Perceptual Studies.[10] He attempts to corroborate the children's memories, and to determine whether their stories demonstrate any knowledge that could not have come from their current lived experiences. He has written a number of books and peer-reviewed articles on the subject, presenting a rigorous analysis to suggest that carrying memories from previous lives might be possible.

Many of Dr. Tucker's reports focus on young children (usually no older than five) who report verifiable details about an individual they believe they might have been in a former life. Dr. Tucker cites examples of young children speaking fluently in languages they'd had no exposure to, expressing food preferences that are unusual in their culture, and even being stubbornly attracted to adult indulgences such as alcohol or cigarettes. Other cases involve phobias, such as a young girl who had been terrified of water since she was a baby, and later believed herself to be the reincarnation of a woman who drowned. Some children exhibit birthmarks or congenital anomalies in places where the deceased had scars or injuries. Often these children ask to be brought to the place where they believe their previous life took place, where details can then be verified. These cases have taken place all around the world, in cultures that believe in reincarnation as well as those that don't.

In addition to these carefully studied phenomena, there are a great deal of suggestive anecdotal incidents that have been reported around the boundaries between life and death. Many hospice workers and other deathcare professionals report that their patients, when death is near, commonly carry on conversations with invisible figures they identify as deceased loved ones. A great number of people report having "visitation dreams," in which they feel a loved one has paid them a postmortem visit. There are also numerous reports of clocks stopping at the time of a person's death, and even phone messages from the dead. These phenomena have not been put through the rigors of peer-reviewed testing—and may not be amenable to it in the first place!—but they represent, for many, fascinating possibilities that challenge our binary understanding of life and death.[11]

> *Of all the gods only death does not desire gifts.*
>
> —AESCHYLUS, GREEK TRAGEDIAN

CHALLENGES TO THE MATERIALIST WORLDVIEW

The possibility of NDEs, past-life memories, or visitation dreams contradicts the fundamental assertions of scientific materialism, the dominant model by which those in the West understand our world. This worldview posits that everything in the universe, including consciousness, can ultimately be explained in terms of physical matter and its natural processes. The idea stretches back to ancient Greece, but was developed into the dominant ideology it is today during the

Age of Enlightenment of the seventeenth and eighteenth centuries, especially by René Descartes and Isaac Newton. For over a century, the established order has presented scientific materialism as the only valid lens for determining what is real and true. But the primacy of this lens is, today, increasingly being questioned.

The first real challenge to scientific materialism came from quantum physics. This branch of science examines matter and energy at their smallest, most fundamental levels, and was established in response to experiments that made it clear that matter at that scale did not obey the commonly understood laws of physics. For example, certain particles, such as photons and electrons, could be studied as both particles and waves, depending on your experiment. And even stranger: they did not take that form—and could not be pinpointed in space—until they were measured in an experiment, thus "forcing" them to be one or the other. Quantum physics also demonstrates a phenomenon called entanglement, in which particles that have once interacted are connected and react as one, even if they are far from each other in space or time. Einstein called this phenomenon "spooky action at a distance."

Another challenge to the paradigm of scientific materialism arose from the so-called mind-body problem. This is an area of inquiry that explores the nature of consciousness and attempts to understand how the two seemingly distinct realms of mind and body are related. One phenomenon that complicates this understanding is found in meditation, which has been demonstrated to lead to changes in brain structure and function. Another is terminal lucidity, in which people with neurodegenerative diseases such as dementia temporarily regain their faculties soon before dying to communicate with their loved one in a way their pathology should make impossible. A further challenge lies in the study of placebos, which are the inactive substances given to a percentage of clinical trial participants to ascertain the efficacy of the tested intervention.

Dr. Mark W. Green, professor of neurology, anesthesiology, and rehabilitation medicine at Mount Sinai, gave a talk on this topic for Morbid Anatomy and, over the course of the lecture, shared some information that truly defied our common ways of looking at the world.

Placebos, Dr. Green told us, are often as effective as the medicine they are meant to test, in ways that can be scientifically verified. As many as 40 percent of people respond to them as if they were the real treatment; in matters of pain mitigation, that number is even higher. He shared more fascinating details: capsules are better than pills, and injections are better than capsules; four times a day works better than one; bitter pills work better than those with no flavor; and if the pill is expensive, or the institution providing the pill is more prestigious, then it is experienced as more effective. Optimists have higher response rates to placebos, pessimists lower, and, most provocatively of all, placebos can still work even if you are told—*and continually reminded*—that they are just a placebo.

Dr. Green also revealed that doctors themselves can function as placebos, and that their words have real power to heal, or to initiate self-healing in the body. Their words can also harm, in which case they function as what are called nocebos. Dr. Green shared a story in which a man was told he had metastasized cancer, leaving him a very short time to live. His one wish was to make it through the holidays, and he did so, dying soon after. A postmortem examination, however, found that he had been misdiagnosed; this man had never had a deadly cancer, merely benign cysts on his liver. It seems it was the man's belief in the doctor's diagnosis that sealed his fate.

Another area in which we see the boundary between mind and body blurred is the case of heart transplants, after which some recipients report changes that seemingly reflect the personalities of the donor. A provocative example can be found in Dr. Imants Barušs's book *Death as an Altered State of Consciousness: A Scientific Approach* (2023). In this case, we learn about a seven-month-old boy named Carter, who inherited the heart of a sixteen-month-old drowning victim named Gerry. When Carter was six years old, he was brought to meet Gerry's family. Carter approached Gerry's mother and rubbed his nose on her, which, she reported, was something her deceased son had regularly done. When Gerry's father, whom Carter had never met, appeared, the boy jumped into his lap, crying, "Daddy!" When Carter was asked why he had done this, he said he had not; Gerry had done it, he had just gone along with him.

Another intriguing story comes from Dr. Jacalyn Duffin, a hematologist, historian, and professor. In her book *Medical Miracles: Doctors, Saints, and Healing in the Modern World* (2009), she details work she conducted for the Vatican, investigating the veracity of an alleged miracle cure performed by a woman named Marguerite d'Youville in the early eighteenth century. The Vatican invited Dr. Duffin to examine some medical specimens related to the healing, taking care not to give her any information about the context. After careful study, Dr. Duffin determined that the healing had been real, and she could provide no medical explanation.

When Dr. Duffin, who is not religious, was asked if she had scientific explanations for the evidence of healing miracles claimed by the Vatican, she replied, "There are lots of things we can't explain, scientifically, and I have no problem whatsoever calling them miracles. But my definition of a miracle does not require it to have been worked by God."[12] On the basis of testimonies, including that of Dr. Duffin, Marguerite d'Youville was declared a saint in 1990. On a related note, research conducted by Tanya Luhrmann, a Stanford University–

based anthropologist, found that faith-based healings do happen. Luhrmann discovered that, in order for them to be effective, the patient needs both a good story and to be a good listener—to have the capacity to make what they imagine seem real to them. The ability to use our imagination this way, she said, is a skill that can be learned.[13]

SYNCHRONICITY

When my opa was diagnosed with terminal cancer, he chose to die at home, in hospice. Soon after he died, my family and I gathered around the dining room table, sharing a quiet lunch. I suddenly realized I was freezing. A look at the thermostat indicated that the heat was still turned on. When someone went down to the basement to investigate, it turned out the pilot light had been blown out. I wondered if this had ever happened before, and was told that no, as far as anyone knew, the pilot light had not gone out once in the fifty-plus years my grandparents had lived in that house. This strange and meaningful coincidence is what is called a synchronicity.

The concept of a synchronicity was developed by Carl Jung and physicist Wolfgang Pauli. They defined it as a coincidence that is meaningfully related in a way that suggests a deeper, underlying connection or pattern, but that seems to have no direct causal connection. Some scholars, such as religious studies professor Jeffrey J. Kripal, assert that synchronicities and other unusual or unexplainable phenomena often occur in situations involving danger or death. Going further, Diana Walsh Pasulka, a religious studies scholar and author of *American Cosmic: UFOs, Religion, Technology* (2019), observes:

> In every religious tradition and spiritual community I've
> studied, synchronicities or meaningful coincidences play

a significant role for practitioners. I call synchronicity "the engine" of religious and spiritual belief, because when practitioners describe these improbable events, they always credit them with supporting their beliefs. Philosopher Friedrich Nietzsche, an atheist, weighs in on this aspect of synchronicity by calling it the "greatest danger." He said that when human beings are confronted with the most amazing coincidences that defy their belief that life is random, they should be careful to not attribute these coincidences to a God or deity. Instead, he suggested we marvel at these spectacular displays of coincidence. I lean toward this view, but cannot help but think that synchronicities reveal aspects of our material world, and space/time, of which we are just beginning to understand.[14]

Some thinkers consider synchronicities emerging in your life to be a sign that you are "on the right path." In my experience, if you give them attention—whether you believe they are all in the mind or have some exterior meaning—they have the power to generate a sense of possibility and meaning in your own life.

One of the most powerful synchronicities I experienced had very direct real-world consequences. I was a graphic designer at the time, with a well-paid freelance job. It was reliable and did not take up too much time, providing me with both financial stability and time to travel and work on my own creative projects.

During an economic recession, the head designer left her post. Because jobs were scarce and the future unclear, I thought it might be wise to interview for the job. But I was very unsure. The idea of being there, day in and day out, chitchatting by the copy machine under harsh fluorescent lights, sounded deeply unfun. Still, practicality won over sentiment. I applied and was invited into the office for an interview.

Intensely conflicted, I asked for a sign of what I should do. And strangely, I got it, loud and clear. On the morning of the interview—all dressed up in my professional interview clothes, portfolio in hand—I walked confidently down the stairs to the front door of my building. When I tried to open the door, it would not budge. I tried and tried, but nothing I did made any difference. I was forced to call a locksmith; it turned out the lock had broken, which had never happened before (or since, as far as I know). I was forced to cancel the interview, and was wise enough to take that as the sign I was asking for. I ended up rescinding my application with apologies, explaining I thought I would make a better freelancer than a full-time employee.

I recently experienced a synchronicity that was directly related to the writing of this book. On the day of my first big deadline, I noticed a huge black butterfly fluttering high up against my window. It was so large—about five inches across—and flying so erratically that at first I thought it must be a small bird or a bat. When I went to eat lunch, it returned, alighting on the glass door, high above my head. When some workmen opened the door, it flew uncannily into the house, hovering around the ceiling for a moment, then flew back out.

When I went online to try to discover the identity of this mysterious creature, I discovered that it was a Majanás moth, which locals call *la mariposa de la muerte* or "butterfly of death." In central Mexico, they are known by a Nahuatl name, *mictlanpapalotl*, meaning "butterfly from the country of the dead." I had never seen one before, but I have seen many since, almost always while I was deeply engaged in the writing of this book.

The world is a big, mysterious place. Have you had your own synchronicities, or other experiences that have challenged our culture's ideas of what is possible? I'll bet you have. You'll have an opportunity to work with some below, and to interrogate how these might open up your sense of possibility for life, death, and the in-between.

EXERCISES

JOURNAL PROMPTS

1. **Received Ideas.** What ideas did you receive from your family or friends about what happens after death? Do your parents believe in God, or ghosts, or the survival of the soul after death? How about your community? Does your family believe in rewards or punishment after death, or maybe nothing at all? Or do you not know—was it simply not spoken of? Is it a subject you feel comfortable speaking about with your family?

2. **Woo-Woo or Magical Worldview Biography.** Write a sort of "alternative biography" in which you list everything that has ever happened in your life that supports a magical, spiritual, animistic, or woo-woo worldview. Add new examples as they occur. I maintain my list in an easy-to-find-and-edit digital file.

3. **Synchronicities.** A synchronicity—according to Carl Jung and Wolfgang Pauli, who coined the term and originated the concept— is a meaningful coincidence with no clear causal connection, or, in Jung's words, a "meaningful coincidence of two or more events where something other than the probability of chance is involved."[15] One example most of us have experienced is when we find ourselves thinking of someone, and the phone rings, and there they are! Have you experienced any synchronicities? If so, note them. Continue to notice them as they happen, and add

them, along with any you remember from the past, to your Woo-Woo or Magical Worldview Biography.

4. **Thought Experiment: Family Choice.** My stepmother, Judy Ebenstein, is a tarot reader who is open to the idea that we might choose when and where to incarnate. Here is a fun thought experiment: What if this were literally true? Why might you have chosen your particular family? This particular era? The place you grew up? This can be particularly useful if you have a complicated relationship with your family, offering a different—and more positive—perspective.

5. **After Life.** Free-write (described on page 15) on the topic of what happens after death. Let your imagination take the lead here, and be fanciful and fun; just write, with as little thinking as possible, and see where it takes you. Is there a psychopomp to lead you to the next destination? Is there a space of judgment or welcome, punishment and reward? Are you reborn into another form? Is there a liminal, in-between state? Is there a divinity of any sort? Added bonus: Try a meditation or relaxation technique from addendum three, page 243, before beginning.

6. **Fairy Tale.** Write a fairy tale or short story exploring your own afterdeath experience or that of a fictional character. Added bonus: To bypass the rational mind, begin with a meditation or relaxation technique from addendum three, page 243.

7. **Dream Afterlife.** If you were the king or queen of the world, what would happen after people died? Would there be an afterlife experience? What would it look like? What deities would oversee these realms, and what guides would take you there? How would knowledge of this afterlife realm make people feel about death?

8. **Dreams and Death.** Many people report what are called visitation dreams, in which dead loved ones seemingly pay a visit. They

say these dreams have a noticeably different feel than normal ones, feeling like a real experience, and that they are often experienced as special gifts, bringing feelings of love, connection, and gratitude. Jung and some of his followers believed these to be different kinds of dreams than ordinary ones. Have you had any such dreams? What did you think at the time? Did the experience change you? Did you talk to anyone about it? For guidelines on going deeper with those dreams, see appendix four, page 246.

9. **Thought Experiment: Indigenous Realities.** Given what science is beginning to suggest, what if Indigenous ideas of an inspirited world, where we live on after death, were actually and literally true? What might that feel like? How would our conceptions of the world be different? How would we think about death? How might the sciences have developed differently? What would our relationships be like? Our political and justice systems? Would people be happier?

ACTIVITIES

1. **Afterdeath Traditions.** Until the past two hundred or so years, most people believed in a soul that survived death and had a particular afterdeath fate. Do some research about what your ancestors would have believed about death, the soul, and the afterlife experience.

2. **Death Is Not the End?** Read a rigorous, well-researched book that challenges a scientific materialist approach to death. I highly recommend *Death as an Altered State of Consciousness: A Scientific Approach* (2023) by Dr. Imants Barušs and *Consciousness Unbound: Liberating Mind from the Tyranny of Materialism* (2023), edited by Edward F. Kelly and Paul Marshall.

3. **Explore NDEs.** Read a credible book about near-death experiences, such as Dr. Elisabeth Kübler-Ross's *On Life after Death* (1984) or Dr. Raymond Moody's *Life after Life* (1975). You might also look up Carl Jung's account of a near-death experience in his book *Memories, Dreams, Reflections* (1962).

4. **Explore Past-Life Memories.** Read a credible book about the scientific study of past-life memories, such as Dr. Jim B. Tucker's *Life before Life* (2005).

5. **Scientific Studies of Life after Death.** Visit websites of credible groups doing research on life after death. I would suggest the University of Virginia School of Medicine's Division of Perceptual Studies (med.virginia.edu/perceptual-studies/) and the Windbridge Research Center (windbridge.org), both of which make available videos, articles, podcasts, and other resources.

6. **Explore Psychopomps.** Psychopomps are figures who guide the souls of the dead to their next destination. Shamans and divine beings—such as Hermes and the archangel Michael—might act as psychopomps. They were also seen to take the form of animals, including horses, crows, and dogs. Research psychopomps in your own cultural traditions or that of another culture that draws you; maybe even invent your own!

7. **Make Your Own Kokdu Doll.** While visiting Seoul, South Korea, I learned about *kokdu* dolls, which are painted wooden figures depicting otherworldly creatures meant to accompany the deceased on their journey through the afterlife. They would be placed on the ornate traditional funeral biers that carried the dead to their final resting places. Some kokdu figures were meant to act as guides, others as protectors; some were even entertainers. I invite you to conceptualize and create your own creature to

aid you in your post-life experience. What kind of helper would you most appreciate? What skills would they have? What sort of help would they offer? What kind of personality? What would they look like? The final piece could take the form of a drawing, a sculpture, a piece of writing, or any other medium that feels right. Added bonus: Look up kokdu dolls on the internet!

8. **Child Mind/Beginner Mind.** What were you interested in as a child? If you were anything like me, you were fascinated by the mysteries of this world—what happens after death, the possibility of ESP. If so, return to some of those interests, with an open, childlike mind, remembering that despite appearances to the contrary, what happens after we die continues to be a mystery.

9. **Altered State of Consciousness.** All of our brains are capable of many modalities, some of them mystic or visionary. Explore a safe, accessible activity that engages other aspects of your consciousness, such as a shamanic journey; you will find guidelines in addendum thirteen, page 261. You might also try prayer, chanting, rhythmic dance, breathwork, or an active imagination; for more on the latter, see addendum twelve, page 260.

10. **Resonance Check.** Did any material in this chapter particularly resonate for you? Is there something that piqued your interest? I invite you to keep track of the things that spoke to you in a special place in your journal. I also encourage you to go further, to do more research on anything that you felt excited about. If you are a visual person, collect images related to things that interest you. Start a folder of these images or create a Pinterest board.

11. **Check In.** What were the biggest surprises this week? Did you learn something new about yourself? Make notes in your journal.

6

LOVE AND DEATH

MOURNING THOSE WE'VE LOST

I was very close with my oma. A deeply curious and adventurous woman, she had studied to be a doctor, but was never able to practice because she was forced to flee Nazi-controlled Vienna before her final exams. She was a lover of art and culture, an excellent host, and made a mean martini.

My oma was also my special friend in the family, the one who best understood me and accepted me for who I was, without judgment. When she died at ninety-four, at the end of a long, relatively healthy and contented life, I cried. She was cremated, and we scattered her ashes. And that was that; I got back to my busy life and never really thought much about it.

A few years later, when I spent a month in Seoul, South Korea, as part of an artist's residency, some of the feelings I had around my oma's death resurfaced. The aim of this program was to take artists

Grief can be the garden of compassion. If you keep your heart open through everything, your pain can become your greatest ally in your life's search for love and wisdom.

—RUMI, PERSIAN POET AND SUFI MYSTIC

out of their comfort zones—not in order to make art, but rather to provide room for life experience outside the world of art production. For me, the experience was much more profound.

Being alone in a deeply unfamiliar locale with an impenetrable visual and spoken language for an entire unstructured month left me alone with my thoughts in a way I had never experienced in my adult life. One of the things that spontaneously emerged for me in that quiet, lonely place were tears I had not yet shed for my grandmother. In my solitude, I spontaneously mourned her. I had no intention of doing so; it just happened.

Her husband, my opa, had died a few years before her. He was the kind of small-town doctor who delivered babies, ushered people to their deaths, and treated everything in between. He made house calls and rarely went on vacation, worried a patient might need him while he was away. When he discovered, in his late eighties, that he had cancer, he opted not to be treated; when his sickness progressed, he chose to die at home with the support of hospice. After he died, the family shared a quiet meal, after which we attended a traditional memorial service for him at a local funeral home. Members of my family stood up and said a few words about him. We cried a bit.

His service was . . . *OK*. It was better than nothing—a kind of, sort of useful act of closure. But it left me wanting.

Such half-hearted memorial practices are the common lot for

most of us in the industrialized West, but this was not always the case. As recently as the 1880s, memorials were often much more lavish and involved affairs, with horse-drawn hearses shimmering with black ostrich plumes, wailing mourners, and tolling church bells. Some funerals would even hire professional mourners, or keeners, whose job it was to cry for the dead; their tears helped others weep, providing catharsis for the community. Over the course of this chapter, we will look at different mourning and grieving practices, and the forms of containment that allow us to fully express them.

LOVE AND LOSS

When we lose something we love—be that a loved one, a home, or a job—we suffer. These losses are an inevitable part of the human experience. To love and to lose is an inescapable part of life. Losing someone you love to death is arguably the greatest of these losses.

My favorite Buddhist parable addresses the inevitability—and gifts—of this universal experience. It tells of a woman whose only child, a young boy, died suddenly. The mother's grief was so profound and enduring that people began to worry she was losing her mind. An old man suggested that she go to the Buddha to ask for help. So she went to him, asking him if he could relieve her suffering and bring her son back to life. The Buddha replied that he would be delighted to do so! But first, she must do just one little thing: bring him a single mustard seed from a household that had not been touched by death.

When you are sorrowful look again in your heart, and you shall see that in truth you are weeping for that which has been your delight.

—KHALIL GIBRAN, LEBANESE AMERICAN ARTIST, POET, AND WRITER

The woman went from house to house in her village, and she

found that, while each of them was happy to provide her with a mustard seed—a common ingredient in Indian cooking—there was not a single household that had not experienced a death. Her visceral realization that no one is spared from death cut through her debilitating grief. She made her way back to the Buddha, where she became his student and ultimately attained enlightenment.

This story illustrates the fact that the grief we feel when we lose someone we love is the common lot of humanity; it is, in fact, a byproduct of love itself. It also suggests that *understanding* this opens us up to the possibility of compassion and enlightenment. As humans, it is our nature to long for things to stay the same; for our loved ones to live forever, our relationships to continue as they are, our youth to endure. When we lose the things we love, we suffer. It's no wonder that the core principles of Buddhism proclaim that the nature of life is impermanence, and that the condition of attachment is a major cause of suffering.

GRIEF

To love and to lose is to grieve. To love that which is impermanent, that which can be lost, is, by its very nature, to make oneself vulnerable to grief. The more deeply we love, the more vulnerable we are to the commensurate pain of loss.

In his book *The Smell of Rain on Dust: Grief and Praise* (2015), author and educator Martín Prechtel—who was raised on a Pueblo reservation and later became an initiated member of the Tzutuhil Maya community—turns a keen outsider's eye to contemporary affluent American culture. From his perspective, this is a culture that has been taught neither how to grieve nor how to praise, one being the flip side of the other.

From the Tzutuhil Maya perspective, he explains, if you are unable to *properly* grieve that which you have loved and lost—and by "properly" he means, in his words, "where you look bad when you're done"[1]—the natural flow of grief can solidify into depression or even physical illness. If you cannot in some way express (literally, "to press out") your grief, you endanger your mental and physical health.

Prechtel goes on to address the despair he sees in the United States. He poignantly notes, "When you have two centuries of people who have not properly grieved the things that they have lost, the grief shows up as ghosts that inhabit their grandchildren." These ghosts, he says, can take the form of disease, even hardening into tumors, which the Maya see as "solidified tears," or manifest as psychological issues, including addiction and depression. He notes that one needs cultural support to mourn well, and that his own Indigenous communities offer the support necessary for the bereaved to completely lose themselves in their grief. Such support is essential to mourning properly, and, as he points out, the United States provides no such container.

Echoing Prechtel's observations is a statement commonly attributed to Sigmund Freud, which proclaims that "unexpressed emotions will never die. They are buried alive and will come forth later in uglier ways."[2] Contemporary science also affirms these ideas. Emotional stress, particularly that resulting from blocked emotions, has been linked not only to mental illness, but also to physical problems including heart disease, intestinal problems, headaches, insomnia, and autoimmune disorders.[3]

The words of Austin Eubanks, a survivor of the notorious Columbine school shooting of 1999, also echo Prechtel's reflections. During this terrifying mass shooting, a seventeen-year-old Eubanks hid under a table in the school library with his best friend. He was shot and forced to watch his best friend die of gunshot wounds before his eyes, all the while having to stay silent to save his own life.

Later in life, Eubanks became a passionate advocate for the proper expression of grief. In his opinion, the opioid addiction crisis in the United States is, at least in part, the legacy of unacknowledged or numbed-out grief. In many articles and a TEDx Talk, he spoke of his own journey from avoiding his pain to leaning into it, leading to, as he put it, "post traumatic growth." He himself struggled with an opioid addiction—the result of a painkiller prescribed after the shooting—and ultimately died of an overdose.

Our experiences of grief often stem from intense personal experience, but it is important to note that grief can also be collective. We are living through a time of deep uncertainty, with a future that is far from clear. The news is rife with stories of cruelty, violent death, and human misery, and we are enduring a very real threat to much of what we love as we observe the unfolding effects of the climate crisis. Many of us are also more keenly aware of the injustices enacted by our hierarchal and patriarchal culture, and more conscious of the brutal legacies of colonization, genocide, and slavery upon which the wealth and plenty of our great nations were built. Indeed, there is much to grieve.

The connections we make in the course of a life—maybe that's what heaven is.

—MISTER ROGERS (AKA FRED ROGERS), AMERICAN TELEVISION HOST, AUTHOR, AND PRESBYTERIAN MINISTER

At the same time, we have inherited the legacy of a culture that has, for several generations, provided no language for—nor satisfying rituals around—death, loss, or grieving. This cumulative, undealt-with trauma is passed down, some scholars believe, through what is called ancestral grief, also known as ancestral trauma, generational trauma, or intergenerational trauma. They define this as the ways in which the trauma experienced by our forebears can continue to have a negative impact on their descendants, undermining their mental and emotional well-being in various ways.

Recent scientific studies suggest that ancestral trauma might be not only a cultural phenomenon, but also a *biological* one. Research suggests that the trauma experienced by our ancestors can be passed down biologically, via our genes, for several generations. In one experiment, mice were trained via electric shocks to fear the scent of cherry blossoms. Their offspring *and* their offspring's offspring had this same fear, despite never having experienced the electric shocks.

THE TREASURES OF GRIEF

Karen Montgomery is an artist in the Morbid Anatomy community. At the time this book went to press, she was caring for her father, who had been diagnosed with progressive supranuclear palsy (PSP). The progression of the disease, in Karen's words, has been "heartbreaking and cruel." As the disease intensifies, her father will be unable to walk and will lose his ability to see and speak. He was given a five-to-ten-year prognosis; when I spoke to Karen, he was in year six.

Karen shared with me that even in the midst of this very challenging situation, she was able to find treasures. When I asked her what these treasures might be, she said she had been surprised to find that she is able to feel joy, to laugh heartily, and to have fun. She also reports moments of deep gratitude, a "peace and acceptance" of her father's disease. She adds that her beliefs about what happens after we die have opened up, and that she finds comfort in the fact that we all will experience death.

She also told me that she's noticed a deepening of her creativity, and finds herself filled with ideas for new sculptures inspired by grief, family legacy, and consciousness. She notes that grief heightened her senses, and she has "many moments of feeling very alive with an awakened heart." She told me she had been brought to tears by "the kindness of a stranger, overhearing a loving conversation between a mother and child, a friendly coffee barista, a caring neighbor, a man petting his dog."

When I asked what she feels she has gained from the experience, she said that she has developed a hard-won confidence that she has the strength to get through long and painful days. She also said, "I have learned that this depth of grief helps express the huge feelings and love I have for my dad. When the burning waves of grief pass, my heart feels a sense of purification that makes room for tenderness and innocence."

Karen's observations about the gifts of grief make me think of *kintsugi*, a Japanese art form devoted to the repair of broken pottery. Rather than repairing these objects to make it seem as if they had never been broken, the wound is *celebrated* by binding the pieces back together with a glue mixed with gold, silver, or platinum, so that its fragments are held together by seams of gleaming precious metal. The final piece is all the more beautiful—strong, idiosyncratic, and unique—for its traumatic history than it was in its previous, unshattered state.

For me, this metaphor of cherishing rather than disguising the cracks is a wonderful one for looking at the concept of grief as a gift. It provides a vision of a self whose wounds never completely disappear, but instead become a celebrated and essential part of who we are. Expressing a similar sentiment in the thirteenth century, the Sufi teacher, philosopher, and poet Rumi said, "The wound is the place where the light enters you." Rumi speaks to the truth, recognized by many spiritual traditions, that it is precisely our places of pain, wounding, and vulnerability that allow in the grace that can engender transformation.

GRIEF AND LOSS IN NONHUMAN ANIMALS

Research suggests that our experience of grief links us not only to our fellow humans, but also to other members of the animal kingdom. Many observers have reported seeing elephants visit and stroke the bones of their dead, sometimes even rocking back and forth in what looked like a "vigil."[4] Scientist Cynthia Moss, who studies elephants in Kenya, has even witnessed elephants covering the bodies of their dead with leaves and branches and watching over their bodies.[5]

Another story comes from naturalist Jane Goodall, who tells of a chimpanzee she called Flint. After his mother died, the young chimpanzee stopped eating and interacting with the community. Eventually he died of what seemed to her like a broken heart. There are other suggestive stories, such as a group of dolphins that slowed down to accompany a mother dolphin carrying a dead calf, and a group of giraffes holding what seemed to be a vigil for a dead infant. In recent years, an orca mother made international news after she was observed carrying her dead calf for seventeen days.[6]

One of the most famous stories of animal grieving was that of Koko (1971–2018), a famous gorilla who was taught sign language, allowing her to communicate her inner world in a way humans could clearly understand. Koko had a beloved pet kitten that died, after which, for a few days, she whimpered sadly and signed about death. Later, when a gorilla companion died, she did not smile for six months. It took a visit from comedian Robin Williams to cheer her up; they had a strong bond, and Williams often spoke about how touched he was by their time together. When Koko learned of Williams's death by suicide in 2014, she signed "cry lip" and bowed her head, with a quivering lip.[7]

DEATH RITES

Mourning and honoring the dead is an important part of all known human cultures. One of the earliest known human burials, created around seventy-eight thousand years ago by Stone Age hunter-gatherers, contains the remains of a child interred in the fetal position. Its head was placed on a pillow and its body wrapped in a shroud, suggesting that death rituals stretch back at least that far, probably even longer.[8]

Cultures around the world have developed a variety of practices that are instrumental in helping survivors transition into a world without their loved one. These rituals often provide those in mourning with a formal, delineated time of withdrawing from the world in order to process their grief and loss. These rites also signify their loss to the community, who can then assist them during this challenging and difficult time.

One of the best known of these is the Jewish tradition of sitting shiva. For a period of time after a death—as long as seven days, *shiva* meaning "seven" in Hebrew—the family is meant to sit together in the home, un-showered and unshaven, on low seats, symbolic of being brought low by grief. Mirrors are sometimes covered to show that this is not a time for vanity. It is also a time when working, sexual relations, and study of the Torah are forbidden. Friends, family, and community members visit to bring food for the bereaved and share stories about the dead. They might also join the nightly mourner's kaddish, a prayer recited in honor of the deceased. It is traditional to mark the end of official mourning by going for a walk with a friend or family member to symbolize their return to the regular world. A related Jewish tradition is the yahrzeit (or yahrtzeit) candle, a special twenty-four-hour candle lit in honor of the dead. These can be burned while sitting shiva, or lit in the home, in the synagogue, or near the grave to commemorate the death anniversary.

What we have once enjoyed we can never lose. . . . All that we love deeply becomes a part of us.

—HELEN KELLER, AMERICAN AUTHOR, EDUCATOR, AND HUMANITARIAN

In Buddhist traditions—in which death is seen as a part of the natural cycles of birth, life, death, and rebirth—mourning rites begin with a visitation in a temple or funeral home. There, one will usually find an altar with a figure of the Buddha, along with candles, incense, fruit, and flowers, and perhaps a portrait of the deceased.[9] The body is generally presented in an open casket, and people are given time to say their goodbyes. The deceased is honored for a certain number of days after death, thought to be the amount of time the soul is in transition before reaching its next destination. In Japanese Buddhism, there is also the tradition of *choji*, a sort of eulogy that encourages people to express things they were unable to express to the loved one while still alive. This might include sentiments of gratitude and love, as well as difficulties one had with the person.

The Christian religion has a tradition called the vigil (literally, "wakefulness"), or wake. This is a period of time after death and before burial when people gather with the body of the deceased to say prayers, light candles, and share memories. Commonly, there will also be a memorial service, where friends, family, and community members can pay their final respects, often with a view of the corpse in an open casket.

There is also an archaic Christian tradition called "telling the bees," which traces back to the ancient Celts. When someone died, a member of the family would share the news with the beehive, sometimes even draping it with black cloth. If one failed to "put the bees into mourning," it was thought you might invite death to visit again. It is interesting to note that this tradition continues to the present day; when Queen Elizabeth II died in September 2022, it was reported that the royal beekeeper paid a special visit to inform the palace bees.[10]

VICTORIAN MOURNING, OR THE CULT OF THE DEAD

In 1861, Prince Albert, the beloved husband of Britain's Queen Victoria, died of typhoid fever at the age of forty-two. Devastated, the queen entered into a state of deep mourning, from which she never emerged. She maintained his room exactly as it had been at the time of his death, and wore nothing but black until her own death nearly forty years later. At a time when royalty set the fashions for the Western world, the queen's display of grief was widely imitated, leading to a lively industry of fashionable mourning for women, complete with guidelines on how—and for what length of time—to mourn different relations.

The popularity of public mourning at this time led to the establishment of vast "mourning emporiums." They sold cloth for making mourning dresses in black, gray, and purple—the only colors appropriate to wear in that state—along with black veils, gloves, and parasols. To convey one's state of grief to the community, one could also purchase mourning jewelry, featuring symbols such as urns, clasped hands, and weeping willows; black ribbons for marking the home; and black-bordered stationery for correspondence.

The Victorians also commemorated their dead loved ones through what are called postmortem or memorial photographs, which were photographic portraits taken of the deceased. The wealthy classes had long commissioned painted portraits of the dead, and the new technology of photography made capturing the likeness of a loved one much easier and more affordable. Because it was common for children to die young, these memorial photos were often the only photo a family would have of the deceased. Typically, the deceased would be posed in bed, on a couch, or in a coffin as if in a gentle and beautiful repose, a style referred to as "sleeping beauties." These photos might then be framed and hung on walls, kept in lockets, or added to the family photo album.

Another Victorian craft related to mourning is called "hairwork." Here, the hair of the dead beloved (or sometimes someone still alive) was used to make cherished keepsakes. This could take the form of jewelry, in which the hair might be artistically arranged and set into a locket or brooch. Sometimes the hair would even be woven or braided into the form of bracelets and necklaces. Others used hair to create large flowery wreaths set in shadow boxes. Hair might even be macerated and mixed with a medium that would then be used to paint melancholic mourning scenes. Popular nineteenth-century women's magazines, such as *Godey's Lady's Book*, provided detailed instructions for how to make these pieces, and they were a common and encouraged pastime for mourning women.[11]

My friend Karen Bachmann teaches the art of Victorian hairwork for us at Morbid Anatomy. To learn the craft, she spent years studying

WHAT HAPPENED TO VICTORIAN MOURNING?

The elaborate mourning made famous by the Victorians came to an end in the early twentieth century. With the mass casualties of World War I (1914–18) and the influenza epidemic (1918–20), there were simply too many lost loved ones to mourn in the old ways. Women, the chief mourners and memorializers, were drawn into the workforce to make up for lost male workers, leaving them with much less time for such activities.

These upheavals and the disillusionment caused by World War I—as well as the birth of consumer capitalism as we now know it—led to massive societal shifts, which we can now identify as the birth pangs of our own era. The early twentieth century also saw the beginning of the generation gap as young people rejected the traditions and values of their parents and grandparents, striving to create new ways of living, thinking, dressing, and expressing themselves.

Many of us now regard Victorian mourning as morbid: a morose and unhealthy obsession with death and loss. This sort of prolonged and rarefied grief is no longer seen as a beautiful expression of love but as a sign that something is wrong. Those mourning a lost loved one too robustly today might be prescribed drugs such as escitalopram (Lexapro), fluoxetine (Prozac, Sarafem, Symbyax), paroxetine (Paxil), and sertraline (Zoloft) to get the mourner back on their feet and back in the workforce. This cultural trend has helped support a multibillion-dollar pharmaceutical industry.

old women's magazines and antique hair art pieces. She even made a pilgrimage to Våmhus, Sweden, a town where the practice continues today. Karen sees these works as personal relics constructed with the non-decaying part of the body most associated with our personality and individuality—our hair.

When I tried to make such a piece in one of Karen's classes, I was deeply struck by how *meditative* the process of transforming human hair into an artwork is. Hair as a medium is very finicky, and to work with it one must move very slowly and deliberately. As I spent hours trying to give artistic form to hair sourced from a local wig shop, I mused on what this experience might have been like if I were instead working with the hair of a dead loved one. It seemed to me that it must have been the *practice* of making hairwork—the slow, repetitive task of focusing on the person you had lost—as much as the final piece that was the key to the art form's popularity. I was struck by what a beautiful, gentle, and contemplative way this was to mourn, to pour your love and sorrow into a focused activity of remembrance, using a precious part of your loved one that would remain forever. Both the process and the final pieces are true arts of bereavement.

MEMORIALS TO THE DEAD

The long-standing importance of honoring our ancestors is made evident by the fact that some of our most lavish and revered monuments were constructed to commemorate the dead. The time, effort, and resources necessary to create such marvels speak eloquently to how important this practice has been for millennia and all over the world. In ancient Egypt, the iconic Great Pyramid of Giza (2589 BCE) was created to serve as a burial vault for the mummies of King Khufu and his wife, Henutsen. It also housed grave goods (now lost) meant to aid them in the afterlife. In Xi'an, China, there is the Terracotta Army, a collection of over eight thousand life-size statues of soldiers along with their horses and chariots. This impressive collection can still be visited in the necropolis—Greek for city of the dead—of China's first emperor, Qin Shi Huang (259–210 BCE). In India, the Taj Mahal was created as a mausoleum to memorialize and house the remains of Mumtaz Ma-hal, the favorite wife of the emperor Shah Jahan (1592 –1666). A dark legend purports that the emperor gouged out the eyes and chopped off the hands of its makers to ensure no structure could ever compete with it. More recent memorials include, in the United States, the Washing-ton Monument and the Lincoln Memorial, commemorating the great founding fathers (or ancestors) of the American republic. Another is Lenin's Mausoleum in Saint Petersburg, Russia, a place of pilgrimage that houses the Russian leader's preserved corpse as its centerpiece.

In 2009, I spent a week photographing urban memorials in Phil-adelphia as part of a university research project. These community interventions are a poignant and common sight in many of the impov-erished and disenfranchised neighborhoods of the United States. Of-ten populated by people of color, they are places where early, violent, and unpredictable death is, sadly, not uncommon.

While exploring these neighborhoods, I came across many touching, large-scale memorials taking the form of wall-size murals featuring portraits of the deceased along with artful text about the individual. I also saw a number of heartfelt memorial shrines that marked the place where a loved one had died. Here, mourners had left behind notes and cards for the deceased, along with photographs, flowers, and lit candles. When the memorial commemorated a child, you would also see colorful balloons, toys, and stuffed animals. Simi-lar shrines—expressions of deeply felt mourning and loss—emerged to commemorate victims of police brutality as part of the Black Lives

Matter movement. Celebrity shrines also spontaneously appear around the world when we lose people who have touched many lives, such as Princess Diana, Heath Ledger, and David Bowie.

Most readers will also be familiar with roadside memorials created in honor of those who died in vehicular accidents at the site of their death. They are often decorated with flowers, candles, photographs, religious symbols, and sometimes the personal belongings of the lost loved one(s). A similar, recently established grassroots memorial tradition is that of the ghost bike. Monuments to individuals killed in cycling accidents, they take the form of white bicycles installed at or near the death sites, which are then augmented by flowers, photographs, messages, and other personal mementos. They are intended not just to memorialize the victim, but also to advocate for safer roads for cyclists and pedestrians.

Another common way to memorialize a dead loved one is to commission a tattoo in their honor. Called memorial, remembrance, or tribute tattoos, these serve as a meaningful way to carry the memory of the deceased permanently on the body. Such a tattoo might take the form of a portrait and/or the name of the lost individual. It might also incorporate symbols, images, quotations, or dates that were meaningful to the deceased. The pain of the tattooing process might also be a cathartic factor in mourning, a way to externalize internal pain and enact a meaningful sacrifice in honor of the beloved.

One of the most moving recent memorial projects I have encountered is the AIDS Memorial Quilt. This project, developed by human rights activist Cleve Jones, was initiated in 1985 to memorialize the millions lost to the disease caused by the HIV virus since it began decimating the San Francisco gay population in 1981. The quilt is constructed from panels sent in by individuals or groups in honor of their dead loved ones. Currently considered the largest piece of folk art in existence, it extends 1.2 million square feet and comprises almost 50,000 panels commemorating over 110,000 individuals. What I find so poignant about this particular project is that the people we see so lovingly and creatively memorialized are the very same people who, at the height of the crisis, many wished to ignore and forget.

Another deeply touching memorial is the "garden of unborn children" at Tokyo's Zojoji temple. Here, one finds neat rows of Jizo statues, which are small stone figures meant to stand in for the unborn, including those lost to stillbirth, miscarriage, or abortion. People decorate the figures and leave toys and other offerings, both to assist the grieving process and to help the souls of the deceased move into the afterlife. Occupying similar territory are *omokage bina*, which are mourning aids in the form of dolls, laboriously crafted to resemble beloved individuals who were lost in the deadly Tohoku earthquake and tsunami of 2011.[12] In the US, sculptor Jennifer Stocks-Dearborn creates similar, hyperreal pieces out of clay for those who have lost babies; she began doing so after her own daughter died of SIDS in 2000.[13]

The contemporary memorial tradition that I find most exciting and inspiring is the Temple at Burning Man. Burning Man is a secular festival that takes place annually in the Nevada desert. It attracts artists, makers, entrepreneurs, and freethinkers who create a temporary city filled with lavishly realized structures and artworks, all of which are ceremonially destroyed at the end of the gathering. In 2000, a structure called the Temple was erected in memory of a friend who had recently died in a motorcycle accident. Other participants began to leave notes and objects to commemorate their own lost loved ones. It was so well received—so *necessary*, you might say—that it has been a central and beloved part of Burning Man ever since.

On the final night of Burning Man, this memorial monument is sacrificed in what is called the "Temple burn." This is intended to be a cathartic community ritual that symbolizes letting go, release, and closure. I see in the Temple a new, spontaneously formed, vital, and meaningful death ritual. A wonderful and hopeful intervention, the Temple offers a contained space where people can engage with death, loss, and mourning. Here, they can ritualize and express their grief in a way that is deeply meaningful, both personal and collective, and outside the confines of established religious belief.

EXERCISES

JOURNAL PROMPTS

1. **Family Grief.** How did your family express grief? Was it hidden? Shared? Denied? Shamed? Transmuted into another, more acceptable emotion? How do you express grief now? Is there a way you wish you had expressed or could express grief?

2. **Grief in Your Life.** Have you mourned the loss of something in your life—a person, a job, a relationship, a dream? Write about one or more of the most impactful experiences. Do you feel you grieved that which you lost properly? If not, is there something you can do to remedy that? Perhaps enact a ritual (see addendum six, page 248). You might also consider designing a monument, making a pilgrimage to a place special to your lost loved one, creating an artwork, or writing about the experience.

3. **The Treasures of Grief.** Have you experienced grief? Did the experience bring you any unexpected gifts? If so, write about your experience and how you would characterize those gifts.

4. **In Honor of the Dead.** In the movie *Coco*, the protagonist visits the land of the dead, where he meets a number of family members who died before he was born. They are loving but complicated, neither all good nor all bad; to me, they feel like honest portraits of real humans, foibles and all. Write about someone you loved and lost, in such a way that it includes their foibles, doing the dead justice by portraying them as they really were, in all their complicated, paradoxical humanity. This could take the form of a drawing, a poem, a short story, or a eulogy or obituary.

5. **Ancestral Grief.** Is there anything that was very traumatic in your family line? For me, it would be the Holocaust. For you, it might take the form of abuse, addiction, social injustice . . . Write about any ancestral grief you can identify. Where did it come from? Is it still alive? Is there something you can do to express or resolve it so it does not get passed down to another generation? If this prompt resonates with you, I highly recommend reading *The Body Keeps the Score: Brain, Mind, and Body in the Healing of Trauma* (2015) by Bessel van der Kolk and/or *It Didn't Start with You: How Inherited Family Trauma Shapes Who We Are and How to End the Cycle* (2016) by Mark Wolynn to explore these ideas further.

6. **Mourning Rituals from Your Own Culture.** Research mourning rituals from your own religious or cultural ancestry or a culture that has fascinated you. Imagine how you might think about death differently if you had been brought up in such a culture.

7. **Burial and Memorial Traditions.** Look into a burial or memorial tradition that comes from your family tree, or simply one that interests you. What speaks to you about this tradition? How does it open up your ideas about grieving and loss?

ACTIVITIES

1. **Grief and Love.** Listen to First Nations author and educator Martín Prechtel's lecture "Grief and Praise" on YouTube, or read his book *The Smell of Rain on Dust* (2015, discussed on page 92), in which he discusses the links between grief and love. Write about your response to it.

2. **Memorial Portraiture.** Photographs of the dead were very popular during the Victorian era. Today, with the ubiquity of camera phones, they are making a comeback. If you lose someone you love, consider taking a photo of them after death, or creating a postmortem portrait of them.

3. **Make a Home Memorial.** In Puebla, Mexico, I found, at the local flea market, memorial objects created for the home. Taking the form of carved wooden crosses about a foot high, they included the name of the deceased and the dates they had lived along with religious imagery and decorative flourishes. I invite you to create your own memorial object to someone or something you have lost. As you plan your object, think of the colors, symbols, and kind of imagery that would be meaningful to the deceased. Make it a proper craft project. It can take any form that seems right. Have fun!

4. **Express Your Grief.** Columbine survivor Austin Eubanks had practical advice for working with grief: he urged people to take an inner inventory of the grief they are holding and express it in some way. This could be as simple as calling a friend, talking to a therapist, or even speaking your truth to a stranger. If you have some unexpressed grief, consider finding a way to get it out of your system.

5. **Fantasy Memorial Service.** Plan the perfect memorial service that would express and celebrate someone—or something—you've lost. Plan the music, readings, location, guest list, and so on. This can stay in the realm of fantasy, or you could put it into

action. This can be done even if the loss is abstract or happened long ago.

6. **Memorial Tattoos.** Design (and perhaps even execute!) a tattoo in honor of someone or something you've lost. If this is commemorating a person, it could draw on something that was important to them, something the two of you had in common, their name, portrait, a date, a relevant symbol, or whatever feels like it expresses something you love about them.

7. **Try Your Hand at Hairwork.** Make something out of the hair of someone you love, dead or alive. It could be as simple as some hair in a locket, or worked into a larger artwork.

8. **Let Go of Grief.** In *A Healing Touch: True Stories of Life, Death, and Hospice* (2008), edited by Richard Russo, Susan Sterling writes, "Our fast-paced American culture isn't kind to those who mourn. You have the funeral, flowers, a flurry of letters, and then—slam bang—you're expected to get on with your life as if nothing has changed. But this isn't how grief works . . . grief takes work, attention, and time, but that sorrow can be eased by sharing your loss with others and by creating meaningful rituals."[14] If you are mourning something or someone, can you create boundaries that allow you to take the time you need to process the experience? Is there someone you trust with whom you can share your feelings? You might also consider creating your own ritual; see addendum six, page 248, for guidelines.

9. **Shed a Tear.** Crying is therapeutic. If this is hard for you (as it is for me), watch a movie (in a private place) that never fails to make you cry and just let yourself go. You might also consider drawing or free-writing as you do so. For me, *Charlotte's Web* (1973), *The Royal Tenenbaums* (2001), and *The Black Stallion* (1979) always do the trick.

10. **Feel the Music.** Play a song that expresses an emotion that you feel might be stopped up in you—anger, sadness, regret—and dance it out. You might also, while listening to the song, either free-write or make a mandala (for instructions, see addendum three, page 243). You could also simply use clay, crayons, or paints to sculpt, draw, or paint your emotions. Follow your intuition and allow yourself to be as free as possible.

11. **A Solitary Journey.** Plan and execute a trip for yourself completely alone, for a weekend or more; I have found that space creates an impetus to spontaneous mourning.

12. **Museum in a Box.** Make a "museum in a box" or shoebox diorama that expresses the personality of your lost loved one, perhaps even using objects they left behind.

13. **Time to Mourn.** Create a mourning schedule, with special rituals to mark important anniversaries. Look to other traditions or your family heritage for ideas. If you have created an altar, you might consider activating it for this purpose.

14. **Grief as a Door.** A poem by Jungian analyst and *cantadora* Clarissa Pinkola Estés called "Abre la Puerta! Open the Door!" speaks eloquently of the gifts of death and grief. If you would like to explore this idea further, listen to her read the poem as part of her audiobook *Theatre of the Imagination, Volume One* (2005), or look it up on the internet.[15]

15. **Send a Note.** One way to mourn the loss of someone less is to feel that you have fully appreciated them before they die. If you have any thoughts of love or appreciation you would like to share with someone, call them or write them a letter (or email) and send it.

16. **Acts of Devotion.** Visit a house of worship that appeals to you and light a candle, say a prayer, or leave an offering in honor of your dead loved one. You do not need to be a practitioner of this religion

for it to be effective; in my experience, such places can help us focus our energy and emotions. This can also be done in a place in nature, or another place that has meaning for you. You might also, if it is within your means, consider visiting Burning Man and leaving a photo or symbol of your loved one, with a note, in the Temple.

17. **Together for the Holidays.** Make Christmas tree or holiday ornaments using drawings or photos of your lost loved ones, so they can celebrate with you.

18. **Capture Memories.** Work with a parent or grandparent to create an oral history, so that their memories live on after they are gone. There are many resources on the internet for actualizing this.

19. **Create Your Own Ritual.** Using guidelines found in addendum six, page 248, design a ritual to grieve a lost loved one.

20. **Create a Memorial Portrait.** Make a portrait of your lost loved one in any medium you like; include things that were important to them, their name, and dates of birth and death. You don't need to be a great artist. Have fun!

21. **Create a Memorial Shrine.** Spontaneous shrines are a common form of collective mourning. If the spirit moves you, create a shrine mourning a lost loved one in a public or private place. Include photos of the person, notes to them, candles, and so on.

22. **Resonance Check.** Did any material in this chapter particularly resonate for you? Is there something that piqued your interest? I invite you to keep track of the things that spoke to you in a special place in your journal. I also encourage you to go further and do more research on anything that you felt excited about, and if you are a visual person, to collect images related to things that interested you. Start a folder of these images or create a Pinterest board.

23. **Check In.** What were the biggest surprises this week? Did you learn something new about yourself? Make notes in your journal.

7

COMMUNING WITH THE DEAD
RITUALS AND CONTACT

I have a friend who lives in a beautiful small town in Mexico's Sierra Norte. When I visited him a few years ago, he took me to meet his parents. In their living room, they had a large, prominently placed altar. It featured framed photos of deceased family members, a small bowl of water, religious prints, prayer cards, and votive candles. When he saw me admiring it, he remarked that whenever his mother was going through a difficult time, she would go to the altar, light a candle, and ask her deceased mother for advice.

Ancestor altars like this one are used by people all over the world. And the practice of communicating with the dead in this way is more common—even in the industrialized West—than you might think. Psychologist George Bonanno, head of the Loss, Trauma, and Emotion Lab at Teachers College, Columbia University, studied bereavement in depth. In his book *The Other Side of Sadness: What the New Science of Bereavement Tells Us about Life after Loss* (2019), he reports that a majority of people in his study felt that their lost loved one was still with them; some even felt they were being watched over by them. As many as *a third* of participants reported that they had a regular practice of speaking with their deceased loved ones, or to a photograph of them. Another study revealed that between 30 percent and 60 percent of elderly widowed people experience what feels like contact with their lost spouses, while in a Japanese study, as many as 90 percent of widows reported having experienced the presence of their dead partner.[1]

> There is a land of the living and a land of the dead and the bridge is love, the only survival, the only meaning.
>
> —THORNTON WILDER, AMERICAN PLAYWRIGHT, NOVELIST, AND ESSAYIST

When Bonanno asked the participants of his study whether they believed they were *actually* communicating with their dead loved ones, many responded that this was not important to them; it *felt* real, and that was enough. This continuation of their relationship helped them not only heal from their grief, but also find meaning in it.[2] Bonanno determined that such behavior was healthy, so long as these communications did not take place too soon (before the death had truly been accepted) and the person was not overly reliant on this bond (that they still had a meaningful life outside this contact).

In this chapter, we will turn our eye to ways that the living have maintained relationships with the dead, from practices to festivals to individuals thought to be able to mediate between the lands of the living and the dead. Whether we believe that spirits of the dead exist in a *literal* way is unimportant. As Bonanno found in his studies, there is a benefit to staying in contact with the dead, whether or not you believe these communications are objectively "real."

ANCESTOR VENERATION

In my family, we celebrate Thanksgiving the way some families do Christmas. My oma and opa started this tradition when I was a child. My oma, a wonderful cook, would lovingly prepare special holiday dishes that we looked forward to all year round, including her signature cranberry sauce with orange marmalade and slivered almonds and sweet potato soufflé. Today, many years after my grandparents' deaths, my family continues to gather at Thanksgiving, usually in my grandparents' former home, to spend time together and enjoy my oma's beloved recipes.

Our family Thanksgiving might be seen as a modern incarnation of the ancient practice of ancestral veneration, once called ancestor worship. Mallorie Vaudoise, in her book *Honoring Your Ancestors: A Guide to Ancestral Veneration* (2019), describes ancestor veneration as "any ritual or spiritual practice that reconnects you with the people who came before." In this tradition, one's relationship with a dead loved one is not understood to end with their death, but rather it continues on, sometimes even deepening and healing.

The dead never stop talking and sometimes the living hear.

—MARLON JAMES,
JAMAICAN AUTHOR

Ancestor veneration—practiced for millennia all around the world—developed in response to the long-standing belief that the soul, or one of the souls, of the dead can go on, after death, to evolve into an ancestor spirit, or to move to an afterworld, where it can still communicate with those it left behind. Many cultures assert the importance of maintaining strong relations with those who have died. The living take care of the dead with offerings such as food and drink, incense, and prayer. If the dead are pleased, they are thought to become powerful allies to the family or community, providing guidance and assistance from the other world. Studies also suggest that cultures practicing ancestor veneration tend to experience fewer problems with anxiety and depression after the loss of a loved one.[3]

Our dead are never dead to us, until we have forgotten them.

—GEORGE ELIOT, ENGLISH NOVELIST AND POET

At the heart of the tradition of ancestral veneration is gratitude. We venerate our ancestors because we acknowledge, in all humility, our reliance on them. Without our ancestors—our parents, our grandparents, and so on—we would simply not exist. Nor would the culture we inhabit, with its foods, languages, and traditions. And so much of what makes us *us*—our character and personality, gifts, difficulties, complexities, likes and dislikes—stem, whether we like it or not, from our family of origin. Ancestor veneration is also about love. These practices allow us to continue to enjoy the bonds we have with our loved ones after their death. It is for these reasons, among others, that many continue to remember the dead and make offerings on their behalf, whether they do so as part of an instituted religion or community group, at a domestic family shrine, or in a more idiosyncratic manner.

Some cultures believe that the souls of the dead can be materially helped by those still living, at least for a certain amount of time after death. Some Jewish traditions assert that after a person dies, their soul moves to a place where they appraise their life from the elevated spiritual perspective death provides. There, they must purge the pain of their regrets and the ways they fell short in life, after which they will ascend to heaven. The deceased's time of purgation can be mitigated by mitzvahs, or meritorious acts, performed by loved ones still on earth. These include reciting certain prayers and doing good deeds on behalf of the soul of the deceased.

Similarly, some Catholics believe that after death all but the most holy must spend time in a place called purgatory, in order to purge their sins before they are fit to enter heaven. The soul's time in purgatory can be shortened by what are known as indulgences. These can be earned through special sanctioned acts such as reciting certain prayers or orations, giving to the needy, making a pilgrimage, or praying for the deceased at their grave.*

Another way to speed up one's time in purgatory was to employ the services of a so-called sin eater. In Welsh and northern English Christian folk tradition, a sin eater was a person who agreed to take on the sins of a dead person so that their soul would be able to ascend to heaven more rapidly. Typically, this role would be filled by a homeless wanderer. In exchange for beer or money, they would consume bread or milk left near the body of the deceased, which was believed to have absorbed their sins.

In the Tibetan Buddhist tradition, some believe that after you die and before you reach your next destination, you will spend time in what is called the bardo, a liminal, dreamlike state between life and death. According to the *Bardo Thodol*, a collection of fourteenth-century Tibetan sacred texts published in the West in 1927 as *The Tibetan Book of the Dead*, there are several bardos that one passes through after death, each with its own unique phenomena and opportunities for liberation. The length of time one spends there depends on their karma, as well as their spiritual and mental state at the time of death. For the period of time your loved one's soul lingers in the bardo, you can help them by doing good deeds on their behalf,

---

* Indulgences were also, notoriously, once sold to raise money for the Church, leading to the bitter dissension of Martin Luther, who left Catholicism and founded the Protestant Church.

such as making offerings to monks or monasteries or engaging in formal remembrances, both of which might aid the soul in its afterlife journey.

Many cultures use the physical remains of the deceased as a way to maintain a strong relationship with them. In the Peruvian and Bolivian Andes, people once mummified their most important dead as a means to retain and cultivate relationships with their ancestor spirits. These mummies would be specially dressed and brought out to attend meetings and weigh in on community affairs.

Similarly, in pre-Columbian Mesoamerica, it was customary for families to keep the bodies of their loved ones or important leaders close to them. The Maya believed that one of the souls continued to reside in and empower the bones after death. Families, then, would commonly bury their ancestors beneath the hearth of their homes. They might also create ancestor bundles, in which reeds and fabric were wrapped around the bones of their relative. Scholars tell us that this was a cultural tendency the Spanish found difficult to eradicate; Indigenous Mesoamericans were deeply upset by the idea of consigning the ensouled bones of their loved ones to a bleak, dark cemetery far from their homes, and continually broke that rule, regardless of punishment.[4]

Bodily remains also serve as a locus of communication in the Catholic world, in what is called the cult of the saints. Here, a relic of a saint—often taking the form of a bone or preserved body part—is understood to be able to connect the living to the soul of the saint in heaven. There, the saint can intercede with God or Christ on the petitioner's behalf. Sometimes a whole body is judged to be a religious relic, as with incorruptible saints. This is a phenomenon in which the body of an individual does not decay after death, taken as a sign that the person might be a saint. Sometimes, it is reported, the body even emits a beautiful fragrance.

Some traditions make statues of their ancestors intended to serve as a vessel for their soul. In ancient Egypt, ideally two souls would be preserved in the tomb. The first was the *ba* soul, that which makes each of us unique, believed to reside in one's mummified body after death. Another soul, the *ka* soul, the locus of our passions and physical nature, would be invited to inhabit a portrait or statue of the individual. The dead were believed to be able to interact with the living through this enspirited representation.

In many African cultures, ancestor statues are crafted from wood, stone, metal, or other materials, and then used in rituals and ceremonies to honor and communicate with the spirits of the ancestors. In Polynesian and Maori cultures, intricately carved wooden sculptures known as tiki represent ancestral figures. And in many Asian countries, ancestor tablets or plaques, which bear names and symbols of deceased family members, or portraits are often displayed in ancestral shrines.

TALKING TO THE DEAD

Techniques to communicate directly with the souls of the dead have been practiced for millennia. Often this is achieved through the intercession of a medium. Mediums are individuals (usually women) who are believed to possess special skills that allow them to communicate with the invisible world, including the realm of the dead. Some of these individuals, called necromancers, communicate with the dead in order to divine information about the future. In the Hebrew Bible, Saul visited the Witch of Endor to communicate with the spirit of the prophet Samuel. And in ancient Greece, mediums who had a special expertise in talking to the dead could be found at the Necromanteion, or "oracle of the dead." Located in a temple honoring Hades and

Persephone—king and queen of the underworld—they could be consulted to make contact with the dead on your behalf.

A contemporary oracle of the dead can be found at Japan's Osore-zan, literally Mount Dread, a volcano some believe provides an entrance to the underworld. Today it is a popular pilgrimage destination, especially during a yearly festival during which those in mourning visit to make contact with the dead. This communication is facilitated by the Itako; these are specially trained mediums, often blind women, who can communicate on your behalf with souls of the recently deceased, including those of stillborn or aborted children.

The figure of the medium is also central to Spiritualism, a religion rooted in the idea that the soul survives death and can be communicated with in meaningful ways. Spiritualism originated in upstate New York in the 1840s, prompted by the demonstrations of the Fox sisters, three girls who became famous for their supposed ability to communicate with the dead. At its height, Spiritualism was practiced by as many as eleven million Americans. Practitioners engaged in varioys means to communicate with the dead, including séances and planchettes, the predecessors of today's Ouija board. Historical records suggest that President Lincoln and First Lady Mary Todd Lincoln held Spiritualist séances in the White House in an attempt to communicate with their dead son. The religion also attracted luminaries including biologist Alfred Russel Wallace, writer and physician Sir Arthur Conan Doyle, and physiologist Charles Richet, who won a Nobel Prize for his work on anaphylaxis in addition to coining the word *ectoplasm*.

Spiritualism was largely a nineteenth-century phenomenon, but

Death ends a life, not a relationship.

—MITCH ALBOM, AMERICAN AUTHOR, JOURNALIST, AND MUSICIAN

it experienced a resurgence in the early twentieth century in response to the trauma caused by the mass deaths of World War I (1914–18) and the influenza epidemic (1918–20). Today, the religion lives on; one can study to become a Spiritualist medium at Arthur Findlay, a Spiritualist college in Essex, England. It is also possible to visit towns—such as Lily Dale in upstate New York and Cassadaga in Florida—where Spiritualist mediums continue to live and work. Here, visitors can attend message circles, which are free public events where mediums share communications from the dead with audience members. You can also attend Spiritualist church services, receive spiritual healings, hire a medium to help you communicate with the dead, or take part in a séance.

The inception and popularity of Spiritualism coincided with a historical moment in which technology was uncovering hidden worlds not discernible to the unaided senses. Microscopes and telescopes were showing us previously unsuspected organisms and stars, X-rays were exposing the body's interior, the invisible power of electricity was illuminating cities, and people were communicating by telegraph and radio waves. It followed that perhaps, with the right technology, we could create a bridge between the land of the living and the land of the dead.

For the last ten years of his life, Thomas Edison was hard at work on a new invention he called the "mechanical medium," a device he hoped would allow us to unequivocally communicate with the dead. He never achieved his goal, but in the 1920s he told *Forbes* magazine that he was confident such a thing could be achieved "not by any occult, mystifying, mysterious or weird means, such as are employed by so-called mediums, but by scientific methods."[5]

A related project emerged in Japan in the wake of the great Sendai (or Tohoku) earthquake and tsunami of 2011, which killed nearly twenty thousand people. In Japan, it is considered vitally important to care for *butsudan*, which are altars kept in the home that house a family's *ihai*, or ancestor memorial tablets. The tsunami swept away many of these altars, as well as a number of cemetery plots. To complicate the situation, many in Japan (as in numerous cultures around the world) believe that when people die suddenly or traumatically, they are likely to be stranded on earth as despairing and confused spirits. And in the wake of this tragedy, there were, indeed, many reports of encounters with so-called tsunami ghosts.[6]

The *kaze no denwa*, or the "phone of the wind," is a creative grieving tool that was created by garden designer Itaru Sasaki in the Japanese town of Otsuchi. It takes the form of a phone booth, located on a picturesque hill above the sea; inside is a phone that has no connection. Visitors can go into the booth, close the door, lift the receiver, and say anything they wish to their lost loved ones. Sasaki created his phone of the wind as a way to retain contact with a beloved cousin who had died of cancer; in the aftermath of the tsunami, it began to attract scores of people who lost loved ones in the disaster. Sasaki says, "There are many people who were not able to say goodbye. There are families who wish they could have said something at the end, had they known they wouldn't get to speak again."[7]

Itaru Sasaki's memorial intervention was so useful that people around the world have followed his lead and created wind phones in their own countries. These are used primarily as a means of providing survivors of the COVID-19 pandemic a way to speak, at least symbolically, to their deceased loved ones. Today, one can make use of a wind phone in such diverse locales as the US, Ireland, Canada, and Wales.

FESTIVALS OF THE DEAD

In many cultures around the world, there are special times of year when the veil between the lands of the living and the dead is understood to be uniquely permeable, and the dead are thought to be able to return home to spend time with their surviving loved ones. These times are marked by festivals in which the souls of dead family members are welcomed home. During the festivals, families gather, often in cemeteries and homes, making offerings of food, drink, and other things the dead might miss.

In the Celtic world, Samhain (pronounced sow-een) was the festival celebrating the time of year when "the summer goes to rest." It was viewed as a borderline festival, commemorating a time when one was understood to inhabit the liminal space between summer and winter, lightness and darkness, the land of the living and the land of the dead. During this festival, it was believed that the souls of the dead returned to visit their homes and loved ones. It was also the time when those who had died over the course of the year were thought to make their journey to the otherworld. Samhain was later combined with Catholicism's Allhallowtide—the official time to remember the dead, comprising All Saints' Eve, All Saints' Day, and All Souls' Day—to become today's Halloween, a contraction of "All Hallows' Eve." Halloween's trick-or-treating traces back to a medieval European tradition, in which children would dress in costumes and knock on doors asking for food or treats in exchange for songs or prayers, often in honor of the dead. They might receive a soul cake for their efforts, which represented a purgatory-freed soul.[8]

In Japan, Obon, or Bon, is the festival that welcomes home the returning souls of dead loved ones. At this special time of year, families visit and clean familial graves and light lamps to guide the spirits of departed ancestors back home. Also in Asia is the Hungry Ghost Festival, which commemorates a time of year when some Buddhists and Taoists believe the gate to the underworld is open, allowing souls of the dead to spend a month on earth. They welcome the spirits with gifts of food, candy, incense, and other offerings. They also light lanterns to mark homes and temples, and lay lanterns in the water to commemorate those who died from drowning.

In China many celebrate the Qingming Festival, also known as Tomb-Sweeping Day or Ancestors' Day, which takes place soon after the spring equinox. Families visit the tombs of their ancestors to clean the grave sites, pray to their ancestors, and make ritual offerings. Some also burn paper representations of things their ancestors might need in the afterlife. This tradition began by writing what the dead might need on paper and burning it, allowing the deceased to symbolically eat and drink. This was later replaced by mass-produced spirit money, also called joss paper or sometimes "hell money,"* to be used for bribes and purchases in the afterlife. Today, one can purchase not only spirit money, but also sleek paper representations of homes, smartphones, cars, sunglasses, and pretty much anything else you think your deceased loved ones might desire. These are burned in the belief that the smoke and its symbolic gifts will be received by the souls in the afterworld, which is a conviction held by many diverse cultures.

In the West, the best-known festival of the dead is Mexico's Day of the Dead (in Spanish, Día de Muertos or Día de los Muertos). Día de Muertos is celebrated in Mexico and in places with sizable Mexican populations, including many cities in the United States. At this

---

* The name "hell money" is a product of Western misinterpretation. Spirit money was indeed intended for souls in the underworld, but, for the Chinese, this was not a place of eternal damnation as it was for the Christians.

centuries-old festival—a syncretization of pre-Hispanic traditions honoring the dead and the Catholic holidays of All Saints' and All Souls' Days—it is common for families to gather at the cemetery to clean the grave sites of their ancestors. They also decorate them with sugar skulls and other festive ornaments, along with photos of the deceased. Most incorporate marigolds (a holdover from Mesoamerican times) and candles, whose scent and light are believed to guide the dead back to the land of the living. It is not uncommon to see food vendors of every sort, along with roving mariachi bands who, for a small fee, will play a favorite song of the dead. One also sees, in towns and cities alike, adults and children milling through the streets, faces painted into colorful, flowery skulls. Families gather to enjoy special foods, including *pan de muerto*, literally "bread of the dead," a pastry decorated with bones and covered with sugar.

Many families also create *ofrendas*, which are beautiful home altars covered with photographs of the deceased, candles, marigolds, sugar skulls, traditional copal incense, and festive, death-themed *papel picado* (cut paper banners). Here, they leave offerings of the deceased's favorite food, drink, and indulgences, such as tequila or cigarettes. The idea is to enjoy a few precious days with the ancestors before their souls must inevitably return to the land of the dead.

Mexican writer and scholar Salvador Olguín has led a number of trips for Morbid Anatomy to Mexico for Day of the Dead. In each one, we visited a region in which the holiday was observed in a unique way. The different celebrations were all deeply moving—joyous yet solemn—and communicated great meaning and emotional depth. These trips changed my own life, and those of many who joined us.

In 2019, our Day of the Dead destination was a small Mexican town called Pomuch. At the small local cemetery, people practice a tradition known as the Brushing of the Bones, which is a local variant of Hanal Pixán (literally, "food for the souls"), or Maya Day of the Dead. In the Brushing of the Bones, the bodies of the dead are buried long enough for the flesh to disintegrate, after which the bones are exhumed and delivered to the family. They are then moved to the family ossuary, which is an open-fronted receptacle that houses the bones of the dead. Every year, the family reconvenes at the cemetery to wipe the bones clean. Following this ritual, they neatly arrange the bones in metal boxes lined with embroidered white cloths—the skull placed on top so the dead can see their visitors—which they place in the ossuary. The tiny cemetery is filled with candles, incense, flowers, and the sound of prayers.

That day, we had been invited to join a family for their annual Brushing of the Bones ceremony. As we watched, three generations of family members took turns drawing a human bone from a large burlap bag. They would slowly and solemnly wipe each bone with a soft cloth, and then carefully stack them into an orderly pile. As we watched them do so, an old woman in a traditional Maya *huipil* appeared. She was around eighty years old, and had a very beautiful smile. She looked at us and she began to speak.

She told us that in her world, people were taught not to fear death. Everybody dies; every *thing* dies. The bones, she said, are the part of us that is earth; the other part of us is spirit. The dead, she said, are not ghoulish or scary. They are nothing to be afraid of. Then, with a warm and wise smile, she turned and continued on her way.

At the completion of the ceremony, the family invited us to share some locally made Day of the Dead bread with them. As we ate, they informed us, with evident pride, that although their family now lived all over the world, they all returned to Pomuch every year for this celebration. It was the younger family members, they said, beaming, who were the most eager to keep the tradition alive. I felt deeply moved by the bonds of love that united these family members, dead and alive, and the strength and depth of this tradition that bound them all together. I also found myself touched by the fact that these old ways continued to live on, even in the face of modernity, and despite the tenacity and violence with which the Spanish had attempted to eradicate the old Maya ways.

I must admit I felt a touch of envy that day, and found myself slightly resentful that neither my family nor my culture had provided me with practices such as these, that might have allowed for a gentler and less combative relationship with death, and given me the forms to say goodbye to—and yet retain meaningful contact with—my own dead loved ones. If I had been born in Mexico, I realized, I might very well never have been afraid of death in the first place.

In *The Labyrinth of Solitude* (1950), Nobel Prize–winning author Octavio Paz wrote, "The word death is not pronounced in New York, in Paris, in London, because it burns the lips. The Mexican, in contrast, is familiar with death, jokes about it, caresses it, sleeps with it, celebrates it; it is one of his favorite toys and his most steadfast love."⁹ And indeed, if you spend time in Mexico, you will quickly realize that Day of the Dead is no anomaly. Death in Mexico is ever present, and approached with respect, warmth, solemnity, even eroticism and humor. Images of skeletons and skulls are ubiquitous, a part of everyday life. One sees them in the murals covering city walls, in signage for restaurants, in children's games and toys, and on T-shirts and key chains. They populate the works of Mexico's most revered fine artists, such as Frida Kahlo and Diego Rivera. They are also a common theme of the popular arts; at any artisan market, you will find life-size glittery papier-mâché skeletons, leering skull masks, and shadow

Though lovers be lost, love shall not; And death shall have no dominion.

—DYLAN THOMAS, WELSH POET AND WRITER

boxes containing tiny clay skeletons engaged in prosaic human activities ranging from giving birth to dancing at a strip club.

It is clear that people do not shy away from reminders of death in Mexico. If you flip channels on Day of the Dead, you will see news footage of people brushing bones or decorating cemetery plots, mini documentaries about Catholic miracle-working bones, and old black-and-white movies in which mediums make contact with the dead.

Death is also a prosaic sight at the open-air *mercados* (markets), where many do their daily shopping, and where it is not uncommon to see a pig carcass hanging from a hook, blood dripping from its mouth and pooling on the floor, or a pile of goat heads with milky, half-closed eyes. You encounter daily reminders of death, as when you see a home marked by a black or gray bow, signifying a recent death in the family. You might even happen upon, as I did one day a few years back, the corpse of a middle-aged man displayed in a glass-topped coffin as part of an impromptu memorial service staged at a busy Sunday flea market. When I later asked a friend about this strange sight, he laughed and said, "The man was probably a vendor, and that's where all his friends were!"

Death in Mexico even takes the form of a hugely popular new skeleton folk saint called Santa Muerte, literally Saint or Holy Death. A female grim reaper, she is venerated as a loving mother and powerful miracle worker by millions in Mexico, in the United States, and throughout the world. We'll take a deeper dive into this figure in chapter twelve.

Overall, it seems to me that we in the affluent, industrialized West have a lot to learn from Mexico when it comes to death, life, and the relationship between the two. Perhaps on some unconscious level, many of us intuit that Mexico still possesses something our culture has lost, something we still long to experience, if only for a moment.

In Mexico, death feels more like a simple, sometimes laughably absurd fact of life rather than a terror-filled tragedy. And I, for one, find it difficult not to wonder if the intense love for life one witnesses in this country—with its deep appreciation for good food and drink, beautiful artisanal objects, and quality time spent with family—is in some small (or not so small!) way related to their easy intimacy with death.

EXERCISES

JOURNAL PROMPTS

1. **Contact with the Dead.** Did your family or culture have any traditions for maintaining contact with the dead? If so, what are they, and do you find them useful? If not, how might your life have been different if you had grown up with practices around honoring and maintaining communications with the dead? If your family and/or culture had no such traditions, or the one it provided was not useful for you, design and enact one of your own.

2. **Communicating with the Dead.** Have you ever felt you were communicating with a dead loved one? Write about your experience. Did you believe it was really happening, or did you think it was your imagination? Did it change your beliefs in any way? Did it ease your grief? What are your thoughts about it now?

3. **Special Family Friend.** Did you have a special friend in your birth or chosen family, an ancestor you had a special relationship with? Write about them here. What were they like? How did they shape your life? What did you learn from them? What about them are you grateful for? How might you be different if they had

not been part of your life? Consider writing a (never to be sent) letter to them in which you express your appreciation.

4. **Festivals of the Dead.** Did your family have a yearly tradition in honor of the dead? If so, what was it like? If not, how might your life have been different if you'd had one? Have you ever taken part in a festival of the dead? Where and when? What was the experience like for you?

5. **Mediumistic Communications.** Have you ever used the services of a medium? What was it like? What surprised you? Did you learn anything new? Fascinatingly, there are peer-reviewed, double- and triple-blind studies demonstrating that mediums can, in at least some instances, provide testably specific or accurate information.

6. **Ashes of Those We Lost.** Do you keep the ashes of a loved one or a pet in your home? Does it make you feel closer to the deceased?

7. **Hidden Ways We Venerate the Dead.** In my family, we might be understood to continue to venerate our ancestors—my paternal grandparents—by continuing the Thanksgiving traditions they started. We never explicitly discuss this as a means of venerating the dead, but it is clear it functions this way. Do you have any similarly stealthy means of venerating the dead in your life or your family? If so, write about them.

ACTIVITIES

1. **Ancestral Veneration.** Look into a form of ancestral veneration that comes from your family tree, or simply one that interests you. What speaks to you about this tradition? What benefits might it provide?

2. **Ancestral Death Festival.** Did your ancestors take part in a death festival or other ritual to remember their lost loved ones? If so,

learn more about it, and see if there is an element you might bring into your life.

3. **Ancestral Food.** Cook—and perhaps share!—a favorite dish you associate with a deceased loved one, something they made or something they loved to eat. I often make my grandmother's Caesar salad and schnitzel, and I always think of her when I do, and talk about her when I share the dishes with others.

4. **Keeping Memory Alive.** My friend, the artist Mary James Ketch, has a lovely family tradition. She and her husband make a meal that reminds them of a particular deceased family member. They decorate the table with framed photos of the individual, and share the meal with their children, telling them stories about this ancestor they never met or hardly remember. If this sounds interesting to you, try it yourself, with your birth or chosen family! Added bonus: Play some music that the deceased enjoyed! Another added bonus: Plan the meal for a significant day, such as your ancestor's birth or death day, or a holiday that was important to them.

5. **Take Part in Day of the Dead.** Find a local Day of the Dead celebration to attend, or if possible, travel to Mexico for Day of the Dead. Leave a candle or flower for your dead loved one; you also might write them a message, or imagine speaking your message to them. Failing that, watch Pixar's Academy Award–winning film *Coco* (2017), a beautifully researched and realized ode to Day of the Dead that captures its otherworldly feel and poignantly expresses many of its core ideas.

6. **Speak to the Dead.** Visit the grave of a deceased ancestor, or spend time with their ashes or a photo—or even just a memory!—and speak to your lost loved one. Whether or not you believe you are *really* speaking to them is unimportant, but try to use the idea of "sincere pretending" discussed in chapter one.

7. **Communicate with the Dead.** Write a letter to someone you love who has died. Burn it, or leave it in nature, at a shrine or other holy place, or another place that is meaningful for you.

8. **Artwork for the Dead.** Make an artwork dedicated to a deceased loved one. While you make it, listen to some of their favorite music and think about them. Keep the finished artwork in a special place.

9. **Go on a Pilgrimage for the Dead.** Take a trip in honor of the dead to a place that had meaning for them—perhaps the place they grew up in, or their gravestone—or any other place that will help you focus on your relationship with them. Think of them throughout the day, then say a few words—if only in your head—when you arrive. Write about the experience after the fact. How did it make you feel? Did it bring up anything interesting or unexpected?

10. **Create Your Own Wind Phone.** This might be as simple as speaking into a turned-off phone; you might also find an old phone at a junk store, or go to a disconnected phone booth. Use this phone to tell your loved one anything you might wish you'd had a chance to say before they died, or tell them about your life, or anything else you want to share. Again, belief is not important here.

11. **Develop a Relationship with Your Ancestors.** Hannah Haddadi is a spiritual death worker and death doula in the Morbid Anatomy community. As someone who helps people with ancestral work, I asked her what advice she might offer people who wish to develop a relationship with their ancestors. She suggests getting to know them as best you can. Find out all you can about them, and look at photos or portraits. She also recommends that, if possible, you talk to people who knew them in life. Pick someone from your ancestral line whom you know little about, and apply Haddadi's advice. Added bonus if this is a person who has been actively ig-

nored, disdained, or looked down on by the family; by taking this on, you are also helping bring to light your family shadow.

12. **Ancestral Ways.** If you have been estranged from your older family traditions, spend some time getting to know them. Perhaps study an ancestral language, cuisine, literature, or traditional dance. You might also do research on folklore, or mythological or religious traditions, and try to incorporate elements of this heritage into your life.

13. **Create an Ancestor Altar.** For guidelines on creating an altar, see addendum five, page 247. Add photos of, or mementos relating to, your dead ancestors and loved ones. You might also put out some of their favorite food and drink, especially on important days, such as the anniversary of their birth or death. If it feels right, light a candle and speak to them, or ask for guidance. You need not believe, only practice, and see how it makes you feel.

14. **Explore Spiritualism, the Religion That Speaks with the Dead.** Spiritualism is a religion that began in 1848 and is based on the idea that the souls of the dead live on and can be communicated with after death. Visit Lily Dale, New York, or Cassadaga, Florida—extant Spiritualist towns in the United States—or attend a service at a Spiritualist church. You might also read a book on the topic, such as *Radical Spirits: Spiritualism and Women's Rights in Nineteenth-Century America* (1989) by Ann Braude, or *Talking to the Dead: Kate and Maggie Fox and the Rise of Spiritualism* (2004) by Barbara Weisberg, to explore their beliefs and practices. For a visual introduction to contemporary Spiritualists, check out *Séance* (2019) by photographer Shannon Taggart.

15. **Hold a Modern Séance.** Tiffany Hopkins is a modern-day Spiritualist medium. In her forthcoming book *Beyond*, she shares a number of accessible techniques for communicating with the

dead. She speaks at length about the séance, where a group of people sit with a medium to bring through communications from the "other side." Hopkins also provides a simple séance that can be done over video chat, without the need for a medium. Simply gather your group and invite them to "bring through" one of their ancestors by sharing a photo, telling a story, playing a song they loved, or going into character and giving advice as if they were that person.

16. **Make an Ancestor Artwork.** Draw or sculpt a representation of your dead loved one, and invite their essence into the work. Put it on your altar and use it to communicate with the dead. (Remember, you need not believe this is literally true, but engage with the idea with seriousness and humility.)

17. **Design Your Own Death Festival.** If your family has no meaningful festivals or celebrations that honor the dead, or if the ones they practice fail to resonate with you, invent your own, perhaps drawing from the examples above, along with further research. For more inspiration, you might read *From Here to Eternity: Traveling the World to Find the Good Death* (2018) by Caitlin Doughty, and/or *This Party's Dead: Grief, Joy and Spilled Rum at the World's Death Festivals* (2021) by Erica Buist.

18. **Resonance Check.** Did any material in this chapter particularly resonate for you? Is there something that piqued your interest? I invite you to keep track of the things that spoke to you in a special place in your journal. I also encourage you to go further, to do more research on anything that you felt excited about, and if you are a visual person, to collect images related to things that interested you. Start a folder of these images or create a Pinterest board.

19. **Check In.** What were the biggest surprises this week? Did you learn something new about yourself? Make notes in your journal.

8

FEAR OF DEATH AND THE
QUEST FOR IMMORTALITY

O ver the years, I have given many talks on death-related topics at museums, libraries, and universities around the world. On more than one occasion, in the Q and A session, a man has raised his hand and asked, "What do you think about the idea of uploading our consciousness to the cloud?" This idea of a machine-enabled immortality is a core tenet of trans- or post-humanism, a movement that advocates using technology to augment the human body in hopes of, ultimately, vanquishing aging and death.

To me, the idea of living forever sounds like its own kind of hell, as does the idea of living without a body! I personally find it comforting to think that one day, at least this incarnation of my life will end. But to many of us, in a culture that prides itself on its ability to control life, to transcend nature, to reduce risk and do everything in its power to ensure a long, healthy life, death is the ultimate insult. It reminds us that despite our awesome technological accomplishments and our mighty civilizations and monuments, we are still animals, and as such, we are subject to the humbling laws of nature. We may have managed to immerse ourselves in our own constructed world, but regardless, in the end, we all die.

Fear of death is often asserted as a universal human characteristic, part of the human condition. But a look at the historical record—and even the world today—makes it clear that this is not the case. How we feel about death has a great deal to do with when and where we were born, and the culture in which we were raised. In the matriarchal societies that many scholars believe predominated before 4000 BCE, it is purported that people did not fear death. Rather, they saw death as a movement from one state to another, part of the repeating cycles of life, death, and rebirth. In these cultures, the lands of the dead were welcoming places of lush abundance where you would happily tarry until the time came to be reborn into your original clan.

There are also extant cultures that provide their members with a sense of serenity in the face of death. When the Mount Kilauea volcano erupted in Hawaii in 2018, some in the Indigenous community understood it to be a manifestation of Pele, goddess of fire, lightning, and wind. They welcomed their goddess with offerings and sacred hula dancing. One can watch deeply moving footage of the women singing and dancing a welcome to Pele as emergency helicopters hover and the lava sparks and flows toward them, threatening their lives and communities. Speaking to their response, Dr. Jonathan Osorio, dean of the University of Hawaii at Manoa's Hawai'Inuiākea School of Hawaiian Knowledge, observed,

Those who are afraid of death will carry it on their shoulders.

—FEDERICO GARCÍA LORCA, SPANISH POET, PLAYWRIGHT, AND THEATER DIRECTOR

"We have learned to live with her and to be intimate with Pele and these forces. It doesn't mean that life is always going to be smooth. From time to time, it's dangerous and from time to time it's tragic, but it's a part of being in this place to live with it."[1]

In their book, *The Myth of the Goddess: Evolution of an Image* (1991), Jungian psychoanalysts Anne Baring and Jules Cashford trace the history of the goddess as it changed form and evolved from the Paleolithic era to our own histor- ical moment. In their opinion, the fear of death so many of us today consider an inevitable part of the human condition can in fact be traced back to a par- ticular historical moment—specifically, around 2500 BCE, during the Bronze Age. They assert that the fear of death emerged at this time in response to a deep societal in- stability, when people suffered under the constant threat of invasion and unpredictable violent death. At this time, the great matriarchal goddesses—who represented in one unified figure the attributes of life and death, creation and destruction, fertility and rebirth—were di- vided into *two* goddesses, splitting her characteristics into positive and negative aspects of the divine female archetype. The first of these fig- ures, a sort of loving mother figure, brought "hope and joy"; the other, envisioned as a devouring mother, brought "terror and despair." At this same historic moment, the land of the dead, long conceived of as a place of fertility and regeneration, began to be imagined as a dark and dreaded place, "a barren underworld of dust and darkness."[2]

It was at this point, according to Baring and Cashford, that we in- herited a new cultural vision of death that continues with us to this day. Death began to be understood as the opposite of light and life, rather than just one part of the cycle of life, death, and rebirth. A new fear emerged: that of death at the hand of others, and with it, the

> *People living deeply have no fear of death.*
>
> —ANAÏS NIN, FRENCH-BORN AMERICAN DIARIST AND WRITER

If you realize that all things change, there is nothing you will try to hold on to. If you are not afraid of dying, there is nothing you cannot achieve.

—LAO-TZU, CHINESE PHILOSOPHER CREDITED AS THE FOUNDER OF TAOISM

emergence of goddesses of war. As death became thought of as horrible and final, the authors explain, humans developed a concomitant need to achieve a sort of symbolic immortality through heroism, an "extraordinary act that elevates the idea of human nature."[3]

One of the first literary works in recorded history, *The Epic of Gilgamesh*, details this dark view of death and the afterlife, as well as the solace of a symbolic immortality achieved through fame. Written around 2100 to 1200 BCE in ancient Mesopotamia, this epic tale traces the adventures of Gilgamesh and his close companion, Enkidu. Gilgamesh was a real historical figure, king of the Sumerian city-state Uruk (now Warka, in southern Iraq), and is thought to have ruled at some point between 2900 and 2350 BCE. In *The Epic of Gilgamesh*, he is portrayed as a demigod, the son of a goddess and a mortal man.

In the story, Gilgamesh's best friend, Enkidu, is killed by the gods as punishment for his part in the killing of a sacred bull. Driven by his despair—and subsequent terror over the prospect of his own death—Gilgamesh embarks on a quest to find the key to everlasting life. After a long journey, he meets Utnapishtim, the sole survivor of the Great Flood, who has been rendered immortal. He tells Gilgamesh about a magical plant that possesses the power to bestow everlasting youth and immortality. Gilgamesh manages to locate the plant, but before he is able to eat it, it is swallowed by a snake. Our protagonist, resigned to his own death, returns home and goes on to become a great king. He achieves a symbolic immortality through his good governance, and through his story that reaches down to us thousands of years later.

In his Pulitzer Prize–winning book, *The Denial of Death* (1973), anthropologist Ernest Becker (1924–1974) calls quests like that of Gilgamesh "immortality projects." Such endeavors are a means of *symbolically* defeating death, creating or associating ourselves with something that will outlast our physical life on earth. Immortality projects, says Becker, can provide people's lives with a sense of meaning, purpose, and significance. For some, this might take the form of achieving something for which you will be remembered in history, long after your death, such as being a great king, becoming a famous artist, or walking on the moon. For others, this might mean having children, who will bring a part of you into the future, or being an esteemed member of a powerful nation or religion.

Ernest Becker had an unusually close relationship with death. An American Jew, he was part of an infantry troop that liberated a Nazi concentration camp during World War II. He wrote his most famous work, *The Denial of Death*, during the dark days of the Vietnam War, and under the shadow of terminal colon cancer. He died at only forty-nine years old, the same year his book won the Pulitzer Prize.

In *The Denial of Death*, Becker posits a theory of human behavior, the core tenet of which is that we are torn by a paradox central to our nature. On the one hand, we know that we are animals, who will one day die and whose bodies will rot. On the other hand, we have the godlike ability to use our imagination to manifest our own realities and control the world around us. He sums up this central problem with the pithy proclamation that we are "a god who shits."[4]

Becker hypothesizes that in order for us to survive day-to-day—to be able to make a living, feed ourselves, and reproduce effectively—most of us repress the knowledge of our own death in order to avoid overwhelming existential angst. Managing this fear of death is, in his opinion, at the core of much of what we do, impacting—unconsciously—our thoughts, behaviors, and beliefs. In turn, this affects the way we live, make decisions, and interact with one another, especially with those who are different from us.

In his opinion, many of us minimize our fear of death by subscribing to worldviews and value systems that give our lives greater purpose and meaning. By investing in these systems of meaning—which could include religion, political affiliation, career, family, and so on—we are able to reduce our death anxiety by building our self-esteem and feeling that we are not adrift as individuals, but rather are a part of something larger than ourselves. The dark side of this tendency is that challenges to our thought or belief systems can make us cling to people we perceive as belonging to the same groups that we do, and evoke negative reactions toward individuals we perceive as different, such as those of different races, religions, genders, or nationalities.

Becker's *The Denial of Death* was an unlikely hit in its time. It makes an appearance in Woody Allen's *Annie Hall*, where Alvy Singer, played by Allen, purchases a copy of the book for his new girlfriend to help her understand his obsession with death. The book also had a profound influence on the way many in the West have come to think about our relationship to death, in large part due to what is called terror management theory. Social psychologists Jeff Greenberg, Sheldon Solomon, and Tom Pyszczynski developed this theory when they found ingenious ways to experimentally test—and confirm—Becker's thesis that, when reminded of their mortality, people who have not developed a conscious relationship with death become demonstrably hostile toward out-groups, or people they perceive as different. On the world stage, this can play out as xenophobia, nationalism, misogyny, racism, and violence against others, and helps create conditions ripe for genocide and dictatorships.

The core hypothesis of Becker's book is that it is our denial of death—the fact that we have repressed it—that creates this dangerous situation that can lead to so many personal and societal ills. From a psychological perspective, when we repress something, it does not just go away; rather, it is pushed out of our conscious awareness and into the unconscious. Once it's out of sight, it can manifest in our lives in strange and troubling forms. That which remains unconscious—in other words, that which is not looked at squarely—can also create fear. Terror management theory suggests that when people have not brought death to consciousness, they use various defense mechanisms, including projection onto other individuals and groups, to reduce the anxiety associated with mortality. By projecting their fears onto others and strongly identifying with their own cultural worldviews, these individuals can maintain a sense of security and significance, mitigating the existential anxiety triggered by thoughts of death.

Columbia University psychologist George Bonanno has demonstrated that there is an antidote to the problems caused by the denial of death. If we can bring death from our unconscious to our consciousness—via a sustained reflection on death, such as the one we are engaging in over the course of this book—we can make ourselves healthier and less vulnerable to manipulation. Such contemplation, Bonanno found, goes even further, reducing our fear of death and helping us forge stronger connections to others.

Another way of mitigating our fear of death might be the cultivation of the right side of the brain. In her bestselling book, *My Stroke of Insight: A Brain Scientist's Personal Journey* (2008), Harvard-trained neuroscientist Jill Bolte Taylor details her experience of a stroke that debilitated the left side of her brain. She notes that when that side of her brain—associated with logic, analytical and linear thinking, detail, and achieving goals—went offline, she experienced the world entirely from the perspective of the right side of her brain, associated with a holistic view and a focus on connection, emotion, and metaphor. In this state of pure right-brain existence, fear of death, she reveals, simply did not exist. In her own words:

> My left mind thinks of me as a fragile individual capable of losing my life. My right mind realizes that the essence of my being has eternal life. Although I may lose these cells and my ability to perceive this three-dimensional world, my energy will merely absorb back into the tranquil sea of euphoria. Knowing this leaves me grateful for the time I have here.[5]

The kind of right-brain cultivation championed by Jill Bolte Taylor comes more easily to some cultures than others. This has been the observation of my husband, Bryan Melillo. Recently, Bryan trained to be a death doula, which is someone who guides a person through the dying process. He had previously spent many years in India practicing meditation. When studying for his death doula certification, he was struck by the number of similarities between what he was being taught in his doula training and what he had learned in India. Bryan noticed that among the many ways an end-of-life doula is taught to serve the dying is by the sharing of awareness.

Awareness, a state of being cultivated by the act of meditation, is not much valued by the Western world, which favors rationalism—or, in Bolte Taylor's parlance, the left brain. Awareness is a feeling disposition that can provide profound relaxation and insight into something greater and more expansive than everyday consciousness. From the Eastern perspective, the fear of death we experience in the West is mostly based on a misunderstanding that is culturally reinforced. Once awareness is felt, one can begin to relax beyond the mind, and to release the fear that resides there.

Awareness in Eastern spirituality influences how people relate to one another in everyday life. When one is in a state of awareness, there is no sense of being separate. Instead, much as in Bolte Taylor's description of being in the right brain, there is a tacit understanding that we are all one, sharing in this life experience.

Bryan teaches a death meditation class for Morbid Anatomy, where cultivating awareness is one of the main goals. He explains that in the Eastern traditions in which he was trained, preparing for death is a central, even primary, concern. Meditation itself can be seen as a means to prepare for death, as it trains us to stay focused, centered, and conscious in any situation, including the challenging and unfamiliar one of dying. The goal of the death meditation is to guide participants through what can be a profound experience of awareness, and also to help neutralize the fear surrounding death. Bryan teaches that, in Eastern traditions, death itself is not something to fear; it is just another experience that we all share. It is only our discomfort of the unknown and our inability to control the outcome that create fear. The hope is that by familiarizing people with awareness and what happens when we die, we can release that fear and begin to really practice living.

> *Death is seen as an enemy only by those who set themselves in opposition to nature.*
>
> —JUNE SINGER, JUNGIAN ANALYST AND AUTHOR

CHASING THE SPECTER OF SECURITY

Over the course of my life, I have had many close brushes with death. I was in my first year of studies at UC Santa Cruz when the Loma

Preita earthquake decimated much of the downtown; we were forced to evacuate and, pre-internet, huddled around transistor radios trying to figure out if "the big one" had destroyed San Francisco. I was also living in New York City during the 9/11 terrorist attacks. For months, we saw (and smelled) the plume of smoke that rose from the wreckage, and picked up the bits of charred paper from the destroyed buildings that littered our backyards. In the aftermath of the attack, the news was filled with stories of anthrax poisonings and threats of follow-up attacks. The sense of anxiety on the streets and subways was palpable.

During this very difficult time, I was not sure what to do. Was it unwise to stay in this city, which was sure to be the target of future attacks? I tried to make an intelligent, informed choice, and watching the news was not helping me in any way. It was just making me more anxious.

I decided to call my father—a judge with a great mind for political science—for advice. When I asked if he thought I should leave New York City, his response was, "You can run but you can't hide." His words cut to the heart of my question, and the heart, it seems, of our quest for security more generally. No matter what you do, no matter what precautions you take, how safe you are, or how much you exercise and eat the "right" foods, there is no way to escape death, or even know we can postpone it. Death will come for us all, and we don't know when or how. There is no possibility of total security, no way to guarantee our safety and survival.

It was only by spending a good amount of time in countries other than the United States that I began to notice how uniquely obsessed my home country is with security, safety, and control. To me, the single-minded pursuit of security seems like a fool's errand because it is, at its heart, an attempt to avoid death. Perhaps the reason that we

FEAR OF DEATH IN DIFFERENT DEMOGRAPHICS

In my experience, men seem to have more anxiety around death, and a concomitant fascination with the possibility of immortality, than women. I should also note that the majority of the Morbid Anatomy community—and the majority of people drawn to compassionate death care, such as hospice workers and death doulas—are female. Why might this be?

Over the years, I have discussed many theories about this with friends, colleagues, and students, and here are a few of our thoughts. Women, historically, have been the keepers of memory and overseers of death rites. In matriarchal cultures, it was usually women who maintained relationships with the ancestors; from the time I have spent in Mexico, it seems that this country's ancestor altars are also largely created and maintained by women. Women, as bearers of children, regularly had to face the possibility of death when giving birth, especially before the advances of modern medicine. Further, the act of giving birth, as well as monthly menstruation, requires a surrender to the body's processes, ego (or will!) be damned. Women also make up the majority of the "care economy"—the unpaid or low-paid sector that focuses on the physical and emotional well-being of others; this includes compassionate death care as well as childcare, elder care, education, health care, and other personal, social, and domestic services.

My good friend Dr. John Troyer—former director

of the Centre for Death & Society at the University of Bath—has also noticed that the fear of death seems stronger in men. When I asked him what he thought about this, he replied, "Wasn't it Margaret Atwood who said 'Men are afraid that women will laugh at them. Women are afraid that men will kill them'?" In other words, while many men in our culture have the luxury of repressing awareness of their own impending death, for women, along with other nondominant communities—such as people of color and the LBGTQ+ community—death is more a part of our everyday awareness, and so perhaps we're not able to push it into our unconscious quite so readily.

in the United States are so preoccupied with security stems from the fact that so many of us have been protected from the realities of death. We are a relatively young and geographically isolated nation, and most of our wars—with their destruction, bloodshed, and carnage— have taken place overseas. We also ghettoize the likelihood of violent death to our marginalized communities and turn a blind eye to those realities. It seems to me that this quest for security is also directly related to our lack of conscious engagement with the idea of death.

In *Sand Talk: How Indigenous Thinking Can Save the World* (2019), Australian author Tyson Yunkaporta, a member of the Apalech clan and professor of Indigenous knowledges at Deakin University in Melbourne, notes that in his own language, there is no word for either *safety* or *risk*; there are, however, many words for *protection*. These in-

volve two protocols: to watch out for yourself,
and to watch out for those around you. Similarly, in Mexico, a place decidedly less obsessed
with security and predictability than the US,
there is a saying I have come to take to heart:
"There is always a way." Things in Mexico often do not work easily or predictably, but when
things go wrong, there is a great deal of com-
munity support and flexibility that allows one to find effective and
amenable solutions. One learns to trust that although things cannot
be controlled, they tend to just work out.

*The fear of death follows
from the fear of life. A man
who lives fully is prepared to
die at any time.*

—MARK TWAIN (AKA SAMUEL
LANGHORNE CLEMENS), AMERICAN
WRITER, SATIRIST, AND LECTURER

I learned this lesson very powerfully on a Morbid Anatomy Day
of the Dead trip. On November 1, 2016, we paid a visit to Janitzio
Island—the so-called Island of the Dead—in Mexico's Lake Pátzcu-
aro. Around one a.m.—after a stimulating night full of stunning cemetery displays and magnificent home altars—a few dozen of us piled
onto several small boats and pushed out into the water with great
mirth and anticipation.

It was very cold out and the black skies were filled with stars. As
our boat sped silently over the lake, great sheets of mist began to form
on the surface of the water. They lifted, slowly, ghostlike, swirling into
a thick fog that began to surround us. It was deeply uncanny, mysterious, and spellbinding. Soon, through the thick mists, we saw, off in
the distance, what truly looked like an island of the dead. It was covered in lights, gaily and eerily beckoning to us. It felt for all the world
like Charon—the mythical boatman who delivered the dead to Hades in ancient Greece—was silently navigating us over the river of the
dead. All of us were reverent, enrapt, and silent.

The fog grew yet more dense, and the island faded from view.

Before long, it became clear that our ferrymen had lost their way. They conferred nervously, phones out, pointing in different directions. Soon after, without a word, they extinguished all the lights on the boat and cut the engine. We sat, unmoving, silent, in the dark, cold night. There was a feeling of being lost on this lake, in deepest night, with no idea of where we might find shore. We did not know how—or *if*—we'd make it to our destination. Every once in a while, we would hear or spy the shadowy shape of a ghostly boat passing us in the gloom.

As we sat in this space of danger and unknowing, some people on that boat began to worry. I closed my eyes and plumbed my own depths. Was I afraid? No, I realized, I was not. I did not think we were going to die on that lake. I contemplated the fact that there was no one we could call to fix this, no "big daddy," as there would be in the US, who could come and rescue us. We were very truly in a situation beyond our control. But if I was honest, it did not feel frightening to me, but rather . . . *exhilarating*.

Eventually, still without a word, the ferrymen got the boat moving again. We did, ultimately, make our way to the island, and then uneventfully back home. The whole event felt like a very deep, moving, and powerful experience at the time. It made me realize in a visceral, embodied way the power of danger, the draw toward places or situations that offer the thrill of the unknown, of lack of domestication, of a world outside our own controls. Yes, this experience had a hint of danger. It also made me feel very deeply alive in a way that I would not have traded for the world. It was one of the most profound experiences I have ever had, and I know that others on that boat felt the same.

It seems to me that there is some way in which an overzealous mitigation of risk—motivated by fear of injury or death—cuts us off from something necessary; that only by sitting in death's proximity can we truly feel the fullness of life. I am not at all suggesting that one should rush into dangerous activities for their own sake. But in my own life, I try to carefully, consciously choose what risks I wish to take with my eyes wide open, and remain open to their transformative gifts.

WHAT DO WE FEAR WHEN WE FEAR DEATH?

No one knows what will happen when we die. And, of course, it is natural to fear the unknown. But might it not also be possible for us to see the unknown as *exciting*? If death is such a great mystery, if dying is an experience that all humans who ever lived had or *will* have, might we not cultivate a sense of *curiosity* about what happens next? Would it be possible to look forward to death, as did J. M. Barrie's Peter Pan, as "an awfully big adventure"?

Many people are anxious about death because of fears about what happens—or *doesn't* happen—after we die. As previously discussed, our dominant culture provides us with the model of death as the end, based on the tenets of scientific materialism. The Stoic philosophers of ancient Greece and Rome, like so many of us today, were not convinced about the reality of an afterlife. They were nevertheless deeply concerned with death, and how the fear of death impacted our ability to live full lives. They urged a practice of preparing for death through a regular contemplation of one's own death, and consciously living each day as if it were your last. As the Stoic Marcus Aurelius put it, "It is not death that a man should fear, but rather he should fear never beginning to live."[6]

From the point of view of the Stoics, it was illogical to be afraid of death. In Marcus Aurelius's words, death was nothing to fear, for it was either "a dispersion, or a resolution into atoms, or annihilation . . .

extinction or change."[7] His fellow Stoic Epicurus said that death should mean nothing to us, for "when we are, death is not come, and, when death is come, we are not."[8] In other words, if death is nothingness, then after death, there will be no "me" to lament the loss, to feel grief or pain, so all worry is merely preemptive and will disappear at our death, along with everything else.

For some, a fear of death stems from dread of the possibility of postmortem punishment. Many religious traditions purport that, after death, the soul is sent to a place where it must undergo a temporary mortification in order to purge any impurities before moving on to the next stage. In the Christian tradition, there is also hell, which some see as a place of *eternal* punishment. Although this idea did not enter official Christian theology until the twelfth century, the fear of hell—even by the most rule-abiding Christians—understandably creates a very strong fear of death for many.

All fears are one fear. Just the fear of death. And we accept it, then we are at peace.

—DAVID MAMET, AMERICAN PLAYWRIGHT, SCREENWRITER, AND DIRECTOR

Many people I know are less afraid of death itself than of what happens to the body as death approaches. For some, this manifests as a fear of aging, with its concomitant possibility of losing one's mobility and independence, or suffering from dementia or a related mental impairment. This, of course, could happen to any of us. But it's important to note that it's also very possible these things will never happen, and there are many, many examples of happy, healthy older people living beautiful and meaningful lives.

I was lucky to witness this in my own family. My paternal grandparents enjoyed contented, self-sufficient, active lives into their nineties. But when my oma was about ninety-four, a few years after her partner of over sixty years had died, she began to tell me she was ready to die. She was still relatively healthy, but had outlived most of her friends and was losing her beloved ability to read. She felt she had lived long enough and was ready to go already! Although it made me sad when she told me this, I am very grateful to have learned at such a young age that, at least for some, there comes a time when one is simply ready to die, and death feels more like an overdue friend than a frightening intrusion.

It seems to me that the reason many now fear aging in the contemporary affluent West is that our culture has so little appreciation for its elders. In other countries where I have been lucky to spend extended periods of time—including South Korea, Mexico, Bolivia, and Hungary—it seemed to me that the elderly were respected and catered to, and held a place of honor where they were valued for their hard-won wisdom and broader perspective. The same is also true for many Indigenous cultures around the world, who revere the "grandmothers" and "grandfathers," understood as wise advisers whose many years on this planet give them a unique and elevated perspective.

How deeply we devalue our elderly population in the United States was laid bare during the recent COVID lockdown when Dan Patrick, lieutenant governor of Texas, made headlines by asserting that we should be willing to sacrifice the old to get people back to work and preserve the integrity of the economy. He said that he "would rather die than see public health measures damage the US economy, and that he believed 'lots of grandparents' across the country would agree with him."[9] A farther cry from the Indigenous valuation of the wisdom of elders is hardly imaginable.

For some, anxiety about death stems from a fear that pain and suffering—both physical and psychological—might precede it.

Recently, when reading Giuseppe Tomasi di Lampedusa's *The Leopard* (1958), I came across a passage that put this fear in a different light. The protagonist, an Italian nobleman, is musing on a new medicine discovered in the United States that could "prevent suffering even during the most serious operations and produce serenity amid disaster. 'Morphia'," he says, was what they called "this crude substitute for the stoicism of the ancients and for Christian fortitude."[10] Before reading this book, it had never occurred to me that there might have been a debate about whether, given the opportunity, we would choose to eliminate pain. But, as made clear by this passage, there were at least some who found pain mediation a dangerous development, one that might make people weaker and undermine their stoicism and ability to endure.

As is also clear from the preceding quote, our ancestors were much more familiar with pain and suffering than we are today. It was not until around 1850 that we discovered the painkilling properties of ether and chloroform. Before this, surgeries—as well as prosaic medical and dental procedures—were often not only painful, but often life-threatening.[11] And before our modern understanding of germ theory, many people died—often at a young age, and in a great deal of pain—from epidemics of diseases such as cholera, smallpox, typhus, and scarlet fever.

Before the overwhelming triumph of scientific materialism, many turned to mythology and religion to make sense of the problem of human suffering. The ubiquity of suffering is itself central to Buddhism, whose first noble truth is "The Truth of Suffering," with the other three truths focusing on its causation and solutions. In the Christian tradition, it is *fortitude*—courage in the face of pain or adversity—that is the key to enduring the vicissitudes of life, with Christ's suffering as a model. This is considered so important that there are practices designed to cultivate a personal experience of Christ's suffering, including that on the cross.

Jewish Viennese psychiatrist Viktor Frankl, former inmate of the Auschwitz concentration camp and pioneer of existential psychology, asserted that in a post-religious world, *meaning* was the key to the fortitude necessary to endure suffering. His theory, based on his own experience in the camps, was that life is essentially a quest for meaning, and that what we call despair is the result of "suffering without meaning."[12] The philosopher Nietzsche concurred, writing that the problem is not the suffering itself, but rather "the meaninglessness of suffering," and that "he who has a why to live can bear almost any how."[13]

Carl Jung, who understood the importance of experiencing the opposites in life—both pleasure and pain, joy and sorrow—also saw great value in suffering. For him, suffering was "a great teacher," and in his opinion, "every real solution is only reached by intense suffering."[14] In a similar sentiment, Tenzin Gyatso, the fourteenth Dalai Lama, stated, "It is worth remembering that the time of greatest gain in terms of wisdom and inner strength is often that of greatest difficulty."[15] If we can look at suffering in this way, then perhaps even an atheist can find meaning in the inevitable suffering of life, transforming it into something that opens us up to wisdom and transformation.

Death continues to be the great mystery, and it is natural to fear what is unknown. By looking at what we fear more closely—by bringing it into conscious contemplation—we de-potentiate its power over us. In the following exercises, we will work to do just that, so we can live with less fear, and become comfortable sitting with—*and maybe even learn to relish*—the mysteries of life and death.

EXERCISES

―――

JOURNAL PROMPTS

1. **Fear of Death.** What is your greatest fear about death? Is it your own death you fear? Losing a loved one? The unknownness of it? The lack of control? The bodily degradation of old age? Decomposition of your body? Write about what scares you in as much detail as possible, knowing that making something conscious often makes it less frightening.

2. **Dreams Unrealized.** In his book *Staring at the Sun: Overcoming the Terror of Death* (2008), psychiatrist and Stanford University emeritus psychiatry professor Irvin David Yalom says, "The death anxiety of many people is fueled . . . by disappointment at never having fulfilled their potential. Many people are in despair because their dreams didn't come true, and they despair even more that they did not make them come true. A focus on this deep dissatisfaction is often the starting point in overcoming death anxiety."[16] If you died tomorrow, might you feel this sort of passionate regret for not having accomplished your dreams? What would those dreams be? Write about them in detail.

3. **A Life without Fear.** If you are afraid of death, what might it feel like not to be? What would it feel like in your body? How would it impact the choices you had made? How might your life be different?

4. **The Quest for Immortality.** If you could live forever, would you? Why or why not?

5. **Danger and Death.** What are your thoughts about the relationship between security and death? Have you had a dangerous ex-

perience that made you grow? If so, write about the experience and reflect on how it changed you.

6. **Growing Up with Hell.** Did you grow up afraid of the Christian hell or some other frightening afterlife tradition? What did that feel like when you were a child? Did you believe it? Do you believe it, or fear it, even slightly, now? How, if in any way, does it continue to affect your life?

7. **Age and Beauty.** Are there any old people you have encountered who give you a sense that there might be a decent—even beautiful—life to be had in old age? If so, write about them and note the ways you may wish to be like them, and how you might achieve that goal.

8. **Suffering.** Was there a time in your life when suffering led to a positive outcome? Write about the experience.

9. **The Gifts of Aging.** In her audio recording *The Crown of Age: The Rewards of Conscious Aging* (2011), Jungian analyst Marion Woodman points out that aging brings many gifts. As the body loses its strength, there is more time for working with one's creativity and imagination. For many, age also bestows a sense of balance and wisdom that allows them to live full and vibrant lives and offer valuable perspectives to their families and communities. With no career to keep them busy, many are gifted with the time to explore sidelined interests and talents and go deeper into their dreams and inner life. What do you think you might like to explore as you get older? How might you imagine serving your community?

10. **Worth Dying For.** Martin Luther King Jr. said, "No one really knows why they are alive until they know what they'd die for."[17] The ancient Greek philosopher Socrates, when given the option to recant his teachings, chose to drink a cup of hemlock poison

rather than abandon his principles. Is there something—a principle, a place, a person—you can imagine choosing to die for?

ACTIVITIES

1. **Get to Know Terror Management Theory.** Terror management theory is a sociological theory based on Ernest Becker's Pulitzer Prize–winning book, *The Denial of Death* (1973). It posits that much of human culture is a means of staving off awareness of our existential fear of death, and that it is only by facing this fear and coming to terms with it that we can live lives that are truly free. To learn more about these ideas, read Becker's book, watch the documentary *Flight from Death: The Quest for Immortality* (2003), or read *The Worm at the Core: On the Role of Death in Life* (2015) by Sheldon Solomon, Jeff Greenberg, and Tom Pyszczynski. Added bonus: Enroll in the free online class about terror management theory produced by the Ernest Becker Foundation at udemy.com /course/existential-anxiety-and-the-human-experience.

2. **Ponder Immortality.** Read Anne Rice's *Interview with the Vampire* (1976) and reflect on what it might be like to live forever. Do you identify more with Louis or Lestat? What, if anything, appeals to you about the idea of living forever? What do you find unpleasant?

3. **History of Afterdeath Punishment.** If you grew up as part of a tradition that focused on a punitive afterlife such as the Christian hell, read a scholarly book about the history of this afterlife or its prime figures to learn more about how these ideas developed, the individuals who shaped them, and their historical context. A few suggestions: *Heaven and Hell: A History of the Afterlife* (2020) by Bart D. Ehrman, Diana Walsh Pasulka's *Heaven Can Wait: Purgatory in Catholic Devotional and Popular Culture* (2014), and *The*

Origin of Satan: How Christians Demonized Jews, Pagans, and Heretics (1996) by Elaine Pagels.

4. **Cultivate the Right Brain.** In this chapter we talked about the work of Jill Bolte Taylor, who found that living with only the right side of her brain allowed her to feel a deep inner peace with no fear of death. This internal state, potentially accessible to us all, is habitually undermined by the chatter of the left brain. Spend some time this week cultivating the right side of your brain. Some methods include meditation (see addendum eight, page 256), yoga, working with dreams (see addendum four, page 246), spending time in nature, painting, drawing, dancing, or writing poetry. Added bonus: This week, if you find yourself feeling stressed out, try to notice and take a short time-out with a few conscious breaths.

5. **Quiet the Left Side of the Brain.** One way to move out of the dominant rational brain is to work with our unconscious. This week, consider trying a session of Jungian active imagination (more on which is in addendum twelve, page 260) or embark on a shamanic journey (see addendum thirteen, page 261). You might also take time to work with a dream this week; for guidelines, see addendum four, page 246.

6. **An Antidote to the Fear of Aging.** If the fear of aging resonates with you, I offer a powerful antidote: the documentary film *Ballets Russes* (2005). In it, we meet a number of lovely individuals in their eighties and nineties who are teaching what they love—the rigorous, athletic art of ballet. In their youth, they were lucky to be part of an exciting and artistically fertile period of ballet history, when impresarios teamed up with the likes of Claude Debussy, Salvador Dalí, Pablo Picasso, and Coco Chanel to create beloved productions. When you see these octogenarians and

nonagenarians moving with such grace and so full of joy, you cannot help but realize that there are other possibilities for aging than those our culture offers, and that old age can certainly be a vibrant, creative, and full time of life. Anytime you feel a fear of aging coming on, watch this film. Added bonus: Write about what it evoked for you.

7. **Resonance Check.** Did any material in this chapter particularly resonate for you? Is there something that piqued your interest? I invite you to keep track of the things that spoke to you in a special place in your journal. I also encourage you to go further, to do more research on anything that you felt excited about, and if you are a visual person, to collect images related to things that interested you. Start a folder of these images or create a Pinterest board.

8. **Check In.** What were your biggest surprises this week? Did you learn something new about yourself? Make notes in your journal.

JUNGIAN DEATH MEDITATION

There is a Jungian death meditation I have found very useful and surprisingly soothing. It was written by Jungian psychologist June Singer, and is found in her book *Modern Woman in Search of Soul* (1998). I recommend reading it very slowly into the Voice Memos application of your cell phone, then playing it back with your eyes shut. Repeat as often as is helpful.

Begin by closing your eyes and taking four very deep breaths. Relax each body part one after the other, moving from your toes to the top of your head. I like to do this part aloud, and sync an exhale to each body part relaxed. Next:

> Close your eyes and imagine that you are on your deathbed. You feel yourself drifting. You don't have any more energy to do anything. Your desk is piled high with unanswered letters, bills to be paid, unfinished projects. Either someone else will pick them up for you or they will remain undone. It doesn't matter much. No one will know that the idea you meant to work out never came to expression. No one will feel the poorer for it. Then there are the people in your life. If you loved them well, they will miss you and grieve for you. Over time the poignancy of your absence will fade and only a warm remembrance will be left. There will be those for whom you did not care enough, those you rejected, those with whom

there is still some unfinished business. It doesn't matter now. There is nothing you can do about it.

There is only one thing you can do, and that is to let go. Let the tasks of the world slip away. Let your very identity slip away. Let your loved ones mourn a little while for you and then go on their way. Let go of everything—your home, your possessions, your feelings, and your thoughts.

Allow yourself to float. You begin to feel lighter. You have shed the heavy load you have been carrying. What was the heavy load? It was your sense of self-importance. It was your belief that everything you did had intrinsic importance, therefore you had to do it fully and perfectly no matter what it cost. Or, conversely, it was your belief that your work was so important that you couldn't possibly do it well enough, so the burden you carried was the unfulfilled responsibility. But either way, don't you see how temporal it is when you are facing your own death? This practice can help you learn to do a little less, do it a bit more slowly, do it with care, and do it with love.

9

PREPARING FOR
YOUR OWN DEATH

People often ask me what kind of funeral I would like, or what I want done with my body after I die. Such questions always surprise me a bit, because to be honest, I don't really think about it. I'm more concerned that whatever ritual ushers me out should serve my loved ones. But it is clear that these decisions are very important to many people.

While teaching my Make Your Own Memento Mori class, I was continuously moved and inspired by my students' thoughtful and creative ideas around how they would like to ritualize and memorialize their own deaths. One student, an older woman with a terminal disease, designed (and created!) the room she wished to die in; it was beautiful and inviting, full of sunlight, with fluffy blankets and pillows in an exuberance of colors and textures. Another student began to embroider a burial shroud to cover her when she died; she planned to continue working on it for the rest of her life.

I also had a number of students who created projects designed to live beyond them. One, saddened by the lack of heirlooms in her family, created one of her own as her final project, which she planned to leave to her son, who, she hoped, would then pass it on to his children. Another wrote a series of letters for his loved ones to be sent out after his death; he planned to update them throughout his life as a sort of ongoing memento mori practice.

Many of my students were very passionate about what they wanted done with their bodies after they died. A number were interested in natural burials, also called green burials, in which one's body is returned, in some way, to the ecosystem. This might include being buried in a memorial forest, with a tree serving as a headstone. Another option is what is called human composting, in which your body is transformed into soil that can be used in the gardens of your loved ones. I am very drawn to these ideas, which feel like powerful correctives to our cultural tendency in the affluent, industrialized West to take from nature and give nothing in return. For most of history, humans gave back to the earth in a variety of ways, and, at the end of life, many buried the bodies of their loved ones in the soil, where they could, like countless other dead organisms, nurture new life. Today, in contrast, many of us elect to fill our bodies with embalming chemicals and bury them in impenetrable coffins. Not only is this damaging to the environment, but it also seems to me like a kind of refusal to acknowledge our role in the life cycle, and a final rejection of the opportunity to give back to the natural world that gave us life and sustenance.

Dying is nothing to fear. It can be the most wonderful experience of your life. It all depends on how you've lived.

—DR. ELISABETH KÜBLER-ROSS, SWISS AMERICAN PSYCHIATRIST

Many Indigenous cultures understand humans as a part of a larger web that unites all life-forms. Similarly, many members of the Morbid Anatomy community have shared that they see reentering the ecosystem as a beautiful and heartening form of immortality. A quote by the artist Edvard Munch, who painted *The Scream*, sums up their sentiments beautifully:

> From my rotting body, flowers shall grow and I am in them and that is eternity.[1]

THE CREATIVE POSSIBILITY OF A MEMORIAL

Plenty of my students in Morbid Anatomy classes express an intense dissatisfaction with typical Western funerals and memorials. They are interested in rethinking what a funeral could be, and use their projects as a way to plan aspects of their own memorial service in such a way that it can communicate their sense of self and breathe new life—so to speak—into what they see as a stale tradition. Invariably, they are interested in making the ceremony less somber and more joyous—truly a celebration of life rather than a traditional service. One student designed a cocktail to be served at her funeral, which we made for the last class (it was delicious!). Another chose the readings she'd like her friends to recite, and another created a playlist of songs to be played at her memorial service.

In their reimagining of what a meaningful or satisfying memorial ritual might entail, my students drew on a rich history of remembrance traditions that have, over the centuries, managed to be useful, cathartic, and even *fun*. Perhaps the best known of these is the Irish wake, the name of which derives from its origin as a late-night prayer vigil over the body of the dead. During an Irish wake, loved ones watch over the body for one or more days, usually in the home, where they receive friends and family members who drop in to say their goodbyes. In these often drunken and rowdy affairs, attendees share memories of the dead, often in an irreverent manner, along with laughter and tears, dancing and singing.

A similarly joyous memorial tradition can be found in the New Orleans jazz funeral. A combination of West African, Haitian, and European traditions, these are high-spirited musical celebrations performed to honor the deceased. The funeral procession is led by the "first line," a brass band, behind which follows a hearse containing the body of the deceased and then their family. Next comes the "second line," made up of community members and mourners, who trail the band to enjoy the music, dance, and companionship. At the outset of the procession, the music is somber and dirgelike; by the end, it becomes joyous and rousing, with uplifting spirituals such as "When the Saints Go Marching In" that encourage the bereaved to lose themselves cathartically in music and dance.

> *While I thought that I was learning how to live, I have been learning how to die.*
>
> —LEONARDO DA VINCI, ITALIAN ARTIST, SCULPTOR, ARCHITECT, AND ENGINEER

Another lively memorial practice stems from Ghana, where the dead are often laid to rest in what are called "proverb" or "fantasy" coffins. These are playful, colorful, and often humorous coffins sculpted into images that had meaning to the deceased. They might allude to their former profession, such as a giant shoe for a shoemaker; something they love or identify with, such as a lion or an eagle; or something aspirational, such as a Mercedes-Benz. The options are unlimited; a quick Google search turns up a Coke bottle, a camera, a hot pepper, a mermaid, and a Nike sneaker! These coffins are so popular now that they are exported around the world, especially to the

US.[2] In the playful, irreverent words of Lawrence Anang, a carpenter who makes such coffins for Kane Kwei Carpentry Workshop in Teshie, Ghana, "If you want to have fun in the land of the dead, then you need to get your coffins here."[3]

Another fascinating memorial development took place at Marin Funeral Home in San Juan, Puerto Rico, which made headlines in 2014 when it began posing the bodies of the dead in life-size dioramas meant to express their personalities.[4] Called "nontraditional wakes," as the website explains, these are meant to "honor the life of a loved one in a more personalized and unique way."[5] One tableau featured an old woman who was, per her request, wearing her wedding dress and seated in her beloved rocking chair. Another was a murdered boxer, who was posed in costume in a boxing ring. Yet another displayed a man positioned as if speeding on his favorite motorcycle.

A visit to the San Francisco Columbarium & Funeral Home, which houses cremated remains, also offers a fun, expressive, and unusual way to capture the idiosyncrasies of the dead. The columbarium is filled, floor to ceiling, with small glass-fronted boxes that house the ashes of lost loved ones. Some of these showcase brass urns, religious symbols, and other traditional funereal imagery. A whole section of the Columbarium's vaults is dedicated to victims of the AIDS epidemic of the 1980s and '90s. Many of these treat the space like a shadow box or diorama, and fill it with photos, keepsakes, toys, and other objects and artifacts that express the personality of the deceased in ways that are direct, amusing, and extremely touching.

MEMORIALS FOR THE NOT YET DEAD

Today, some people choose to hold memorial services *before* they die. Called "living funerals," "pre-funerals," or "living wakes," this tradition began in Japan in the 1990s, and was initiated by elders who did not want to burden their families with the planning and expense of their funerals. In 1993, Takiko Mizunoe, a seventy-eight-year-old Japanese actress, made headlines when she produced a living funeral for herself. A lavish and festive affair, it garnered a great deal of international attention and inspired others around the world to stage their own.[6] The aim of living funerals is to take advantage of the opportunity to celebrate the life of the subject *with* them, before their death. Much like a traditional memorial, attendees are invited to bring mementos and stories, and there is often food and drink. The subject might even give a speech, sharing stories about their life and the people who touched them.

South Korea has adopted a similar practice, albeit for a different purpose. In 2012, the Hyowon Healing Center began to offer free pre-funerals in an attempt to reduce the number of suicides, which is the leading cause of death for young people in that country.[7] Since the center began producing these pre-funerals, over twenty-five thousand people have chosen to take part in the practice, which involves saying goodbye to your loved ones, having a funerary portrait made, writing a will, and, finally, being draped in a funeral shroud and lying in a closed coffin for around ten minutes while reflecting on your life. The aim of these ceremonies is to help people find gratitude for their lives and work out unfinished business with loved ones before it's too late. Seventy-five-year-old Cho Jae-hee, who went through the experience, said, "Once you become conscious of death, and experience it, you undertake a new approach to life."[8]

Maybe all one can do is hope to end up with the right regrets.

—ARTHUR MILLER, AMERICAN PLAYWRIGHT, ESSAYIST, AND SCREENWRITER

PREPARING YOURSELF FOR DEATH

In every class I have taught, I have had students who either worked with—or wished to work with—the dying. What I found the most fascinating is that these students were often drawn to this kind of work after helping a loved one transition through the dying process. They reported finding this experience so beautiful and powerful—an honor for which they felt immense gratitude—that they wished to devote their lives to serving people in this way.

One of my students, Diana Muñoz, is a hospice chaplain who works with terminally ill people from a variety of cultural and economic backgrounds. When I asked her about her experiences, she said that although some of her patients are afraid of death, most are more at peace with it than their families; some of her older patients even say that they want to "go home." A lot of her work centers on helping the families of the dying prepare for the death of their loved one.

Love and death are the great gifts that are given to us; mostly they are passed on unopened.

—RAINER MARIA RILKE, CZECH WRITER AND POET

Many of my students express a strong desire to work as a death doula. A death doula is an end-of-life version of a birth doula, who, much like a midwife, helps mothers give birth and assists them in transitioning back into everyday life. A *death* doula guides a person—physically, psychologically, spiritually, and emotionally—through the process of dying. Their duties also often include assisting the families and friends of their client. One might consider the death doula as a secular incarnation of the psychopomp, those "soul guides" who assist the souls of the dead as they transition to the next stage of existence.

What exactly does a death doula do? Kristina Golden, a member of the Morbid Anatomy community who practices this line of work, says:

> A doula provides support and care during the last phases of life, recognizes that death is a part of life, and focuses on quality of life for individuals and their family/caregivers. Death doulas are companions, and can help facilitate family meetings to have open discussions about end-of-life wishes. Death doulas reduce burnout and emotional fatigue for the families and caregivers they support, initiate conversations about the dying process, educate, assist with life planning and advanced directive paperwork, and can even assist with funeral planning.[9]

One of the main roles of the death doula is simply to listen deeply and without judgment to anything the dying person wants to share. Another is to help them work through the psychological blocks that might be making them reticent to surrender to death. These issues, doulas note, often fall into the categories of regret, unfinished business, guilt, and shame. With this in mind, the doula works with their client, helping them resolve any issues that might be holding them back from a calm, peaceful death. They might also help them create a legacy project, which sums up or expresses their life—perhaps a written work, a video, or an oral history—to be shared with their loved ones.

GUIDES TO A GOOD DEATH

In the past, when people wished to prepare for death, they might have consulted a shaman, rabbi, or priest. There were also a variety of so-

*Death not merely ends life, it also bestows upon it a silent completeness,
snatched from the hazardous flux to which all things human are subject.*

—HANNAH ARENDT, GERMAN AMERICAN PHILOSOPHER AND POLITICAL THEORIST

called Books of the Dead, which were textual guides meant to help
one achieve a good death and afterdeath experience. These guides offered advice, rites, and practices aimed at ensuring the best possible
death and post-death experience.

One such book, from the Tibetan Buddhist tradition, is the *Bardo
Thodol*. Published in the West as *The Tibetan Book of the Dead*, this
famous work offers guidance for navigating the various stages of death,
dying, and the afterlife, and is designed to help individuals achieve a
positive rebirth and ultimately attain enlightenment. Passages are often read aloud to the deceased in the days immediately following their
death, in the belief that the teachings can benefit their afterdeath journey. The book also contains guidelines on preparing for death while
still alive, familiarizes the reader with the process of the death of the
body, and provides a map of—and guide on how to negotiate—the different bardos, or liminal states between death and rebirth.

In ancient Egypt, the *Egyptian Book of the Dead: The Book of
Going Forth by Day* served a similar function. This is a collection of
spells, prayers, and instructions used to help the dead make their
way successfully through their complex afterlife journey in order to
successfully achieve immortality. Passages were often painted on objects in the tomb, such as coffins, statuettes, and mummy wrappings.
The text also includes instructions for making offerings, performing

rituals, and reciting spells that would help sustain the deceased in the afterlife and ensure a successful transition.

A similar tradition, called *Ars Moriendi*, or "The Art of Dying," developed in Christian medieval Europe in response to the mass deaths of the black plague. An important element of a good death at this time was to receive the final rites, in which a priest would come to your bedside to hear your last confession and administer a final communion and the sacrament of extreme unction, or the "last anointing" with blessed oil. Due to the sheer numbers of those dying from the plague—in some places, as much as two-thirds of the population—there were simply not enough priests to tend to the dead and the terminally ill; the *Ars Moriendi* filled the gap left by the lack of traditional rites. These books were intended to serve as a guide for the dying, as well as their caregivers and families, helping them navigate the emotional and spiritual complexities of the dying process without the benefit of a priest. They were also meant to ensure that the deceased would enjoy the best possible afterlife experience.

PREPARING FOR THE
PRACTICAL ASPECTS OF DEATH

The book *The Gentle Art of Swedish Death Cleaning* (2017), by Margareta Magnusson, was an unlikely publishing sensation. It asserts the value of preparing for one's death by decluttering and organizing one's possessions, to make the afterdeath process easier for family members and friends. In the author's native Sweden, this practice—regarded as both caring and practical—is commonly undertaken when one reaches a certain age. Over the course of the book, Magnusson provides guidelines for mindful decluttering, urging readers to keep only that which has value—sentimental or otherwise—or

JAPANESE DEATH POEMS

In the United States and Europe, it is customary to write a will when we sense death is near. In Japan, one might also write a *jisei*, a legacy project created for loved ones and the world at large, which takes the form of a brief poem in which one bids a formal farewell to life. The tradition stretches back to ancient times, but really flourished during the Meiji period (1868–1912). *Jisei* were originally written by the nobility and the warrior class, but over time, the practice trickled down to the larger culture. Yoel Hoffmann's book *Japanese Death Poems: Written by Zen Monks and Haiku Poets on the Verge of Death* (2018) details this tradition and shares a number of examples, running from the poignant to the poetic to the humorous.

A few standouts: from Setsudo, who died in 1776 at the age of sixty-one:

> Now then,
> for my journey to the yonder world
> I'll wear a gown of flowers.

Renseki, who died in 1789 at eighty-eight years:

> I cleansed the mirror
> of my heart—
> now it reflects
> the moon.

Saikaku, who died in 1730 at seventy years of age:

> I borrow moonlight
> for this journey of a
> million miles.[10]

brings joy. The book presents the process of decluttering as liberating and even pleasurable, as you create space for the things that truly matter and remove the burden of things you no longer need or love.

Death doula Kristina Golden has her own practical advice for preparing for death. She urges people to create an advance directive. This is a legal document that communicates what sort of medical care or interventions you would (or would not) like if you were no longer able to express your wishes. This might also include specifying a health-care proxy, or power of attorney, which designates who will express your will if you are unable.

Golden also suggests that you compile all your important information in one physical location while you are still healthy. She recommends that you get a notebook or binder and fill it with all your account logins and passwords, including your financial information, medical information, business information, and your bills, and store it in a fireproof safe or file cabinet. Make sure your next of kin or designated proxy knows where to find everything, and share your end-of-life wishes with your loved ones.

Dr. John Troyer at the University of Bath urges people to fill out a funeral-planning worksheet. This is a practical way to look your death in the eye—and plan for it—by writing down your explicit desires for what you would like done after your death. See addendum seven on page 249 for a form that will guide you in creating your own. Added bonus: Share it with a friend, family member, or loved one when it's complete.

EXERCISES

JOURNAL PROMPTS

1. **Memorialize Yourself.** Write about the things that will be lost with your death—mannerisms, voice, habitual phrases, and so on. Ask your friends and loved ones about things they have noticed that are particularly *you* and what they would miss most about you.

2. **What Do I Want to Do with My Body?** There are many options today for what we would like to have done with our remains. Some choose to be buried in a family vault, while others elect to have their cremains transformed into memorial diamonds or shot into space. What would you like done with your body when you die? Would you like to be buried or cremated? Would you prefer to be embalmed and put in a coffin? Or perhaps have a green burial, such as human composting? Maybe something else entirely? Laws vary by country and even state to state, so research whether what you desire is legal in the place you live. Added bonus: Share your preference with a loved one.

3. **Write Your Own Epitaph.** An epitaph is a short inscription or statement memorializing the deceased. Often found on a tombstone or a monument, they can vary in content and tone, ranging from heartfelt messages or poetic verses to humorous anecdotes. They might also take the form of descriptions of what the person did during life, or what they were like. Write your own epitaph, one that sums up who you are and how you lived.

4. **Funerals I Have Known.** What kinds of funerals have you experienced? Are there any you felt were really great, or any that were

really awful? Write a bit about these experiences. What worked? What didn't? Why? Be specific.

5. **Plan Your Dream Funeral.** Write the menu, playlist (or the kind of music you'd like), readings, guest list, venue, and anything else you can think of. Share it with someone you trust.

6. **Write Your Own Eulogy.** A eulogy is a speech or piece of writing created to honor and remember the dead, often read at the memorial or funeral service. Write one in your own honor.

7. **Psychological Preparation for Death.** Many death doulas say that the biggest roadblocks for the dying fall into the categories of regret, unfinished business, guilt, and shame. Answer the following questions in your journal:

   ⬦ If I died tomorrow, what might I regret? What business might I consider unfinished? What might I feel guilty about? What might give me shame?

   ⬦ Are there actions you could take to remedy those situations so they will not become deathbed regrets?

   ⬦ Is there someone you could talk to about these things?

8. **Death Poems.** Write a death poem based on the Japanese death poems in this chapter. If you were dying now, how would you sum up the experience of life and death in a brief piece of verse? This could take the form of something playful or somber.

9. **Your Final Days.** Envision the final days of your life. What would you want this time to look like? Be as specific as you can. Who are you with? Where are you? What are you doing? How are you feeling?

10. **How I Want to Die.** How would you like to die? Alone or surrounded by family and friends? At home or in a hospital? Something else entirely? Why?

11. **Share Sentiments.** Is there something you'd like to tell a loved one before you die? Write a list of people and the things you'd like to tell them. If you can, try to express these things to them, in person, by letter, or with a recording.

12. **Leave a Message Behind.** Write a letter or record a video or audio message to your loved ones to be shared after your death.

13. **Like Tears in Rain.** In Ridley Scott's film *Blade Runner* (1982), as the cyborg Roy, played by Rutger Hauer, is dying, he laments that his memories will be lost with his death. In his poetic last words, reportedly ad-libbed by the actor,[11] "All those moments will be lost in time, like tears in rain."[12] What are the moments that you cherish that will be lost with your death? Make a list of the most meaningful events and memories of your life. Perhaps share it with someone you trust.

14. **Your Legacy.** Imagine you were going to die tomorrow. Looking back, consider the scope of your life. What was most important to you? Where did you find meaning? What were you proud of? Not so proud of? Where did you find joy and fulfillment? Do you have any regrets? Imagine looking at your life from an expanded perspective. What do you see? What gave your life meaning? What were the most important relationships? What did you learn? Record this in some way, perhaps as a written document or other media you can share with your loved ones.

ACTIVITIES

1. **Your Own Living Funeral.** Stage your own living funeral. Plan the menu, pick the space, make the guest list. Invite your friends and family to read eulogies. Prepare your own speech, detailing who and what was most important to you, and how you would sum up your life.

2. **Memorial Traditions around the World.** Do some research into burial and memorial traditions in other countries; some suggested books on the topic are *From Here to Eternity: Traveling the World to Find the Good Death* (2017) by Caitlin Doughty, and *Making an Exit: From the Magnificent to the Macabre—How We Dignify the Dead* (2011) by Sarah Murray.

3. **Your Own Gravestone.** Make your own gravestone, complete with an epitaph. Added bonus: Keep it in a place you can see every day!

4. **Design Your Own Funeral Shroud.** A funeral shroud, also known as a burial shroud or winding sheet, is a cloth used to wrap a deceased person's body before burial or cremation. It is a traditional garment that has been used for centuries in various cultures and religions as a way to prepare the body for its final resting place. Design one of your own, which expresses something about who you are and your values. You might even consider constructing it!

5. **Your Final Room.** Design and/or create the room you would like to die in.

6. **Legacy Project.** Create a legacy project to leave to your friends and family, something that sums up your life. It might take the form of a formal (or informal) autobiography; a recorded video or audio oral history, in which someone interviews you about your life; a poem summing up your thoughts on life; a scrapbook; or anything else that seems right.

7. **Make an Heirloom.** Create an heirloom to be left to a family member (birth or chosen) after you die, and ask that person to leave it to someone at their death.

8. **Funeral-Planning Worksheet.** A practical way to look your death in the eye—and plan for it—is to write down your explicit desires

for what you would like done after your death and with your body. See addendum seven, page 249, to fill out a funeral-planning worksheet. Give a copy to a loved one who can help make sure your afterdeath wishes are honored.

9. **Afterdeath Secrets.** Are there any secrets that you might want to share from beyond the grave? If so, write them down and put them in a sealed envelope to be opened upon your death.

10. **Hidden Possessions.** Are there any possessions you want hidden from your family or friends before you die? If so, arrange for them to be hidden upon your death by a trusted loved one.

11. **Heal a Relationship.** Do you have a relationship that needs healing? If so, can you take a small, gentle step in that direction?

12. **Practical Preparation.** Seek resources about writing your will. Research how you would manage access to your bank accounts and other legal and bureaucratic concerns. (There are many free online services for this.) You might also take the advice of death doula Kristina Golden, who urges people to create a binder or notebook containing all your online accounts with usernames and passwords, medical information, business info, and information on bills (including those set up for automatic payment). If you create one, store it in a safe place, and inform a trusted loved one of its location and how it can be accessed.

13. **Clean House with Some Swedish Death Cleaning.** Do you feel overwhelmed by stuff? Try divesting some of your possessions, per the suggestions of Margareta Magnusson in *The Gentle Art of Swedish Death Cleaning.* As you sort through your things, ask yourself: Does it improve my life or bring me happiness? Does it have sentimental value or tell a story about my life? If not, consider giving it away to charity or a friend, or letting it go in some other fashion.

14. **Resonance Check.** Did any material in this chapter particularly resonate for you? Is there something that piqued your interest? I invite you to keep track of the things that spoke to you in a special place in your journal. I also encourage you to go further, to do more research on anything that you felt excited about, and if you are a visual person, to collect images related to things that interested you. Start a folder of these images or create a Pinterest board.

15. **Check In.** What were your biggest surprises this week? Did you learn something new about yourself? Make notes in your journal.

10

PLAYING WITH DEATH
DEATH AND POPULAR AMUSEMENT

When I lived in the San Francisco Bay Area, I loved to go to the
Musée Mécanique. The tiny museum—located in a small,
dusty room overlooking the sea—was filled with a private collection
of penny arcade toys, which are coin-activated, mechanized amusements that were popular in the nineteenth and early twentieth centuries. By dropping a quarter in the slot, you could activate these
antiquated amusements, bringing the miniature scenarios they depicted to life.

As a young person, I was fascinated by the fact that so many of the
penny arcade toys exhibited at Musée Mécanique revolved around
death and disaster. You could, for example, see San Francisco destroyed by the 1906 earthquake courtesy of moving 3D images and
a stereoscope. You could also view tiny, crudely modeled figures

If we're honest with ourselves, we have to admit we enjoy our tears just as much as we enjoy our laughter. The only moments of life that are a bore are when we don't care one way or another.

——VINCENT PRICE, AMERICAN HORROR MOVIE ACTOR, ART HISTORIAN, AND COLLECTOR

enacting an English execution, a French execution, and a beheading by guillotine.

These penny arcade attractions are just a few of the death-themed amusements that proliferated in Europe and the United States in the nineteenth and early twentieth centuries. Perhaps this is because, as theater historian Mel Gordon, author of *The Grand Guignol: Theatre of Fear and Terror* (1988), asserts, one of the main purposes of popular entertainment is the exploration of the taboo. The spike in popularity of death-themed amusements, then, might be seen as speaking to the changing needs of a culture in which the traditional ways of making sense of death were disappearing. With death moving offstage from home to the hospital, and from the realms of religion and mythology to that of science, it was, perhaps for the first time in history, being hidden, and thus becoming uncanny and frightening. In Jungian terms, death was moving out of our cultural consciousness and into our cultural shadow. There, like other unacknowledged or suppressed psychological material, our imaginings of death emerged in furtive, disreputable forms, expressed in the unpoliced realms of popular culture.

THE BIRTH OF DEATH-THEMED AMUSEMENTS

The Age of Reason, also known as the Enlightenment, was an intellectual and cultural movement of the seventeenth and eighteenth centuries that had a great influence on the world we live in today. Adherents strove to eliminate superstition and the power of religion and elevate reason and scientific inquiry in their stead. These thinkers believed that if we could cultivate a democratic society based on the principles of reason, people would naturally become free, just, happy, and peaceful. Sadly, this has not been the case, and in our enthusiasm for this new utopia, we jettisoned the wisdom, traditions, and rituals that once helped us meaningfully make sense of death.

Death-themed amusements as we think of them today emerged during this era, at a historical moment when the newly dominant scientific worldview was challenging millennia-old beliefs in ancestor spirits, ghosts, and the supernatural. It was a time when the old death ways were beginning to be derided as quaint and superstitious, and questions related to death and the hereafter—a realm once overseen by priests—were moving largely into the world of popular culture, where entrepreneurs created attractions that explored these ideas as for-profit, immersive amusements.

A rich flowering of death-themed amusements emerged in Paris in the wake of the French Revolution (1789–99). The revolution was animated by Enlightenment ideals, and was activated by a financial crisis, resentment over class inequality, and what was seen as a decadent monarchy. During this turbulent period, the people rose up and dethroned and executed the king and queen. They established a new, secular, democratic society that went on to inspire the modern rational self-governing societies of today.

One period of the French Revolution has been dubbed "The Reign of Terror." During this time, in a little under a year, seventeen thousand "enemies of the revolution" were publicly beheaded by guillotine. Many would attend these executions as a form of macabre entertainment.

When I try to imagine what it might have been like to live through this historical moment—a time when ancient ideas about God and the immortal soul were being challenged, when the future seemed deeply unclear, and all this was against the backdrop of thousands of spectacularly staged public deaths—it seems to me no wonder that Paris was the birthplace of modern death-themed attractions. The first such amusement we see mentioned in the historical record were what were called *bals des victimes*, or victims' balls. These (probably apocryphal) spectacles were described as lavish affairs that could be attended only if you had lost a loved one to the guillotine's blade. It was said that guests would attend in mourning costume, and women would wind red ribbons around their throats (suggesting a bloody decapitation) and style their hair as if it had been chopped by the guillotine's blade.

Give death a better name or die trying.

—TIMOTHY LEARY, AMERICAN PSYCHOLOGIST, AUTHOR, AND PROVOCATEUR

Right around the same time, we have the inception of the phantasmagoria. These were frightening, immersive ghost shows in which moving magic lanterns—a precursor of the slide projector—were used to project images of ghosts, skeletons, and demons onto smoke, making it appear as if they were darting around the room. Hugely popular in Paris and much of Europe in the eighteenth century, these spectacles were often produced by men who claimed to stage them in order to disprove superstitious beliefs in ghosts and the supernatural. Their performances, however, were—in at least one instance—attacked as demonstrations of witchcraft and necromancy.

By the nineteenth century, Sarah Bernhardt, a Parisian actress, had become a worldwide superstar, primarily on the strength of her tragic roles. Her death scenes were so beloved that the audience would commonly demand encores, and she would happily oblige! Playing to this macabre reputation, some of her publicity photos showed her lying in the coffin she was said to sleep in while preparing for her tragic roles.

Nineteenth-century Paris was also home to the Grand Guignol, conceived as a sort of puppet show for adults. As theater historian Mel Gordon explains, what would make adults laugh and cry, as children did in puppet shows? Sex and death![1] The Grand Guignol, which opened in a former chapel in 1897, presented short plays that alternated between sex farces and horrific melodramas. The latter were replete with scenes of excruciatingly graphic violence; on a given evening, you might see a woman's face burned with acid, or a man's eyes being gouged out. It is said that the violence was so realistic that at least two people fainted every night, sometimes as many as fifteen, and that the fainters were usually men, as they did not cover their eyes. For decades one of the biggest tourist attractions in Paris, it was rendered obsolete by horror films in the 1960s.

Nearby, one could pay a visit to the Cabarets of Death. These were immersive cabarets and theme restaurants that were, in the words of Mel Gordon, "devoted to bardo-like journeys into the hereafter."[2] You could choose between three different venues: the Cabaret du Néant (cabaret of death, or nothingness), the cabaret of heaven, or the cabaret of hell (hell was said to cost more, but be more fun!). Each presented thematic food and drink, performances, and displays of nudity, and allowed you to thumb your nose at death and recently discounted ideas of Christian sin at the same time.

Death will be a great relief. No more interviews.

—KATHARINE HEPBURN, AMERICAN ACTRESS

From the late nineteenth to the early twentieth century, similar attractions were common sights in Europe and the United States, where

CULTURAL WHITEWASHING

As the close experience of death receded from life in the late nineteenth and early twentieth centuries, the United States began to practice a sort of cultural whitewashing. Dark, scary, or death-related parts of a story or practice began to be removed in order to render them more appropriate for children and polite consumption. Many old stories and traditions were defanged, so to speak. Death, violence, and the negative were expunged, leaving only the positive in their stead.

When I lived in Budapest, Hungary, I was shocked one December to see—at the local Burger King, no less!—a frightening red demon standing next to a costumed Saint Nicholas. When I asked my local friends about this curious sight, they told me that this was Krampus, the Christmas demon! Had I really never heard of him? I found myself struck by the disparity between our cultures: in the United States, a naughty child might be punished with a lump of coal in their stocking; my Hungarian friends had grown up afraid that if they misbehaved, they might be kidnapped by a demon who would beat them with a birch switch!

From the eighteenth to the early nineteenth century, there were many illustrated children's books—often quite brutal by our standards—designed to teach children social and moral lessons. The best known of these is *Der Struwwelpeter*, or "Shockheaded Peter" (1845). The book, originally written by Heinrich Hoffmann as a Christmas gift for his three-year-old son, is an illustrated collection of cautionary tales meant to teach children moral lessons. In one story, the heroine, despite the warnings of her parents, plays with matches; she ends up setting herself on fire and dying. In another, a young boy, despite the admonitions of his mother, sucks his thumb, and is punished by having the offending digits cut off with giant shears.

Disney is famous for its whitewashing of traditional fairy tales. In the canonical version of "Cinderella," published by the Grimm Brothers in their *Children's and Household Tales* of 1812, the stepsisters were forced to cut off parts of their feet to fit them into the glass slippers. In the same book, the evil queen in "Snow White" was forced to dance in hot iron shoes at the protagonist's wedding. Similarly, in Hans Christian Andersen's original "The Little Mermaid," published in 1837, the titular heroine is forced by the Sea Witch to give up her voice to become human; when she does so, every step she takes causes her deep pain. And because she fails to win the prince's love, she is ultimately cursed to be reduced to sea-foam.

This elimination of violence from children's tales was not without its critics. Austrian psychologist and writer Bruno Bettelheim (1903–1990) bemoaned this cultural shift, asserting that children loved fairy tales in part because of their extreme situations and violence, which helped them cope with their fears by presenting them in a symbolic and controlled manner in which all was resolved with a happy ending. They allowed children to encounter frightening situations in

> a safe context, letting them process and understand their fears without exposure to real danger.

death- and afterlife-themed spectacles drew enthusiastic crowds at world's fairs and amusement parks. At New York's Coney Island— the world's first amusement park—people could take part in immersive, multi-actor theatrical spectacles that allowed them to experience the apocalypse as described in the New Testament's book of Revelation, Pompeii being destroyed by a firework-activated Mount Vesuvius, and San Francisco's decimation by earthquake. In 1907, there was even an attraction called "Night and Morning: or, A Journey through Heaven and Hell," in which one could enjoy an immersive simulation of being buried alive in a glass coffin, followed by a lighthearted trip through heaven and hell.

THE BENEFITS OF PLEASURABLE FEAR

There have been many studies investigating why so many of us find it so pleasurable to experience death and violence, so long as they are simulations or we are at a safe remove. A few years back, I interviewed Dr. Margee Kerr, sociology professor and author of *Scream: Chilling Adventures in the Science of Fear* (2015). We talked about a study she had conducted about people who love going to haunted houses. She found that these individuals generally reported feeling better after the experience, but for different reasons. Some observed that they had learned about themselves by challenging their fear. Others disclosed that they had left with a feeling of confidence, knowing they could master something that frightened them.

Many, she remarked, also observed that they enjoyed the experience because it quieted their minds. When I noted that this sounded suspiciously like meditation, Dr. Kerr laughed and said that yes, in fact, she and a friend who teaches yoga often joke that they help people get to the same place, albeit from very different starting points. It turns out that some people who enjoy scary entertainments find that, like meditation and yoga, these experiences quiet their inner chatter and put them completely in the body. Dr. Kerr explained that when you are in a situation that is as completely visceral as a haunted house, there is no space or time to worry about the past or the future. These experiences center you and put you entirely in your body, in the moment—or, in the parlance of Dr. Bolte Taylor, in the right side of the brain.

Studies also suggest that laughter can neutralize the sting of that which we fear, including death. In psychiatrist Viktor Frankl's book *Man's Search for Meaning* (1946)—based on his experience as a prisoner of a Nazi death camp—he describes humor as one of the "soul's weapons" in transcending despair. And Freud, in his 1927 essay "Humour," postulated that humor allows the release of psychic energy through the expression of repressed thoughts or feelings, and asserted that jokes and humor provide a socially acceptable way to talk about forbidden or taboo topics, including death and sexuality. In this context, humor could be seen as a way to indirectly confront and cope with the reality of death, and neutralize its fear, by transforming it into a subject of laughter.

More recent studies tell us that a sense of humor is also a great benefit when coping with the vicissitudes of life. Psychologists tell us that laughter reduces pain, stress, and mental suffering; strengthens our immune systems; makes us more alert; lowers blood pressure; and raises our endorphin levels. Studies in grief

Most people die at 25 and aren't buried until they're 75.

—BENJAMIN FRANKLIN, AMERICAN SCIENTIST, INVENTOR, DIPLOMAT, AND STATESMAN also suggest that bereaved individuals who are able to laugh or smile as they recall their lost loved one report lower levels of anxiety and depression.[3] Shared laughter in groups can also create a sense of social bonding and support, which can be valuable for coping with difficult topics, including death.

Studies have also demonstrated the benefits of black humor, also called gallows humor, in which one finds amusement in dark or morbid situations. Researchers suggest that this sort of humor may help individuals mentally distance themselves from traumatic events, aiding in emotional regulation and resilience. Fascinatingly, recent studies have shown that those who most appreciate black humor had lower scores for bad mood or aggression and high scores on IQ tests.[4]

Similar benefits have been discovered for those who possess what is termed "morbid curiosity." The morbidly curious are defined as individuals interested in topics such as death, violence, disaster, and the macabre. Researchers have found that exploring morbid topics can help individuals regulate their emotions. By confronting fears and anxiety in a controlled manner, people may experience a sense of catharsis or relief. Those with morbid curiosity also tend to exhibit other personality traits, including curiosity more generally and openness to experience.

An intriguing study led by behavioral scientist Coltan Scrivner examined the fact that morbidly curious people and horror fans fared better during the COVID-19 pandemic. This speaks to a phenomenon that I had noted, anecdotally, in the Morbid Anatomy community: that those who are interested in death—the morbidly curious—seemed to fare much better in the strange, uncertain times of the pandemic, and expressed far less of the anxiety and despair I noticed in many of those who do not share this predilection. Scrivner and his colleagues report that morbid curiosity promotes "positive resilience," which is the possibility of having positive experiences even when encountering a threatening or frightening situation. Because people who are morbidly curious were able to find the pandemic not only scary but also *interesting*, they were able to "experience less psychological distress."[5] Morbid curiosity has been shown to foster empathy and compassion by helping people connect, on an emotional level, with the suffering of others. It also prompts one to explore the darker aspects of human history, leading to a more inclusive view and understanding.

One activity that tends to draw the morbidly curious is the viewing of human remains. The most famous impresario of the dead human body is German anatomist Gunther von Hagens, who launched his infamous Body Worlds exhibitions in 1995. In these touring shows, staged at science museums and exhibit halls around the world, he displays human bodies preserved through plastination—a technique of his own invention that replaces the liquids and fat in a cadaver with plastic, rendering them durable and sterile. Von Hagens presents preserved cadavers in everyday poses, such as a basketball player shooting a hoop, men playing poker, or a woman dancing. More recent exhibits feature cadavers in increasingly charged scenes, including some engaged in sexual acts.

Gunther von Hagens's exhibits have made him millions of dollars. They are also deeply controversial. His spectacular staging of dead human bodies offends some people's sensibilities, who see his works as disrespectful or in bad taste. There are also ethical questions regarding some of the bodies he has used, said to be sourced from Chinese political prisoners.

Dead bodies had been used for entertainment purposes long before Gunther von Hagens started making headlines. In the eighteenth century, when dead bodies were still an everyday sight, the artist and anatomist Honoré Fragonard (cousin of the famous Rococo painter Jean Honoré Fragonard) made artworks from preserved human and animal bodies. The themes of his pieces were often drawn from the Bible, with figures such as Samson with the ass's jaw and a horseman of the apocalypse. Long before plastic, it is thought that Fragonard preserved his pieces with a mix of mutton tallow, essence of turpentine, and essential oils, along with a special varnish to keep insects at bay. It is said that he sold these anatomical écorchés—or flayed bodies—as artworks to members of the French aristocracy before the revolution.

For centuries, dead bodies have been exhibited in ways that blended entertainment and education. In the seventeenth century one could, for example, visit custom-built anatomical theaters where one could witness the dissection of an executed criminal. Often staged as part of wider carnival festivities, these spectacles taught the audience about the anatomy of the human body, often to the accompaniment of drinks and music. There were also popular anatomical museums, where the general public could see preserved human cadavers and anatomical models that displayed the body inside and out, in sickness and health. These museums often featured—as their centerpiece—beautiful, dissectible, life-size women. Called "Anatomical Venuses," they were usually made of wax and augmented with real human hair and glass eyes.

Less educational exhibitions of the dead body were also prevalent. In the eighteenth century, one could visit London's Tyburn gallows, where public executions were a popular entertainment that drew picnicking families and other onlookers. And in a horrifying twentieth-century practice, lynching postcards were produced as souvenirs of the public murders of Black people by vigilantes in the United States. On the front one finds a photo of the lynching, often surrounded by smiling white men, women, and children. Many of these were sent to friends and family, and included messages such as "Token of a great day."

It was also not unusual to seek entertainment in cemeteries. Usually located in churchyards, from the Middle Ages through to the seventeenth century, these were not just places to bury the dead, but also venues in which you could play games, buy wares from a variety of merchants, and seek romantic adventure, sometimes with professionals. Later, in the nineteenth century, the new rural or garden cemeteries—with rolling hills, manicured grounds, beautiful funeral monuments, and permanent interment—became fashionable leisure destinations. Brooklyn's Green-Wood Cemetery, founded in 1838, was New York City's first garden cemetery. At one point in the nineteenth century, it was the state's most popular tourist attraction, second only to Niagara Falls. One would visit the cemetery to appreciate its natural splendor, marvel at the tombs of the rich and famous, and enjoy a lovely picnic.

One might also frequent a cemetery in order to cultivate a sense of melancholy, which novelist Victor Hugo defined as "the happiness of being sad."[6] As many of us have no doubt experienced, there is, at times, a delightful aspect to sadness in a certain measure. It invites a poignant, heightened quality to one's awareness, and produces a calm, introspective, and reflective state. It is a solitary feeling that can be nurtured by spending time in moody spaces such as cemeteries, or by certain seasons, such as autumn. Melancholy is a pleasurable pain, one that often inspires people to express themselves creatively, in forms such as poetry, music, or painting.

The "cult of melancholia" was a social phenomenon centered on a celebration of melancholy as a source of creativity, insight, and inspiration. It emerged during the Renaissance, but reached its zenith with the eighteenth- and nineteenth-century Romantics. The

Romantics were a group of artists, writers, musicians, and thinkers who, in defiance of the growing domination of rationality and bourgeois commonsense values, chose to focus on emotion, passion, and the imagination. A classic novel of the genre, Johann Wolfgang von Goethe's *The Sorrows of Young Werther* (1774), tells the story of a young man who kills himself over unrequited love. The book captivated many melancholic young men, who began dressing as Goethe's hero; some even committed suicide with the book at their sides, leading some countries to ban it.

Devotees of the cult of melancholia and the Romantics were both interested in the idea of the sublime, which is the awe, reverence, and sometimes fear that we experience when we encounter something vast, powerful, and beyond our comprehension. The sublime often evokes a mix of feelings, including pleasure, terror, and a sense of insignificance in the face of the immense. It might be inspired by something in nature, such as the snowy peaks of the Alps, or a great work of art. It can also be evoked by an intense personal experience, such as the birth of a child or an encounter with death. The sublime might be understood as a secularized form of religious awe: something that reminds us of our capacity for wonder and our connection to the vast and mysterious aspects of the world around us.

The Gothic genre of the late eighteenth and nineteenth centuries drew on the melancholic, romantic, and sublime, and gloried in death, darkness, mystery, the supernatural, and intense emotions. Its best-known works include *Frankenstein; or, The Modern Prometheus* (1818), *Strange Case of Dr. Jekyll and Mr. Hyde* (1886), *Dracula* (1897), and Edgar Allan Poe's short stories, such as "The Pit and the Pendulum" (1842), "The Tell-Tale Heart" (1843), and "The Masque of the Red Death" (1842). The Gothic style has endured, almost unchanged, into the modern age, living on today in the films of Tim Burton and

Guillermo del Toro; the phenomenal popularity of Stephenie Meyer's *Twilight* series, with its sparkly vampires and hunky werewolves; and the ongoing allure of Wednesday Addams and her unusual family.

The Gothic also lives on in the form of the youth subculture that bears its name. With its members known as "goths" or sometimes "death rockers," this subculture devoted to all things deathly originated in bleak, post-punk, late-1970s London. Goths of all genders tend to dress in black, androgynous clothing and corpse-pale makeup with black eyeliner and dark lipstick. Like the Romantics who came before them, they value the emotions and the imagination, and keep the dark flame of melancholy alive. They read the Gothic classics and cultivate a relationship with death. Goths actively defy the cultural mandate to deny or repress awareness of death, ensuring that death has a cherished and intentional place, if only in a robust counterculture.

DEATH-THEMED AMUSEMENTS IN THE TWENTIETH AND TWENTY-FIRST CENTURIES

If the discussion or awareness of *natural* death is largely avoided in the modern world, *violent* death is a ubiquitous part of popular culture. Violent scenarios are integral to many of our most beloved and critically acclaimed films and television shows, including *The Godfather*, *Pulp Fiction*, *The Sopranos*, *The Wire*, and *Breaking Bad*. There is also a seemingly unending thirst for true crime narratives in a variety of media. This fascination probably stems, at least in part, from the prevalence of violent death (and its concomitant anxieties) on the world stage.

The twentieth century was an extremely violent time, with two devastating world wars, the Russian Revolution, the Nazi concentration

camps, multiple genocides, the nuclear bombs of Hiroshima and Na-
gasaki, and terrorist attacks, all of it reported on by a burgeoning mass
media. Violence has not abated in the twenty-first century, and the
nightly news regales us with stories of wars, random violence, countless mass shootings, a violently charged political discourse, and the
unfolding fallout from the intensifying climate crisis.

In his 1955 article "The Pornography of Death," written in response to a cultural panic about horror-themed children's comics,
British sociologist Geoffrey Gorer argues that death had become
taboo in his own time, just as sex had been during the Victorian era.
Death, he notes, like sex in the nineteenth century, is not talked about,
especially in front of children, and if it must be talked about, it will be
in euphemisms ("passed away," "casualties") or behind closed doors.
Gorer observes that "while natural death became more and more
smothered in prudery, violent death has played an ever-growing part
in the fantasies offered to mass audiences."[7] His solution?

> If we dislike the modern pornography of death, then
> we must give back to death—natural death—its parade
> and publicity, readmit grief and mourning. If we make
> death unmentionable in polite society—"not before the
> children"—we almost ensure the continuation of the
> "horror comic."[8]

A contemporary development that responds to Gorer's call can
be found in what is called the death-positive movement. The term—
coined by *New York Times* bestselling author, funeral director, and
activist Caitlin Doughty—refers to a movement that seeks to change
the way society views and interacts with death and dying by helping
remove its stigma, and by returning it to everyday life and conversa-

Death is there as irrefutable proof of the absurdity of life.

—ANDRÉ MALRAUX, FRENCH NOVELIST, ART THEORIST, AND POLITICAL ACTIVIST

tion. To this end, it provides practical resources, supports alternative forms of death care, and works with legislators and other advocates to protect and expand access to sustainable, affordable, and meaningful death care. In this way, it hopes to reduce death-related anxiety and encourage greater diversity in end-of-life options.

In 2011, Doughty started an organization called the Order of the Good Death, which is made up of a group of individuals—myself included!—who are committed to embracing our mortality and helping others do the same. Doughty's work is very much in the spirit of the woman I regard as the unsung grandmother of the death-positive movement: Swiss American psychiatrist and compassionate end-of-life-care pioneer Dr. Elisabeth Kübler-Ross (1926–2004).

Kübler-Ross grew up in Switzerland, where she was exposed to traditional ways of death, with people dying at home and the children invited in as part of the process. When she moved to the US and began working in its hospitals, she was troubled by the way the medical establishment approached death, especially by their disinclination to inform the dying of their true condition. She interviewed terminally ill patients to ascertain what kind of care they desired, how they wished to be talked to by their doctors and families, and how they dealt with knowledge of their forthcoming death.

Kübler-Ross's research led her to write her international bestseller, *On Death and Dying: What the Dying Have to Teach Doctors, Nurses, Clergy and Their Own Families* (1969), in which she introduces her influential concept of the five stages of grief—denial, anger, bargaining, depression, and acceptance—that often follow a terminal diagnosis. Over the course of her life, she published over twenty books as part of her mission to change how we thought about death. Her work was also pivotal in the acceptance of palliative care for the terminally ill.

Today, we have a number of options for those who want to embrace and cultivate a sense of death positivity. One of these is the Death Cafe, founded in 2011 by Jon Underwood to function as a safe space for talking about death over tea and cakes. Today, there are Death Cafes all over the world, and people are encouraged to start their own. Similar initiatives include Death Over Dinner, which encourages people to host dinner parties where people are encouraged to share death-related stories, thoughts, and experiences while sharing a meal. There is also the Death Deck, a card game designed to initiate conversations about death and dying, prompting players to communicate with others about death and end-of-life matters. At Morbid Anatomy, we also offer a variety of online and in-person classes, lectures, and experiences geared toward thinking and talking about death. Together, these organizations and interventions are all doing their part to challenge societal taboos around death and create a safe space for open, thoughtful, and even *fun* conversations about a part of life many of us would rather avoid.

EXERCISES

JOURNAL PROMPTS

1. **Childhood Frights.** When I was a kid, I loved reading the horror books of Stephen King and watching scary movies. Did your par-

ents let you read or watch scary stuff when you were young? Did you like that sort of thing? If so, what were your favorites? What do you think drew you to such material, and what do you think you got out of it, if anything?

2. **Scary Family Traditions.** Did your family have any frightening cultural figures like Krampus the Christmas demon? If so, describe them. What was the experience like?

3. **Morbidly Curious?** Are you a morbidly curious person or a person drawn to horror? If so, do you think it has helped you in any way? If so, how? If you do not consider yourself morbidly curious, is it something you might like to cultivate in some way? Why or why not? Added bonus: Read up on the characteristics and benefits of morbid curiosity.

4. **Gallows Humor.** Did you and your friends tell death-related jokes when you were children? Do you now? What do you think about the idea of morbid humor? Write down as many dark jokes as you can think of, or look some up on the internet. Write down your favorites, say them aloud (or share them!), and note how they make you feel.

5. **The Human Corpse.** Have you ever seen a dead body, perhaps at a funeral, at a medical museum, or in an exhibition such as Gunther von Hagens's Body World? How did it make you feel? If not, and if it makes you curious, go and see such an exhibit and write about your response.

6. **Cultivating Melancholia.** Does the idea of cultivating a sense of melancholy resonate with you? Are you attracted to that emotion? Do you nurture it in any way? If so, what does it add to your life? Does it encourage you to engage in creative work of any sort?

7. **Thought Experiment: The Age of Rationality.** Do you think

Western culture's emphasis on rationality and the attempt to eliminate religion and superstition has made the world a better place? How or how not? What might the world be like if we had never moved in this direction?

8. **Violence in Entertainment.** How do you feel about violence in TV and film? Is it something you enjoy? Something you are willing to overlook for the sake of a good plot? Make a list of favorite TV shows or movies that you cannot imagine without violence.

ACTIVITIES

1. **A Cute Death.** How might death be made to be cute and/or fun? Write or create an artwork, a doll, or an object to explore this.

2. **Your Own Death-Themed Amusement.** If you had unlimited resources, what death-themed amusement would you create? What would the theme be? What would it look like? What would the experience be? Where would it be staged? Make a drawing of it, or write about it at length.

3. **Have Fun with Fear.** Ride a roller coaster, visit a haunted house, or go see horror movie and observe how your mind and body respond. Write about the experience. Added bonus: Go with a friend and discuss your feelngs afterward.

4. **The Art of José Posada.** In nineteenth-century Mexico, artist José Posada created the iconic image of La Catrina, an elegantly dressed woman who happens to take the form of a skeleton. Spend some time looking at Posada's work, which features jolly skeletons dancing, riding bicycles, and engaging in other common daily activities. Try drawing some amusing skeletal images of your own, for example, of skeletons engaging in contemporary pastimes.

5. **Death Doll.** Make or buy a puppet or doll of death and keep it in your home.

6. **Gallows Humor.** Both Edward Gorey and Charles Addams (of *The Addams Family* fame) were artists and writers who merged dark humor and the macabre to create a sort of alternate universe. Look up some of their best-known work, such as Gorey's *The Gashlycrumb Tinies* (1963), or some Addams cartoons, and spend some time immersed in their worlds.

7. **History of Death-Themed Amusements.** Do some research on death-themed amusements online. To take a deeper dive, read Mel Gordon's *The Grand Guignol: Theatre of Fear and Terror* (1988) or *Cabarets of Death: Death, Dance and Dining in Early Twentieth-Century Paris* (2023). I also recommend the short films of Morbid Anatomy former filmmaker-in-residence Ronni Thomas, many of which explore these topics, at themidnightarchive.com.

8. **Camp Horror.** In the 1960s and '70s, Vincent Price was the master of elegant, fun, tongue-in-cheek, campy horror. A wonderful example of the power of keeping death close at hand as a means of living a fully realized life, he was, in addition to being an actor famous for his dark roles, also an art historian, collector, and gourmet cook! Watch one of his classic films, such as *The House of Wax* (1953), *The Masque of the Red Death* (1964), or *The Abominable Dr. Phibes* (1971).

9. **Classic Horror Films.** In the mid-twentieth century, no one knew what frightened—and simultaneously *delighted*—the Western world quite like Alfred Hitchcock. Watch one of his classic horror films, such as *Psycho* (1960), *Shadow of a Doubt* (1943), or *The Birds* (1963). You might also enjoy other classic horror films, such as *Rosemary's Baby* (1968), *The Night of the Hunter* (1955), *The Innocents* (1961), *The Haunting* (1963), *The Exorcist* (1973), *The Shining* (1980), and *The Silence of the Lambs* (1991).

10. **Visit a Cemetery.** In the nineteenth century, cemeteries were

major tourist attractions. Bring a friend or loved one for a picnic at a historic cemetery. Spend some time admiring the beautiful monuments and landscaping, and enjoy the piquant melancholy.

11. **Laugh at Death.** Watch a death-themed comedy, such as *Harold and Maude* (1971), *The Addams Family* (1991), *The Loved One* (1965), *Beetlejuice* (1988), or the TV show *The Good Place* (2016–20). For absurdist humor mixed with poignant existential angst, you might also enjoy the critically acclaimed television show *Six Feet Under* (2001–5), centered around a family who runs a funeral home.

12. **Embrace Your Inner Goth** . . . and indulge in some melancholic expression! Get yourself into a mood of enjoyable sadness (maybe with the help of the music of the Cure, Satie, or Mozart's Requiem mass) and allow yourself to feel the emotion, then express it in prose, poetry, art, dancing, or whatever medium you like.

13. **Indulge in the Gothic.** Cultivate a Gothic sensibility by reading one of the genre's classic texts, such as *Frankenstein* (1818); *Strange Case of Dr. Jekyll and Mr. Hyde* (1886), *Dracula* (1897), or a short story by Edgar Allan Poe and write about what it evokes for you.

14. **Play with Death.** Spend a night going through the Death Deck with some friends.

15. **Death Cafe.** Have you ever gone to a Death Cafe, Death Over Dinner, or similar? If not, and if you are curious, can you find one to attend? If not, consider starting your own!

16. **Expose Yourself to the Sublime.** Put yourself in a situation that allows you to experience the sublime. You might go out into nature or to the sea, marvel at the nighttime sky filled with stars, or view photos of the cosmos taken by the James Webb Space Telescope. You could also take in the grandeur of a national or state park, such as Yosemite, Niagara Falls, or the Grand Canyon. Al-

low yourself to feel the sense of awe for something so far beyond yourself, something ineffable and outside comprehension that leaves you in thrall to the wonders of nature. Write about the experience when you return home. What was it like? How did it make you feel? What surprised you? If so inspired, you might try creating a poem or artwork that tries to capture the feeling.

17. **Resonance Check.** Did any material in this chapter particularly resonate for you? Is there something that piqued your interest? I invite you to keep track of the things that spoke to you in a special place in your journal. I also encourage you to go further, to do more research on anything that you felt excited about, and if you are a visual person, to collect images related to things that interested you. Start a folder of these images or create a Pinterest board.

18. **Check In.** What were the biggest surprises this week? Did you learn something new about yourself? Make notes in your journal.

II

LIVING YOUR TRUE VALUES

I really hate flying. As I wait in line, I can't help but visualize my fellow passengers, now calmly filing on board, plunged into a state of panic as the aircraft takes a nosedive. Once on the plane, whenever we encounter the tiniest bit of turbulence, I grip the seat with white knuckles, desperately staring out the window for a spot of earth with which to ground myself.

But for every ounce that I hate flying, I love to travel. So, when I was in my adolescence, I developed a little ritual. When I got on the plane, I would close my eyes, sit quietly, and take a few deep breaths. Then I would ask myself, "If I die on this flight, what would I regret? What would I wish I had done differently?" I have been asking myself these questions regularly for around forty years now. Engaging in this ritual—*and making changes in my life in accordance with what I've learned*—has profoundly altered the course of my life.

Using practices like this one helped me clarify my own personal values rather than simply accepting those presented by my family and culture. Such activities, performed over the course of a lifetime, helped me manifest the life I longed for in the here and now, instead of waiting for a future that might never come. And even today, when I am stuck on an important decision—Do I want to accept this new job? Write this book? Move to a new country?—I ask myself a simple but profoundly powerful question: *Is this what I want to do with my time on earth?* Similarly, when anxious, worrying about what the future might bring, and unsure if I am in the right place, I ask myself, *Would I be happy to die here?*

Asking myself such questions immediately cuts through the muddle and makes things crystal clear. It has been my experience that many anxieties, when traced to their roots, stem from a fear of death. When I worry if I made a mistake and follow this concern through to its end point, I often realize that, at its root, I fear that this mistake will in some way lead to death. If we move straight to that point—to the worst possible outcome, which lurks behind so many of our anxieties—if we look death in the eye, we find to our surprise that it brings not fear, but *clarity.*

This is how the memento mori looks when applied to a life. And I'm not the only one who sees the profound power of such tools. Steve Jobs, the mastermind behind Apple computers and the iPhone, revealed in a 2005 commencement speech for Stanford University graduates that he had been using a memento mori–like death awareness practice since he was seventeen. He reported that he would look in the mirror every morning and ask himself, "If today were the last day of my life, would I want to do what I am about to do today?" If he found that for too many days in a row the answer was no, then he would make a change.

Speaking as someone who'd only the year before been diagnosed with a rare form of pancreatic cancer, he said:

Remembering that I'll be dead soon is the most important tool I've ever encountered to help me make the big choices in life. Because almost everything—all external expectations, all pride, all fear of embarrassment or failure—these things just fall away in the face of death, leaving only what is truly important. Remembering that you are going to die is the best way I know to avoid the trap of thinking you have something to lose. You are already naked. There is no reason not to follow your heart. . . .

Death is very likely the single best invention of Life. It is Life's change agent. It clears out the old to make way for the new. . . .

Your time is limited, so don't waste it living someone else's life. Don't be trapped by dogma—which is living with the results of other people's thinking. Don't let the noise of others' opinions drown out your own inner voice. And most important, have the courage to follow your heart and intuition. They somehow already know what you truly want to become. Everything else is secondary.[1]

WHAT DO YOU WANT TO DO
WITH YOUR TIME ON EARTH?

When I was getting ready to open the Morbid Anatomy Museum (2014–16), I asked a curator friend if she could recommend any books on her craft. Although there were a few good ones, she said, in her opinion it was much more important to visit lots of exhibitions and carefully observe what I liked—and, more crucially, what I didn't like. I have found that this valuable lesson can be applied to many situations in life.

When I was in high school, I lived with my father. He hated getting up early. But every morning, he dutifully got up at five thirty for a job he had no interest in, but that gave him a good wage and a secure retirement. His example made it clear to me that working at a job I had no connection to and waiting for my few weeks of vacation to do the things that really mattered to me was very much *not* how I wanted to live my time on earth. It was clear to my young eyes that people spent the majority of their lives at work. For that reason, I knew I wanted to do something I *loved* for a living. It was more important to me to put my energies—my intellect, my creativity, my passion—into something that I enjoyed, and something that, in my opinion, made the world a better place, than to have money and security.

The privilege of a lifetime is to become who you truly are.

—CARL JUNG, SWISS PSYCHIATRIST
AND PSYCHOANALYST

Christina Pratt, a practicing shaman and the author of *An Encyclopedia of Shamanism* (2007), states that from a shamanic perspective, each of us is born with a particular purpose. If we can find a way to express this purpose, it not only makes our life more satisfying, but also benefits our community and the natural world, and makes a unique contribution that no one else could. But how does one ascertain what that purpose might be? She has some advice: ask yourself what you would happily get out of bed at two in the morning to talk about. In an interview in Hillary S. Webb's *Traveling between the Worlds: Conversations with Contemporary Shamans* (2004) she further advises:

It's a big game of hotter-hotter, colder-colder that you play
with the universe, only your soul's purpose is the thing that
is hidden, and your emotions are the language that Spirit
communicates to you through. Your passion is the "hotter-
hotter." When you are feeling depressed and passionless, that
is the "colder-colder."

THE SEARCH FOR HAPPINESS

The idea of happiness is integral to the worldview of the United
States. Indeed, "the pursuit of happiness" is one of the inalienable
rights listed in its Constitution. The US is a relatively young country,
and geographically isolated. The majority of its white, affluent population has not experienced the hardship and trauma suffered by
many in other parts of the world. Of course,
this situation is complicated by our (often
unacknowledged) cultural shadow: the very
real suffering (genocide and slavery) perpe-
trated on others to achieve the wealth and
security some of us now enjoy.

> *If I take death into my life,*
> *acknowledge it, and face it*
> *squarely, I will free myself from*
> *the anxiety of death and the*
> *pettiness of life—and only then*
> *will I be free to become myself.*
>
> —MARTIN HEIDEGGER, GERMAN
> PHILOSOPHER

My oma was a refugee from Hitler's
Vienna, and she experienced a level of personal fear and trauma that I cannot even
imagine. When people asked if she was
happy, she would shrug and say, in her strong Austrian accent, "Happiness? What is happiness?" Happiness, to her, was a fleeting experience, a momentary high in life. *Contentment*, on the other hand . . .
that was a sustainable feeling, and yes, she was indeed content.

Modern happiness studies support my oma's opinion. Finland

I went to the woods because I wished to live deliberately, to front only the essential facts of life, and see if I could not learn what it had to teach, and not, when I came to die, discover that I had not lived.

—HENRY DAVID THOREAU, AMERICAN PHILOSOPHER, POET, AND ENVIRONMENTALIST

has, for a number of years in a row, been ranked the world's happiest nation, and its secret is surprisingly similar to my oma's hard-won wisdom. The people of Finland assert that it is not happiness they seek, but rather *contentment*. Because of this, they are not disappointed that life is not entirely full of bliss.[2]

Striking a similar note is an exchange from *The Sopranos* (1999–2007), a television show that introduces us to Tony Soprano, a rich and powerful mob boss who starts seeing a psychiatrist to treat his panic attacks. Tony is complaining about the difficulties of his life to Svetlana, a hardworking, no-nonsense, one-legged Russian immigrant in his circle. Her response is revealing: "That's the trouble with you Americans. You expect nothing bad ever to happen, when the rest of the world expects only bad to happen, and they are not disappointed."[3]

A few years ago, I came to a similar realization while reading a book by William Leach called *Land of Desire: Merchants, Power and the Rise of a New American Culture* (1993), which traces the rise of consumer capitalism in the United States. One day, as I leafed through glossy women's magazines in my therapist's waiting room, bombarded by images of preternaturally beautiful women and ads for Chanel perfume, Rolexes, and Prada bags, a question suddenly hit me—was there a relationship between the fact that so many of us are dissatisfied with our lives and the fact that we are immersed in a consumer capitalist society that promises that the things we buy can make us happy? Is our sense of dissatisfaction—the feeling of always looking for the next thing—due to frustrated expectations? Is that, in fact, why so many of us entered therapy to begin with? When I asked my therapist what she thought about this, she said, yes, she thought I was right. That was the end of traditional therapy—and the thoughtless consumption of media!—for me.

We live in a culture that bombards us with appeals for our attention, from social media to advertisements. Many of these ads—which are sophisticated pieces of propaganda designed by experts to prey on our base wants and insecurities—create a yearning for things we didn't even know we wanted. This system of inciting desire so we will buy something to *satisfy* that desire runs counter to the tenets of religious and wisdom teachings. In *Land of Desire*, we learn that prominent Protestant, Catholic, and Jewish leaders fought against this new way of life that emerged in the late nineteenth century, seeing it as a threat to spirituality, democracy, and civic life.

The phenomenon of consumer capitalism seems to cultivate the exact opposite of what the Buddhists propose makes a good, healthy, and happy life. For Buddhists, the first principle is that all life is suffering, and their philosophy offers a path to minimize this. Malcolm David Eckel, professor and director of the Institute for Philosophy and Religion at Boston University,[4] cites three different kinds of suffering. There is *dukkha-dukkha*, which is when something clearly causes pain; *viparinama-dukkha*, in which the loss of something we love causes suffering; and *sankhara-dukkha*, in which the things we *think* we enjoy cause suffering because the pleasure is "based on an illusion about the nature of the object or about the nature of the self."[5] As Eckel explains, a car might cause *dukkha-dukkha* if you crash it into a bus. It might cause *viparinama-dukkha* if you drive it during a snowy winter and watch it get corroded by snow and salt. And it might cause *sankhara-dukkha* if you labor under the illusion that there is "something in your sense of self that will be enhanced by attachment to the car." From a Buddhist perspective, it seems that advanced consumer capitalism is designed to make enlightenment more difficult, and to cause greater suffering in exchange for an only fleeting happiness.

Bringing our own death into our awareness can help us chart a clear course in this confusion, and summon a broader and wiser perspective to bear, one that extends beyond our mere ego self and smaller desires and needs. By asking ourselves questions that cut through our confusion, like "Is this what I want to do with my time on earth?" or taking a deep breath and asking, "What does my heart (or 'higher self' or soul) want in this situation?" we can draw ourselves back, again and again, from the small, ultimately unfulfilling pleasures in our lives and focus on what is really important.

Another method to take you out of your simple ego desires is to actively cultivate a connection to something larger. For the religious, this might be done by going to a place of worship or a religious service, or engaging in some way with the divine. For the nonreligious, this might be done by engaging in something that creates a sense of wonder or the sublime, something that helps you feel a connection to the universe and a sense of meaning. It could be spending some time in nature, immersing yourself in a great film you really love instead of whatever happens to be on TV, visiting an art museum, volunteering for a cause you care about, or reading a great piece of literature. It could also be really listening to an awe-inspiring musical piece such as Beethoven's "Ode to Joy" or Mozart's Requiem or watching a truly inspiring and joyful film, such as *Won't You Be My Neighbor?* (2018), a moving documentary about Fred Rogers, creator of *Mister Rogers' Neighborhood*.

If we can be cut off at any moment, why should we postpone what is important to us? Why should we postpone doing and being what we know we are here on this earth to do and to be? Why should we enmesh ourselves in obligations that serve no one, and that stand between our ego and the true nature of our being? Why should we not plunge fully into the life that is given to us as a gift for however long or short it might be? When dying no longer holds any terror, it becomes easier to walk lightly through one's life.

——JUNE SINGER, JUNGIAN ANALYST AND AUTHOR

GRATITUDE

The idea of expressing gratitude for everyday blessings might seem trite. But I have found that cultivating gratitude on a daily basis has shifted my perspective so that I am better able to handle the inevitable curveballs that life throws at me. Gratitude exercises are integral to Buddhist practice; practicing gratitude is also central to Indigenous lifeways. Robin Wall Kimmerer, Potawatomi botanist and director of the Center for Native Peoples and the Environment, writes about gratitude in her bestselling book *Braiding Sweetgrass: Indigenous Wisdom, Scientific Knowledge, and the Teachings of Plants* (2013). She points out that "while expressing gratitude seems innocent enough, it is a revolutionary idea. In a consumer society, contentment is a radical proposition. Recognizing abundance rather than scarcity undermines an economy that thrives by creating unmet desires."[6] There are also numerous studies that suggest gratitude can help individuals become more optimistic and satisfied with their lives.

Cultivating gratitude can be as simple as writing down five things one is grateful for each day in a journal. You might also try your hand at a thank-you letter; psychologist Martin E. P. Seligman of the

USING DEATH AWARENESS TO MAKE DECISIONS

Questions to ask yourself when you're stuck:

* Is this what I want to do with my time on earth?
* What would I regret if died tomorrow?
* Would I be happy to die here?
* Where is my passion?
* What would my heart/higher self/soul want in this situation?
* What am I grateful for?
* Would I regret having (or not having) done this on my deathbed?

University of Pennsylvania found that test subjects who wrote letters to people for a past kindness scored much higher on happiness scores for about a month. If you have a significant other, you might consider jotting down some things you appreciate about them in a journal, or expressing your gratitude to them. Studies demonstrate that when people do so, they end up having more positive thoughts about the partner, and greater ease in sharing concerns about the relationship.[7]

In Japan, there is a Buddhist-inspired therapeutic practice that operates along similar principles. Called Naikan ("introspection" or "looking inside"), it was developed in the mid-twentieth century by Yoshimoto Ishin, a Jodo Shinshu Buddhist minister, and is based around examining your thoughts, feelings, actions, and relationships in a structured and systematic way, with the goal of promoting gratitude, self-awareness, and personal growth. Yoshimoto originally used it to help prisoners in the 1950s, after which psychiatrists began to use it as a form of therapy, which revolves around self-reflection on three particular questions: What have I received from a significant other? What have I given back to that person? What troubles and difficulties did I cause that person?

You don't get to choose how you're going to die. Or when. You can only decide how you're going to live. Now.

—JOAN BAEZ, AMERICAN FOLK SINGER, SONGWRITER, AND POLITICAL ACTIVIST

Taking the time to meditate on the fragility and brevity of existence can also lead us to gratitude. In his book *A Short History of Nearly Everything* (2003), Australian writer Bill Bryson details the ways in which the earth we inhabit so perfectly—and so *tenuously*—supports our existence. He also enumerates the many ways this could change in a moment. One example he shared was that of Yellowstone, the American national park famous for its spectacular geyser Old Faithful. This iconic vacation spot, it turns out, is actually an active supervolcano that, if it were to erupt (and this is very likely), could plunge the world into a yearslong volcanic winter that would kill many and change life as we know it.

My takeaway from reading this book—as from so many memento mori practices—was a deep sense of wonder and gratitude. It feels like a small miracle that I happened to be born here, at this time, on this earth, which is so delicately attuned to our needs. This might change—in fact, it might be changing right now, before our eyes. But realizing this only makes me appreciate the gifts I have been given more, and know that if the world I love comes to an end, if I died tomorrow, I am OK with that, and I am deeply grateful for the rich life I was so lucky to enjoy.

REGRETS

A flip side of gratitude, which can also be used to encourage us to live more fully and before it's too late, is *regret*. Have you ever considered what you might regret having done—or *not* having done—if you died today? Australian nurse Bronnie Ware wondered this, too, and in her book *The Top Five Regrets of the Dying: A Life Transformed by the Dearly Departing* (2012) she summarized the sentiments she heard from her palliative care patients. Their most common regrets were (1) not having had the courage to live a life that was true to themselves, having done instead what their families or cultures expected; (2) working too hard; (3) not having had the courage to express their feelings; (4) not staying in better touch with friends; and (5) not letting themselves be happier. Death doula Kristina Golden says what she has heard the most from her clients is "I should have said 'I love you' more."

In *The Master and His Emissary: The Divided Brain and the Making of the Western World* (2019), psychiatrist and neuroscience researcher Iain McGilchrist discusses the findings of the Eurobarometer life satisfaction surveys. These findings are echoed by those of an eighty-four-year research project conducted by the Harvard Study of Adult Development, which followed the lives of hundreds of people in the United States. Both studies discovered that so long as people have enough to eat and survive on, more money does not make them demonstrably happier. What *really* seems to make the difference is the quality and breadth of their social connections. This social connectedness also improves physical health, and is correlated with lower incidences of sickness, cancer, strokes, and premature death in general. Robert Waldinger, director of the Harvard study, sums up the findings by saying that the secret to a happy life seems to be "being engaged in activities I care about with people I care about."[8]

In fact, psychological studies from all around the world affirm that good social connections are one of the strongest predictors that one will live a fulfilling, long, and healthy life. Studies also demonstrate that good relationships have a positive impact on mood, motivation, and coping skills. They can strengthen your immune system, assist in disease recovery, and even lengthen your life. People with weak relationships are twice as likely to die prematurely, a risk factor greater than for those who smoke fifteen cigarettes a day. People who experience social isolation and loneliness have a greater risk for heart attack, stroke, and premature death.

Keeping these ideas in mind, what might your regrets look like if you died tomorrow? In the exercises that follow, you will be invited to explore these ideas for yourself with some inventive and useful prompts that can help tease out what really brings you joy as a means to help you craft a life with fewer deathbed regrets.

EXERCISES

JOURNAL PROMPTS

1. **What Would You Take If . . .** Once I was woken up in the middle of the night; the house behind us had caught on fire, and we had to get out immediately. Still dressed in my nightgown, I grabbed my photo albums and my purse. That was it. Since then, it's been easier for me to let go of physical objects. If you had to flee your house in the middle of the night and could bring only what you could carry, what would you take? Why? Is your answer surprising?

2. **Daily Gratitude List.** Every day this week, think of five things that you're grateful for. You might list them in your journal; I like to do this as a sort of falling asleep ritual, pairing each thing I am grateful for with a deep in-breath and full exhale. This is a great practice that helps us appreciate our life exactly as it is, right here and now, and helps put difficult things into perspective. If

LOCKDOWN LESSONS

During the COVID-19 pandemic lockdown, I found, to my surprise, that I did not at all miss my social life, which had largely consisted of going out to eat or having drinks with friends. What I really prized, it turned out, was spending time alone in nature. This realization led to some major life changes, including leaving the city I'd lived in for twenty-three years and moving to Mexico. Did you learn anything that surprised you during the pandemic? What were you forced to give up? Were you surprised to find that you were happy to give up some things? Did you make any life changes in the aftermath?

you find it useful, continue working with it beyond the week's end.

3. **A Limited Time to Live.** If you found out you had five years to live, what would you change about your life? What if it were three years? One? What if you had a week? A day?

4. **Deathbed Letter.** Write a letter to yourself from your deathbed. What do you regret? What would you change if you could? What could you do now to reduce these deathbed regrets? What advice does your deathbed self have for you now? Make small steps to implement those changes.

5. **"Is Today a Good Day to Die?"** A tradition with certain Indigenous cultures was to regularly ask oneself, "Is today a good day

to die?" Ask yourself these questions: Is today a good day to die? Do I think I did what I was meant to do with my time on earth? What did I leave unfinished? Allow these answers to shape your decisions going forward.

6. **Appreciate Those You Love.** Express your appreciation to the people in your life whom you love, via a conversation, letter, or email. If there's a book you've read that you think they would like, consider sending them a copy. If a song or movie makes you think of them, reach out. Make a practice of reaching out and saying hello when you are thinking about someone.

7. **Cultivate a Good Partnership.** If you're having problems with a friend or a partner, make a list of all of the things that you really value about them. Keep it at hand to go back to when you are having difficult times, to put things in perspective. Similarly, write a list of things you are grateful for about that person. You might also try the Mudita ("sympathetic joy") meditation in addendum eight, page 256.

8. **Where Do You Put Your Attention?** Zen teacher Deborah Eden Tull says in her book *Luminous Darkness: An Engaged Buddhist Approach to Embracing the Unknown* (2022), "The quality of our life experience is determined by the focus of our attention. That which we give our attention to grows." Where do you put your attention? What do you spend the most time on? Keep track of where your time goes for the week. At the end of the week, review this list and see if it aligns with what you want to cultivate in your life.

9. **Thank Your Body.** Write a letter of gratitude to your body, which will someday be gone. Try to treat it with special care this week. You might even talk to it, pat it, and try to intuit and fulfill its desires.

10. **Clarify Success.** What does success look like to you? For some, it might be fame or money. For me, it is to have my work respected

by people whom I respect. If you can, try to find clarity about what would give you that sense of achievement. Added bonus: Take a step toward your goal. Another added bonus: Consciously celebrate when you reach a milestone or achieve your goal.[9]

11. **Cross Them off the List.** For me, figuring out what I wanted to do with my life was not a straight path, but more like call-and-response. I tried a number of things that I thought I might like to do and then crossed them off the list when it was clear they were not for me. Have you had a similar experience? Make a list of some of the things that you once wanted to do but have since realized are not for you. Do you still have a list of possibilities? Write them down and see if you can put one into motion and try it out.

12. **The Bucket List.** A bucket list details the things you want to do before you die. Make one of your own. Is there an item on it that you can do soon? Added bonus: Ask someone what's on their bucket list as a fun parlor game or conversation starter!

13. **Autobiography.** Write an autobiography detailing the most important and meaningful people and events in your life, as well as your most prized moments and achievements. This could take the form of a written piece, a list, a recording, a story or fairy tale, or something else entirely.

14. **Obituary.** Write an obituary of what your life would have been like if you had lived out your dreams. Allow yourself to be fanciful. Did writing this reveal any dreams you did not know you had? If so, what are they, and how can you honor them?

15. **Your Ideal Getaway.** When you go on vacation, what do you seek—nature or culture? Fast-paced or slow? What are you looking for in these experiences? Can you find a way to bring more of what you seek on vacation into your everyday life?

16. **Time on Earth Chart.** What do you want to do with your time

on earth? Divide a piece of paper into two columns; title one side "Outer" and the other "Inner." On the Outer side, write all the things you are good at, that you have talent, expertise, or skills in. On the Inner side, write the things you love to do. Examine the two lists and see where they correlate. For me, they correlated with writing, travel, emotion, curation, books, lectures, teaching, and image collecting. If possible, come up with an overarching title that unites these common traits. For me, it was "Communication of Ideas and Self-Expression." Use this as a guide to help you make choices about where you want to spend your time and point your energies in the future. Added bonus: To invite the perspective of the unconscious or the right side of the brain, go on a shamanic journey (more in addendum thirteen, page 261) and ask a figure you encounter for advice.

ACTIVITIES

1. **Push Your Comfort Zone.** Is there something you are interested in doing that makes you uncomfortable but might expand your sense of self? If so, what is keeping you from attempting it? If possible, take at least a first step toward trying it out. Added bonus: Enlist the support of a friend!

2. **Expanding Your Sense of the Future.** In my experience, meeting with a tarot reader or psychic—whether or not you believe in their ability to accurately predict the future—can expand your sense of what your life might be beyond your own narrow sense of possibilities. Visit a tarot reader or psychic and reflect on how it made you think about your past and potential future.

3. **Life's Purpose.** Some cultures believe that we are born with certain skills and talents meant to aid us in achieving a purpose that

will not only give our life meaning, but also enrich the community. The way of identifying this purpose is to find where you are most passionate. If there were such a thing as a "soul's purpose," what might yours be? Where does your most heartfelt curiosity and passion flow? What would you get out of bed at two in the morning to talk about, with gusto? What skills and talents do you have? With this in mind, what might your purpose be? Is this something you are on the way to manifesting? If not, what is holding you back? And how might it be changed? Added bonus: Invite the perspective of the unconscious or the right side of the brain via a shamanic journey (more in addendum thirteen, page 261).

4. **Overlooked Talents.** If you died tomorrow, what talents would you feel you had not properly cultivated? Is there an action—small or large—that you could take to remedy that?

5. **Give Thanks with Art.** *Retablos* are artworks made to commemorate a miracle. Often naively painted, they depict the miraculous event, as well as the saint or figure they wish to thank. Look at some examples on the internet, and create one of your own depicting something that felt like a miracle in your life, or something you are grateful for. You might also offer a prayer of thanks while lighting a candle, or make an offering at a church, a temple, or another meaningful space.

6. **Memento Mori Reading.** Read Bill Bryson's *A Short History of Nearly Everything* (2003), which might lead you to more greatly appreciate your life by reminding you how precarious human existence is and how everything could change in a minute.

7. **Spending Time.** Jungian analyst Jean Shinoda Bolen asks us to consider how we would like to "spend the energy of [our] life." Some questions to ask ourselves when we consider an activity we

are about to embark on: Is it meaningful? Is it fun? Is it motivated by love? Note how much of your time is spent doing things you really care about, and how those other things make you feel.

8. **Guilty Pleasure.** When you find yourself conscious that you are engaging in a guilty pleasure (for me, that would be scrolling headlines that make me feel indignant in the *Guardian*, or spending time on Instagram), ask yourself if this activity is *really* giving you pleasure—does it make you feel good? If not, try to find a replacement treat. For me, these replacement treats might be researching something I am really interested in on Google, gazing out the window, going for a walk, dipping into a book, or closing my eyes and resting for a minute or two, paying attention to my breathing.

9. **Consuming Media.** When meditating, I have sometimes noticed hearing whole segments of radio shows heard earlier that day. This led me to the visceral realization that the media I consumed became, in some way, a part of me, which led me, in turn, to become much more deliberate about what I allowed in. This week, I invite you to look at the media that you consume, such as social media, the news, books, music, film, or TV. Consider each example in turn, and ask: Does it add to my life, and if so, how? Does it detract from my life, and if so, how? Does it help me make better and more informed decisions about my life? If you find the negative outweighing the positive in any instance, consider taking a break from that form of media and seeing how you feel.

10. **Thank-You Letter.** Write a letter of thanks to someone who has done something kind for you.

11. **The Inspiring Steve Jobs.** In 2005, a year after he was diagnosed with cancer, Steve Jobs delivered a commencement speech for graduates of Stanford University (excerpted previously). He speaks eloquently of contemplating death to live more fully

and authentically. If his words resonated for you, I encourage you to read and/or view the speech in its entirety at news.stanford .edu/2005/06/12/youve-got-find-love-jobs-says.

12. **Find a Community.** We can achieve so much more as a community than alone! Try to spend more time with people who support your own values, people who encourage and inspire you and don't diminish your view of reality. If you don't have friends who meet this description, make an attempt to meet some like-minded people. Take a class or go to a meetup or club related to something you are truly interested in. Alternately, if there are people in your life who you feel undermine your true values, try to reduce—or eliminate—the time you spend with them.

13. **Choose Where to Put Your Time.** The amount of time we are allotted in this life is limited, so it seems wise to be choosy about how we spend it. To prioritize making time for what is really important, make a list of where you spend your time each week. Ask yourself these questions about each entry:

    ⁘ Do I like this?
    ⁘ Is this necessary for my life?
    ⁘ Do I need it to be happy?
    ⁘ Does it enrich my life?
    ⁘ Does it expand or reduce my sense of self?

14. **Balance.** Create a schedule that allows you ample time to do things you truly value. As time is limited, this might mean having to give up other occupations. You might use the exercise above as your starting point.

15. **Do Something You Really Love.** Take the time to do something you really love, something you have been curious about but never had a chance to do, something adventurous, or something frivolous that sounds super fun.

16. **What Is Really Important to You?** Another way of finding something that is important to you—maybe even without you noticing it!—is to look over your own past. When I did so, I realized that I have been doing yoga off and on for over thirty years. And every time I have written a book—including this one!—I have done yoga several times a week, often followed by meditation. I simply never noticed these things were important to me because I live in a culture that does not value such things. By looking carefully at our histories, we can discover the things we really value in our own lives.

17. **What Motivates You to Do Your Best Work?** What motivates you to do good work? What I know about myself, from paying careful attention, is that I do my best work when I am in small groups with people I like and respect. I do not respond to abstract motivations such as punishment, money, or grades. Your answer might be very different.

18. **Life Is Too Short to . . .** Complete the sentence "Life is too short to . . ." with ten different answers as quickly as possible, and without overthinking. A few of my own examples? Life is too short to . . . not use soap that smells good . . . spend time on Instagram . . . live somewhere ugly . . . spend time with people I don't really like. Added bonus: Use this prompt as a fun parlor game to get to know people on a deep level very quickly.

19. **Make Friends.** If there's someone you think you would like to get to know, invite them to do something that you enjoy. If you have a partner, make an effort to share things that allow you to have fun and step outside of your usual, normal routine.

20. **Heal Complex Relationships.** I have found the practice of Mudita ("sympathetic joy") meditation, from the Buddhist tradition, a useful way to cultivate better relationships. It is designed to act

as an antidote to some of the natural feelings that can complicate our relationships, such as jealousy or competitiveness, by helping us find a genuine sense of happiness in the achievements of others. If this sounds useful to you, try one out! See addendum eight, page 256, for directions.

21. **Gratitude for Loved Ones.** Each day this week, write in your journal some things you appreciate about your partner or a friend.

22. **Naikan Therapy.** Give yourself some Naikan ("introspection" or "looking inside") therapy. Ask yourself: What have I received from a significant other? What have I given back to that person? What troubles and difficulties have I caused that person?

23. **Say Grace.** One simple way to live out gratitude each day is to say grace before you eat. It need not be your standard Christian version; you could instead find a phrase that communicates your appreciation for the sustenance you are about to receive in a way that feels true to you. Try saying grace, in your own special way, before a meal every day this week. You might also consider making an offering of a small portion of your food to the earth before you eat each meal. After the week is through, reflect on the practice. What was the experience like? Did it shift your perspective in any way? Is it something you might like to bring into the future?

24. **Resonance Check.** Did any material in this chapter particularly resonate for you? Is there something that piqued your interest? I invite you to keep track of the things that spoke to you in a special place in your journal. I also encourage you to go further, to do more research on anything that you felt excited about, and if you are a visual person, to collect images related to things that interested you. Start a folder of these images, or create a Pinterest board.

25. **Check In.** What were your biggest surprises this week? Did you learn something new about yourself? Make notes in your journal.

12

BRINGING BACK THE TREASURE

YOUR OWN MYTH OR SYMBOL OF DEATH

Over the course of this book, we have looked at many traditions in which the contemplation of death was considered essential to our psychological health and well-being: the keystone of a life well lived. Of all the modern thinkers I have encountered, it is Carl Jung who most echoes these sentiments, and who, through his thought and work, creates a bridge to the wisdom of the past and other cultures. For Jung, a crucial part of a mature, well-lived life was to come to terms with our own death. "Not to have done so," he says, "is a vital loss. For the question ... is the age-old heritage of humanity: an archetype, rich in secret life, which seeks to add itself to our own individual life in order to make it whole."[1]

Jung encouraged his colleagues and analysands to look death in the eye and develop their own myth about it. Dr. Marie-Louise von Franz, his protégé and colleague, said that for Jung, it was "of tremendous importance, if not absolutely essential" to have a myth about death. She reports that he encouraged all the older people in his circle to ponder if they believed life continued after death, and to come to an understanding of what death meant to them. He urged them to remember that these must be their own ideas, not received ones. She quotes him saying:

> It won't help you when you're lying on your deathbed to recall, "Jung said this or that." You must have your own ideas about it. You have to have your own myth. To have your own myth means to have suffered and struggled with a question until an answer has come to you from the depths of your soul. That does not imply that this is the definitive truth, rather that this truth, which has come, is relevant for oneself as one now is, and believing in this truth helps one to feel well.[2]

The goal of Jungian psychology is individuation, or becoming fully yourself, becoming *whole*. It is a process, facilitated by Jungian analysis, in which we integrate all the contents of our psyche, including that which we have denied and repressed, which Jung called the shadow. Jung believed that by making ourselves whole, by accepting and integrating all parts of our pysche, we would become truly mature adults who could take responsibility for our own inner realities rather than dangerously projecting them outward onto others. This reckoning and integration is necessary not just for individuals, but for a culture as well.

One does not become enlightened by imagining figures of light, but by making the darkness conscious.

—CARL JUNG, SWISS PSYCHIATRIST AND PSYCHOANALYST

Jung also spoke of the need to hold what he called "the tension of opposites." If we have life, we must also have, *in equal measure*, death. Much like the yin-yang concept in Eastern thought, opposites should not be seen as in conflict, but rather as complementary, in *relationship*. Jung said that when the opposites balance each other, it is "a sign of high culture." On the other hand, "One-sidedness, though it lends momentum, is a mark of barbarism."[3]

Such a balance between life and death is, of course, very much lacking in contemporary affluent Western culture. Ours is a culture that tends to see the world through a lens of "either/or" rather than "both/and." It is a culture that privileges light over darkness, happiness over grief, and, as we have seen, life over death. In Jung's opinion, on a personal level, this imbalance could be corrected by individuals who had done the hard work of making their own darkness known and balancing their own psyches. On a cultural level, it could be remedied by our creatives—our artists, writers, filmmakers, musicians, and poets. These individuals, he believed, instinctively restore a sense of balance to their respective cultures by excavating and bringing to light its shadow side—that which is not consciously expressed. By sharing their work with the culture at large, they help restore balance to the collective.

As we explored in the previous chapter, from a shamanic perspective, each of us has a life's purpose for which we have been given certain gifts, and it is our obligation to live out this purpose, not just for our own sakes, but also for the world. Christina Pratt, author of *An Encyclopedia of Shamanism* (2007), says that from a shamanic perspective, everyone is born with their own unique genius. If all goes well in our lives, we have an innate sense of this; we feel more *alive* when we do certain things or spend time with certain people. The thing we are most passionate about is linked to this unique genius, and this feeling of passion naturally moves us toward the things we're most curious about. If we live in this way—and continue to ask ourselves, "Is today a good day to die?"—then we move toward an authentic life that allows us to die without fear or regret. We live a good life, and we die a good death.[4] Some mystical Jewish traditions concur, asserting that each person is born with a particular task we are meant to accomplish with our time on earth, which constitutes our own special contribution to what is called *tikkun olam*, or the healing of the world. We are given the talents, gifts, and proclivities to live this out, and it is intimately linked with what we love to do.

Jung also believed that each of us has gifts we can bring into the world, and that these can only be fully accessed when we have delved into our own psyches. He believed that after we descended into our own darkness, we would emerge with a treasure of sorts. The treasure we found was important not just for us and our own psychological development, but for the community at large. It was thus important for us to bring what we found into the world in some way, for both our own well-being and that of our fellow humans.

Jung also had a lot to say about creativity. He saw this faculty as a deeply important human drive that linked us to the divine—a mysterious inner urge that drove us to, like the gods themselves, manifest something that had once existed only in the imagination. It was also an essential tool for connecting with the unconscious and assimilating its contents. Jungian analyst Marion Woodman asserted that the imagination is what makes life worth living, feeding our psyches and keeping us in touch with our own transformative processes. She said, "Kill the imagination and you kill the soul. Kill the soul and you're left with a listless, apathetic creature who can become hopeless or brutal or both."[5]

Scientific studies have demonstrated that creative expression makes us healthier. It has been found to boost our immune system, increase our sense of well-being, and reduce stress, anxiety, and depression. It provides us with a sense of agency, and can even help reduce the negative effects of dementia. Creative acts such as writing and painting—as well as crafting, gardening, and sewing—have been compared to meditation for their power to focus the mind and generate the release of dopamine, a chemical produced by our brain that makes us feel happy, satisfied, and motivated. The creative arts—which allow us to safely work with darker emotions and express that which is beyond our rational understanding—can also be immensely useful tools as we attempt to engage with the mystery of death.[6]

Jungian analyst and bestselling author Clarissa Pinkola Estés speaks at great length about the importance of using our creativity as we seek to make a relationship with death. She notes that we cannot talk about the ineffable—particularly "the great mysteries of life and death"—without the arts. It is only through the indirect, symbolic language of the arts "that we can talk about things that are too big for our very small minds to comprehend." In her opinion, the existence of these mysteries creates a *need* for art, and is perhaps also behind our drive to create. She said, "If all the mysteries of the universe were known, there would be no need for artists, because that's the artist's work, is to talk about mystery, or to paint about mystery, or to sculpt about mystery, or make music about mystery. And so because there are so many mysteries . . . we need artists more than we need anything else."[7]

I paint flowers so they will not die.

—FRIDA KAHLO, MEXICAN ARTIST

Creative expression can also be seen as a way of asserting the preciousness of life, just as it is, right here, right now. Yes, it is true, we will die. You, I, and everyone we know. And you know what? That's OK. We can use the gift of our time on earth to affirm having been here, by making our own unique marks, to leave a record of that which we valued, that which we loved, to affirm life in the face of—and in response to—death. We can do so with real joy, having accepted—and perhaps even *embraced*—the fact that our lives, and the lives of all we love, will, inevitably, end.

PERSONIFICATIONS OF DEATH

In her book *On Dreams and Death* (1987), Jungian analyst Marie-Louise von Franz notes:

> Whenever man is confronted with something mysterious, unknown (with a question, for instance, of the origin of the universe or with the enigma of birth), his unconscious produces symbolic, mythical—that is, archetypal models, which appear projected into the void. The same is also true, of course, with the mystery of death.[8]

In other words, when we look deeply at a mystery, we see only emptiness, and into this void, we project the contents of our unconscious.

Death is a great mystery that, as a species, we have been projecting into for millennia. The art, traditions, writings, and practices—as well as the myths and deities—we have looked at over the course of this book are all a product of our ancestors' intimate engagement with this eternal mystery. By looking at these cultural projections of death in different times and places, we can glean something about how different cultures understood or imagined life, death, and the relationship between the two.

A common strategy for forging a relationship

No art is possible without a dance with death.

—KURT VONNEGUT, AMERICAN WRITER

with something unknown is to anthropomorphize it—that is, to personify it, or give it human qualities. Doing this allows us to transform abstract forces into active, conscious personalities we can understand and relate to. Psychologically, we might look at the veneration of a deity as a safe way to cultivate a relationship with powerful, larger-than-life archetypal energies. Venerating Hades or Persephone in ancient Greece, for example, might have helped people cultivate a humanized relationship with the unknowable reality of death, one in which the mystery could be, if not understood, then contained, and safely engaged with.

The predominant personification of death in the Western world has been, for centuries, the grim reaper. An anthropomorphized skeletal figure holding a scythe or sickle, he rose to prominence during the mass deaths of the black plague. He is depicted with a punitive and frightening demeanor—no surprise when we consider the historical moment from which he emerged, a time when death must have seemed vindictive and capricious indeed!

But the grim reaper is not only a personification of death; he is also our prime *symbol* of death. A symbol, in Jung's lexicon, is "the best possible expression for something that cannot be expressed otherwise than by a more or less close analogy."[9] A symbol points to something that is ultimately unknowable and inexpressible, something we can only vaguely apprehend and cannot intellectually understand, and that cannot be explained in direct, nonpoetic language. In the words of Jungian analyst Muriel McMahon, a symbol is the best representation of something still unknown; it is a portal to a mystery.

Jung believed that when our psyche is out of balance—when, for example, we focus on life at the expense of

We die. That may be the meaning of life. But we do language. That may be the measure of our lives.

—TONI MORRISON, AMERICAN AUTHOR

death—our unconscious generates images intended to help bring us back into balance, to compensate for the one-sidedness of our conscious awareness. This can happen on an individual level, in which a new image might emerge in a dream or waking fantasy. It can also happen on a cultural level. What kind of image might emerge from the collective unconscious of a culture as a means to restore a much needed balance to light and dark, to compensate for a culture that exalts life and demonizes death? Such an image would surely express the idea of death with nuance and richness, and allow a "both/and" rather than an "either/or" understanding, in which death might be seen as both tragic and beautiful, sad and magnificent, horrific and awe-inspiring. It would enable us to create a relationship with death that transcends fear. There is such a symbol, and perhaps not surprisingly, she has emerged in Mexico. Her name is Santa Muerte.

Santa Muerte—literally "saint death" or "holy death"—is a newly emerged Mexican folk saint who is venerated by millions in Mexico and beyond. She takes the form of a female grim reaper, and is often depicted standing on a globe and holding a set of scales, with an owl at her feet. It is common to see her dressed as a bride, or resplendent in gowns, wigs, and tiaras. Renowned for the power of her miracles, she is also referred to as La Santisima Muerte ("The Very Holy Death"), La Flaquita ("The Skinny Lady"), and La Niña Blanca ("The White Girl"). Many of her

> *Death is the mother of Beauty; hence from her, alone, shall come fulfillment to our dreams and our desires.*
>
> —WALLACE STEVENS, AMERICAN POET

devotees see her as a loving mother and a compassionate psychopomp who will guide you out of this life and into the next realm of existence. They ask her for a good death, one without pain, suffering, or violence; they might respectfully request that she not come too soon, but they will welcome her with love when she makes her inevitable call.

Santa Muerte is believed to be the product of a syncretization between the Spanish Catholic grim reaper and the death-related goddesses venerated by pre-Hispanic cultures. These figures—including Mictecacihuatl, the Aztec queen of the dead, and Coatlicue, the Aztec patroness of life, death, fertility, and rebirth—represent a more complex, positive, and holistic view of death than that presented by the Christian worldview. Despite her pagan roots, most of Santa Muerte's devotees see themselves as good Catholics, and venerate the skeleton saint alongside officially sanctioned figures such as the Virgin of Guadalupe and San Judas Tadeo. The Church, however, has rejected her, condemning her as satanic.

Santa Muerte is hugely popular in Mexico and throughout the Mexican diaspora. In 2012, she was estimated to have about twelve million followers, with numbers on the rise.[10] Her exact genesis is unclear, but many believe that she emerged as a powerful force in late twentieth-century Mexico, at a historical moment when death seemed—much as it had at the inception of the grim reaper—capricious and ever present. This time also marks the beginning of NAFTA, which led to increased poverty, government deregulation, and loss of faith in public institutions. This was also a time of increasing drug-related violence in response to the United States' "war on drugs." For these reasons, the lives of many became more tenuous, and the specter of death more unpredictable and omnipresent.

Eva Aridjis Fuentes, director of the documentary film *La Santa Muerte* (2007), sees Santa Muerte as patroness of "life, death, and everything in between," much like the matriarchal great goddesses we looked at in chapter eight. Her devotees, accordingly, request her aid in a wide variety of arenas. Her powers are especially revered in matters of love, healing, and protection, but she can also be called upon to assist in issues related to money, education, wisdom, and justice.

Because death is characterized by its lack of discrimination—taking rich and poor, young and old, sinful and holy alike—Santa Muerte is understood to embrace and accept all, without judgment. She is also understood to have a special understanding of—and compassion for—the contingencies of life as it is lived by the poor, the oppressed, and the disenfranchised. For this reason, she is particularly popular with individuals not traditionally welcomed by the Catholic Church, such as sex workers, members of the LGBTQ+ community, and criminals.* She is also venerated by those whose lives bring them into close proximity to death and who are vulnerable to injustice and abuse, including prison guards, taxi drivers, the poor, and those who live in dangerous neighborhoods.

I can think of no better symbol of death for our times than Santa Muerte. I see her as a powerful compensatory figure balancing the dominance of the traditional grim reaper. Where he is masculine and punitive, she is feminine and loving: a gentle guide to the next world. While the grim reaper brings with him the threat of hell, Santa Muerte evokes an image of death as just one of the natural and necessary steps in the infinitely repeating cycles of life, death, and rebirth. Santa Muerte brings death from the fearful shadows into the light of conscious awareness, where a true, appreciative, and positive relationship with her can be made. Santa Muerte also renders the image of death—which seems so unmitigatedly ghastly to many of us in the industrialized, affluent Western world—*beautiful.* Like other symbols that emerge from the personal or collective unconscious, she has

---

* Santa Muerte has been vilified by some due to her association with Mexico's infamous *narcos*, drug traffickers known for their ruthless violence. Although it is true that many narcos venerate the Skeleton Saint, this does not mean that all devotees of Santa Muerte are criminals; as Fuentes puts it, in Italy, all members of the Mafia might be Catholic, but it does not follow that all Catholics are part of the Mafia.

the power to rebalance and to heal. I love that her influence is spreading, and can't wait to see where she goes next.

Over the course of this book, we have learned how people have understood and imagined death in different times and places, and we've examined and interrogated our own attitudes. We have been introduced to a variety of ways that people have cultivated a relationship with death and the dead. We have also looked at how people remember the dead, how they grieve, and even how they have had fun with death. In the following exercises, we will consolidate what we have learned, clarify our own understanding of the great mystery of death, and make a plan for how we want to live this out in the world, through the end of this book and beyond.

EXERCISES

JOURNAL PROMPTS

1. **What I Truly Value.** In this book or in your journal, fill out this form quickly, without overthinking it; allow yourself to be fanciful:

My name is _____.

Five of my core values are _____

_____

_____

_____

My ideal pace of life is _____.

My ideal kind of job is _____.

My ideal way to work (for example, at home or in an office, 9-to-5 or open hours) is _____
_____.

My ideal place to live is _____.

My ideal culture to live in is _____.

The talents I have are _____
_____.

The skills I have are _____
_____.

Some things I really love to do with my time are _____
_____.

The things I truly value are _____
_____
_____.

The people who are most important to me are _____
_____
_____.

What I want to do with my time on earth is _____
_____.

2. **Statement of Intent.** Consider your answers to the preceding questions and the information gleaned from the other exercises throughout the book. Use this as the basis for a statement of intent, using your imagination to conjure an image of your life as you would like it to be six months in the future. Write it in the present tense, as in "I am living in . . ." If you have a smartphone or computer, make this an editable document. Read this aloud daily, and edit it when it no longer seems to fit your vision. Write down some concrete steps you could take to move closer to one or more aspects of your dream life. Make sure to celebrate any accomplishments or milestones!

3. **Revisit Your Bucket List.** In chapter eleven, page 217, you created a bucket list of things you wish to do before you die. Choose one of the entries on your list, and take a step toward making it happen.

4. **My Own Myth.** Write a myth for the world as you see it after completing this book, one that encompasses life, death, the role of humanity, and anything else important to you. How does your myth understand death? How does death relate to life? Are these forces personified? If so, what are they like? Does death have any positive aspects? Does it have anything to teach us? Is there an afterlife existence? If so, what is it like? If not, is there a sort of symbolic immortality you envision? Can we stay in contact with the dead? How does the myth make you feel? What would a culture that lived by this myth look like? Would people lead meaningful and contented lives? Is this a myth you can live by? How can you stay in touch with it, and live it into the future?

MAKE YOUR OWN MEMENTO MORI

When I engage in an extended practice, such as the one we have undergone over the course of this book, I like to end with something that helps me consolidate what I have learned, and return with something that helps me reconnect with what I have learned and experienced.

As we have learned, many people around the world found it useful to have a memento mori—an object or practice intended to remind them of their own death so they could live a full, rich life before it was too late. So now I invite you to create your own! This can be anything that reminds you, in a useful, life-enhancing way, of the finitude of life; a way to keep death, as you understand it, close at hand. Your memento mori can take any form that feels right to you; it might be an artwork, a poem, an altar, a musical piece, a manifesto, a film, a letter, a death shroud, a life-and-death self-portrait . . . anything you can think of that will remind you, in a life-affirming way, to live the life you want now.

To begin this process, I invite you to reflect on your journey, and to formulate an image of death that feels true to you, informed by the inner and outer work you've done. I invite you to spend time on this, to not force yourself to commit to a final idea, but to play until you start to sense a thread that feels true—that evokes what you feel—and stick with that, always feeling your way back to that feeling, through asking yourself "Is it true?" rather than "Is it good?"

Some steps if you're stuck:

1) Look at your dreams and doodles.

2) Look at any images you've collected over the course of your journey.

3) Look at your list of resonances from each chapter. Do they fit together into any groupings or categories?

4) Make a mind map (see addendum eleven, page 259).

5) If you're stuck between a few ideas, go with where your passion seems to flow—what sounds the most *fun*?

ACTIVITIES

1. **Get to Know Saint Death.** Watch the film *La Santa Muerte* (directed by Eva Aridjis Fuentes, narrated by Gael García Bernal, 2007), a documentary about this contemporary Mexican folk saint who takes the form of a female grim reaper. I also urge you to look up images of Santa Muerte on the internet. If you are interested in a more scholarly history, I recommend *Devoted to Death: Santa Muerte, the Skeleton Saint* (2011) by R. Andrew Chesnut.

2. **Have a Conversation with Holy Death.** Using the practice of Jungian active imagination (see addendum twelve, page 260) or the shamanic journey (see addendum thirteen, page 261), meet and have a conversation with Saint Death. Try to get to know her;

what is she like? Does she have any special messages for you that help you understand death, or recommendations for how you could live a better life? Write about the experience.

3. **Celebrate Completion.** Undertake a rite of passage to celebrate the completion of this book. This could be taking yourself out for a nice dinner, alone or with friends; it could be taking time to go to a place that you really love, or gifting yourself with flowers or something else that feels special. You might also consider adding a new object to your altar to signify this milestone. If you started this process with a ritual, create a complementary ending. If you drew an eye on a Daruma doll at the beginning of this book, enjoy the warm sense of achievement as you draw in the other. If you started with a note, write an ending note.

4. **Reflect on What You Have Learned.** Respond to the following prompts in your journal:
   - My feelings about death when I started this book were...
   - My feelings about death as I end this book are...
   - Some things I got out of this process are...
   - Some ways this process changed me are...
   - Some of things I found surprising were...
   - Some things that really moved me were...
   - Some things I found really confronting were...
   - Some important things I learned are...
   - Some important realizations I had were...
   - This book changed me in these ways...
   - I would like to live what I have learned into my future by...

Anything else you would like to add?

PHOTO BY THE AUTHOR OF A SANTA MUERTE SHRINE IN MEXICO CITY, 2023

APPENDIX

RESOURCES AND GOING FORWARD

ADDENDUM 1: GOING FORWARD—WHAT NEXT?

Creating a relationship with death is a lifelong process. I encourage you to continue with the good work you have done! Here are some suggestions for how you might do so.

- Revisit this book after three months, six months, and/or twelve months. Engage in some of the exercises and journal prompts you skipped the first time, or revisit some old favorites.
- Keep working with—and fine-tuning—your statement of intent. Is there anything that no longer feels right? Edit accordingly.
- Set alerts on your digital calendar—perhaps at three-month intervals—to review your statement of intent and your bucket list, and assess your progress. Have you taken steps to create the life you want to live? If so, list them. If not, what might you do to remedy the situation?
- Make sure to celebrate your achievements, no matter how modest!

- Join the Morbid Anatomy community of like-minded, death-curious people for online and in-person classes, lectures, and a variety of other offerings at morbidanatomy.org.
- Death doulas are like midwives of death, acting as allies to the dying, helping them prepare for death, and ushering them through the process. Read about death doulas, interview one, or undergo training to become one.
- Volunteer at a hospice or an assisted-living facility, or spend time with an aging loved one.
- Join a Death Cafe, or a Death Over Dinner group (these are groups that meet to discuss death over coffee or food, respectively); if there are none where you live, consider starting your own!
- Visit the website for the Order of the Good Death to find people engaging in death-positive activities around the world: orderof thegooddeath.com.
- If you find there are psychological or emotional blocks keeping you from accomplishing what you wish with your time on earth, seek out therapy, counseling, or some other intervention.
- I have found Jungian analysis to be an irreplaceably transformative process. If Jung's ideas appeal to you, consider engaging in a Jungian analysis of your own. There are many online resources for locating an analyst, and it is even possible to work, at a reduced fee, with an analyst in training.

ADDENDUM 2: A GUIDE TO WORKING THROUGH THIS BOOK AS A GROUP

If you wish to go through this book with one or more other people, I heartily encourage it! There is no one way to do it, but following are some suggestions.

- Pick a time each week to meet, in person or online, for one or more hours. Agree that this will be a safe and supportive space, with no criticism.
- Choose people who make you feel safe, with whom you can open yourself up and make yourself vulnerable.
- Focus on one chapter per meeting. Discuss what came up for you, what resonated, what you loved or hated, what was powerful, what surprised you, and what you learned. You might also encourage bringing images you each have collected, or any artistic or creative responses the material inspired.
- Try to engage in deep active listening with the others in your group. See addendum nine, page 257, for guidelines.
- When prompts consist of activities, consider doing some together, and discuss them during or after.
- Have a party to celebrate completion!

ADDENDUM 3: AIDS FOR DEALING WITH DIFFICULT OR COMPLEX EMOTIONS: MEDITATION/RELAXATION

The material in this book might be challenging for some. Following are some resources to help you navigate and work with difficult emotions that might come up.

- **Mindfulness and Relaxation.** Before doing an exercise, or to deal with difficult material, I encourage you to try a relaxation technique. Following are a few simple ones, all of which should ideally be practiced alone, in a quiet space where you will not be interrupted, and in a comfortable position, preferably lying down or sitting with your back supported. Lighting a candle, lowering the lights, or putting something over your eyes can also be nice.

- **Full-Body Relaxation:** Get into a comfortable position, close your eyes, and take four very deep breaths; make them the deepest, fullest breaths of your day, and notice where you feel the breath at each stage in the process. Next, relax each body part in turn, moving from your toes to the top of your head. Toes . . . feet . . . calves . . . I like to do this part aloud, in a soft voice, and use a full breath cycle to focus on each body part.

- **Alternate Nostril Breathing:** Start by closing your right nostril with your right thumb and inhale through your left nostril. Then close your left nostril with your right ring finger and release your right nostril. Exhale slowly and completely through your right nostril. Keeping your left nostril closed, inhale slowly through your right nostril. Release your left nostril, close your right nostril with your right thumb, and exhale through your left nostril. Continue alternating nostrils, inhaling and exhaling through each, for several cycles. As you practice, focus your attention on your breath and the sensation of the air moving in and out of your nostrils. Keep your breathing smooth, steady, and gentle.

- **Extended-Exhale Breathing:** Inhale slowly and steadily through your nose to the count you've chosen. This could be a count of five, or any number that feels good. Exhale through your nose even more slowly, extending the exhalation to a count that's *double* the count of your inhalation (so if you chose five, that would be ten). Pay attention to the sensation of the air moving in and out of your nostrils. Keep your breath steady and relaxed. Avoid any forceful or strained breathing. The emphasis is on the smoothness and length of your exhalation. This is said to soothe the parasympathetic nervous system, which reduces stress and anxiety.

- **Emotions as Energies, Not Identity.** One strategy I have found for dealing with unpleasant emotions is to think of them as energies running through me rather than who I am. In Spanish, people say, "I have hunger," not "I am hungry." Similarly, when you think, "I am angry," perhaps try to think instead, "I *have* anger." Try to honor the emotions that come up for you and sit with them, and try to understand what they may be trying to communicate to you. The next time you notice what you think of as negative energy, allow yourself to feel it, while also holding the awareness that it is not you, but rather, a transient energy passing through you. Allow yourself to be curious about it, and wonder what its positive aspects might be. For example, anger can be a very strong motivating energy.

- **Express the Emotion:** Many say it is important to *express* (from the Latin for "press out") an emotion rather than keep it within. One great way to express pent-up emotion is through music and dance. I encourage you to make a playlist of songs you love, in many tempos and moods, and choose an appropriate song to dance to that might help you express the emotion you are feeling. You might also draw, paint, journal, write poetry or a letter you never plan to send, or punch a pillow.

- **Personify Your Emotions:** One way of looking at the gods and goddesses venerated by our ancestors is as personifications of archetypal energies, or energies that exist in all of our lives. If you feel a dark emotion emerging, close your eyes, take a deep breath, and center yourself. Try one of the mindfulness and relaxation suggestions on page 243. In a relaxed state, summon up the emotion. Where do you feel it in your body? What does it feel like—is it still or moving? Is it solid or amorphous? Does it feel male, female, or nonbinary? Does it have a color? Can you have a conversation with it? Is there anything it would like from you? (For more, see *Healing through the Dark Emotions: The Wisdom of Grief, Fear, and Despair* [2004] by Miriam Greenspan.)

❖ **Make a Mandala.** One useful tool I have found is to make a mandala each day—or several times a week. This helps with a nonrational, nonverbal connecting with one's emotional state. I make my mandalas by simply using a pencil to lightly draw a circle on a piece of paper, then draw a cross that divides it into four equal parts. Next, I pick up paint, colored pencils, or crayons and, without overthinking, grab a color that feels right, make a mark, and then continue until it feels done. Yes, you can go outside the lines. There are no rules! Date it and keep it, or take a picture of it and keep it in a file.

ADDENDUM 4: WORKING WITH DREAMS

I have been recording and working with my dreams for about eight years, ever since I entered into Jungian analysis. At first, I was a complete skeptic; I thought dreams were nonsense, the detritus of the mind. But as I began to work with them regularly, it was impossible for me to dismiss them in this way. If you begin to document your dreams, you will notice specific figures, animals, and themes that shift and change over time, an inner language all your own. Once you become attuned to their language, dreams can also help you find clarity and suggest unexpected ways forward.

There are many fun, easy ways to work with dreams. My advice is to record them on your phone when you wake up, and later type them out into a word processor. I also like to write down the important things that happened the day before, to see if there might be some relationship between the dreams and the day's activities. You can also give your dream a title, draw an element, or write a haiku based on it. If you want to go deeper, I suggest working with Jill Mellick's fantastic book *The Art of Dreaming: Tools for Creative Dream Work* (2001), which offers dozens of ways you can engage with your dream world. Another wonderful way of working with dreams and dream images is via the Jungian technique of active imagination. For more on that, see addendum twelve, page 260.

I also advise trying to stay as conscious as possible during the liminal states between sleeping and waking. Referred to as hypnagogic and hypnopompic states—the former when you are falling asleep, the latter when waking up—these are times when our conscious mind can really observe the unconscious at work. With practice, it is easier to purposefully linger in this state while still retaining conscious awareness. You might want to work with any images that emerge while in these states, perhaps via writing, dance, artwork, or active imagination (see addendum twelve, page 260).

ADDENDUM 5: GUIDELINES
FOR CREATING AN ALTAR

To create an altar, first identify a space you can work with, perhaps a shelf, or the top of a dresser or bedside table. Cover the surface with a textile of some sort, preferably something you find beautiful. Next, add objects that represent the four elements; on mine, I have feathers, representing air, a lit candle for fire, rocks from meaningful places to me for earth, and a small container that holds water. It is also good to have a mix of natural objects and objects that are human-made.

You might also consider populating your altar with things that hold energy for you at that particular moment. For me, that means a few figures of Santa Muerte, a figure of the Guatemalan folk saint San Simon, a plastic model of a rooster, and a lead figure of a mermaid from the Santeria tradition. You might also include images of your ancestors, or even your own ancestral self. For example, I have a photograph of five-year-old me, full of an energy I no longer possess and would like to cultivate. Tend to your altar, moving objects around, and removing and adding new things. Have a dream image that was meaningful for you? Find some representational object and place it there. Something no longer sing to you anymore? Set it aside for another time.

ADDENDUM 6: GUIDELINES FOR CREATING A RITUAL

Before you begin, decide what you would like this ritual to accomplish.

Next, get into the right mindset. In chapter one, we looked at the advice of Oakley Gordon, who, in his book *The Andean Cosmovision* (2014), recommended using a spirit of intent he described as "sincere pretending." I invite you to try to bring this sincere pretending to bear and concentrate on your intent. Do this with the most passion you can muster, and be as present as possible throughout the ritual. There is no need to *believe* anything, but try to engage in an attitude of sincerity and humility.

You might begin your ritual with a sort of signifier that designates this time and space as special, set aside from normal, everyday life, even sacred (from the Latin *sacrare*, which means "to consecrate," "to dedicate"). This could be as simple as lighting a candle or some incense, taking a few deep and conscious breaths, closing your eyes and saying a few words, or anything else that feels right. It might also be nice to set the space off in some way, through the use of flowers or special textiles or objects. If you have an altar (see addendum five, page 247), you might center the ritual around it.

Begin a ritual with an invocation or by stating an intention, either aloud or in your head. Then undertake a meaningful symbolic action; for example, if you wish to let go of something, you might write (or draw) something on a piece of paper, and (carefully) burn it or bury it, while concentrating your energy on letting it go.

End with a closing of some sort, perhaps some words spoken aloud or in your mind, followed by an act to mark the end of the ritual, such as blowing out a candle, that brings you back into everyday space. Make sure to express your gratitude before returning to regular life.

ADDENDUM 7: END-OF-LIFE
AND FUNERAL PLANNING

This is a slightly edited version of a document originally featured in *Technologies of the Human Corpse* by John Troyer, published in 2020 by MIT Press, used with the permission of the author and publishing house.[1]

Name: _____

Indicate your funeral and end-of-life planning wishes by completing the following sections. Say as little or as much as you want about your choices.

- I want life support used (yes/no/maybe) for the following amount of time and under the following conditions: _____

  _____

  _____

  _____

❖ I would like to be removed from life support for the following reasons. I nominate a specific person, listed below, to make that decision should a decision need to be made: _____

_____

_____

_____

❖ I leave all my funeral arrangement choices to this person or people: _____

_____

_____

_____

❖ I (have/have not) already planned my funeral, and those arrangements can be found here: _____

_____

_____

_____

❖ I request that people not do any of the following things at my funeral or memorial service: _____

_____

_____

_____

❖ The funeral director, cemetery, crematorium, cremation society, or body disposal facility I prefer is: _____

_____

_____

❧ The price range I would like spent on my funeral is: _____

_____

❧ I have no preference for what is done with my body after death, and I want my next of kin to choose my body's disposal method in the event I become incapacitated (yes/no/don't care). _____

_____

_____

_____

_____

❧ I would like my body (embalmed/not embalmed/kept on a cold pad/don't care). _____

_____

_____

_____

❧ I would like my body (laid out at home/taken to a funeral home's visitation chapel/other/don't care), for this long: _____

_____

_____

_____

_____

❧ I would like my body to be dressed in (formal clothes/specific out-fit/don't care) for my funeral. _____

_____

_____

_____

❖ I would like my body to be viewed by (my next of kin only/ extended family/friends/work colleagues/anybody who wants to say goodbye). _____

_____

_____

_____

❖ I would like my body to be transported to (a house of worship/ secular remembrance space/crematorium/cemetery/other) in (a hearse/my own vehicle/other/don't care). _____

_____

❖ If I am buried (or even if I'm not), I would like a gravestone or marker that says: _____

_____

_____

_____

❖ What I would like done with my corpse (burial/cremation/other):

_____

_____

_____

_____

❖ If I am cremated, I want the following done with my ashes:

_____

_____

_____

_____

_____

❖ I (do/do not) want flowers sent by (close family/friends/anyone) to my funeral. _____

❖ I (do/do not) want monetary donations made in my memory. If yes, please donate to these organizations: _____

_____

_____

_____

_____

❖ I would like a funeral or memorial service to be led by (religious minister [state which religion]/celebrant/specific friend/specific family member/other): _____

_____

_____

_____

❖ During the memorial service I would like the following music played (none/hymns/classical music chosen by funeral director/ special piece of music chosen by me/family choice/don't care):

_____

_____

_____

_____

❖ I want my funeral or memorial service to include the following things I have not already discussed in the other sections:

_____

_____

_____

_____
_____

❖ I would like my organs, bones, and tissues donated (yes/no). If yes, please donate these specific ones: _____
_____
_____
_____

❖ I have nominated the following person to manage my online ac-counts and passwords: _____

  ❖ This person has access to (all online accounts/certain ones): _____
  _____
  _____
  _____

  ❖ They (do/do not) have all the necessary log-ins and passwords. _____
  _____
  _____
  _____

❖ The last thing I would like to say is: _____
_____
_____
_____
_____
_____

_____
_____
_____
_____
_____
_____
_____
_____
_____
_____
_____
_____
_____
_____
_____
_____
_____
_____
_____
_____

Signed: _____

Date: _____

ADDENDUM 8: MEDITATIONS

MUDITA ("SYMPATHETIC JOY") MEDITATION

1. **Find a Quiet Space.** Choose a quiet and comfortable place where you won't be easily distracted. You can lie down, or sit on a cushion, chair, or meditation stool in a posture that feels relaxed and alert.

2. **Set an Intention.** Begin by setting your intention for the meditation. Remind yourself that you are practicing Mudita to cultivate genuine joy and happiness for the well-being and success of others.

3. **Focus on a Neutral Person.** Begin by choosing a neutral person—a friend, an acquaintance, or even a stranger—who is experiencing happiness or success.

4. **Visualize Their Joy.** Close your eyes and visualize the person experiencing happiness or achieving a goal. Imagine their smiling face, their feelings of accomplishment, and their joy.

5. **Cultivate Joy.** As you visualize the person's joy, generate feelings of joy within yourself. Imagine that their happiness radiates out to you. Allow yourself to fill with warmth and happiness as you genuinely celebrate their success.

6. **Expand to Loved Ones.** Once you are comfortable with the practice, you can try it using loved ones—family, friends, mentors—by visualizing their happiness and success. As before, generate feelings of joy as you visualize their positive experiences.

7. **Extend to Neutral and Difficult People.** As you feel more confident, you might want to begin to work with people you are experiencing conflict with, or who are evoking darker feelings for you. The aim is to cultivate compassion and joy for all beings, regardless of your personal feelings.

8. **Practice Loving-Kindness.** If you encounter resistance or nega-

tive emotions, you can incorporate loving-kindness phrases into your meditation. For example, silently repeat phrases like "May they be happy. May they be successful. May their joy increase."

9. **Maintain a Gentle Focus.** Throughout the meditation, keep your attention on the person you're visualizing and the feelings of joy you're cultivating. If your mind wanders, gently bring it back to the practice without judgment.

10. **Reflect and Appreciate.** As you conclude the meditation, take a moment to reflect on your experience. Perhaps write about the experience in your journal.

ADDENDUM 9: DEEP ACTIVE LISTENING

In his death doula training, my husband was taught the art of what is called deep active listening. This is a form of focused, nonjudgmental attention to the words of another. It is a useful skill if working with this book in a group. It is also a skill recommended by therapists for maintaining strong relationships. Here are some guidelines for the practice:

1. **Be Present.** Clear your mind of distractions and stay present in the moment. Focus your attention on the speaker. Show through your body language that you are engaged and interested.

2. **Maintain Eye Contact.** Maintain eye contact with the speaker, showing that you are present and paying attention.

3. **Give Nonverbal Feedback.** Utilize nonverbal cues such as nodding or smiling to show that you are actively listening and understanding their words.

4. **Don't Interrupt.** Allow the speaker to finish their thoughts before responding.

5. **Try to Feel Empathy and Understanding.** Put yourself in the

speaker's shoes and try to understand their perspective. Show empathy by acknowledging their emotions and experiences.

6. **Avoid Judgment.** Suspend judgment and refrain from making assumptions or jumping to conclusions while the speaker is talking. Create a safe space for open communication.

7. **Ask Open-Ended Questions.** Ask open-ended questions that encourage the speaker to elaborate and provide more information.

8. **Paraphrase and Reflect.** After the speaker has finished speaking, paraphrase their key points to ensure your understanding. You might also reflect their emotions, which is the practice of observing another's feelings and reflecting them back through body language or words.

9. **Be Patient.** Some speakers may need more time to express their thoughts. Be patient and allow them the space to share at their own pace.

10. **Listen for Feelings and Subtext.** Pay attention not only to the words being said, but also to the emotions and underlying messages. Sometimes what is not said explicitly can be just as important.

11. **Stay Open-Minded.** Be open to hearing perspectives that may differ from your own. Engaging in active listening doesn't mean you have to agree, but it allows you to understand better.

12. **Limit Your Own Talking.** While engaging in deep active listening, limit your own talking and sharing. The focus should be on understanding the speaker's perspective.

ADDENDUM 10: RESOURCES
FOR PROFESSIONAL HELP IN THE US

United States National Suicide Prevention Lifeline: This is a 24-7 toll-free hotline that provides support, information, and local resources for people in distress or crisis. You can call it at 988.

Crisis Text Line: If you prefer texting, you can text "HELLO" to 741741 to connect with a trained crisis counselor. They are available 24-7.

Veterans Crisis Line: This hotline is specifically for veterans, active-duty service members, and their families. You can call 988 and press 1, or text 838255 to speak with trained professionals.

SAMHSA National Helpline: The Substance Abuse and Mental Health Services Administration (SAMHSA) provides a confidential and free helpline for individuals and families facing mental health and substance use disorders. Call 1-800-662-HELP (1-800-662-4357).

National Alliance on Mental Illness (NAMI) Helpline: NAMI offers information, support, and resources for individuals and families dealing with mental health issues. You can reach its helpline at 1-800-950-NAMI (1-800-950-6264).

Trevor Project: This hotline provides support for LGBTQ+ youth who are in crisis, feeling suicidal, or in need of a safe and judgment-free space to talk. Call 1-866-488-7386 or text "START" to 678678.

Teen Line: This hotline is staffed by trained teen volunteers who provide support and a safe space for other teens to talk. Call 1-800-TLC-TEEN (1-800-852-8336) or text "TEEN" to 839863.

ADDENDUM 11: MIND MAPS
Mind maps are a visual way to organize nonlinear and complex ideas.

CHOOSE YOUR TOPIC: DECIDE ON THE MAIN TOPIC OR CENTRAL IDEA
On a large piece of plain paper, write the central idea or main topic

in the center of the page—for example, "death"—and draw a circle around it. From this central idea, create branches that connect to other main concepts related to your topic; in this case, those might include cemeteries, memento mori, fear. From there, add subtopics or details related to these ideas, and link them via a branch; for example, from cemeteries, you might add links to tomb monuments, tourist attractions, ossuaries. There are many online resources to help you create your own.

ADDENDUM 12: ACTIVE IMAGINATION

Active imagination is a technique developed by Carl Jung that involves the exploration of the unconscious through the creation and contemplation of inner images. Jung believed that utilizing active imagination could lead to a deeper understanding of the self and facilitate psychological growth. It is often used in analytical psychology as a means of integrating unconscious material into conscious awareness. It's important to note that any information you receive should not be passively accepted; use your judgment to ascertain what feels useful to you.

The following are some guidelines. If you choose to work with this technique, I highly recommend Jungian analyst Robert A. Johnson's *Inner Work: Using Dreams and Active Imagination for Personal Growth* (1986); you can find a free PDF of it at archive.org.

> **Preparation:** Find a quiet and comfortable space where you can relax without distractions. I like to light a candle and do some relaxation excersies—such as five concious deep breaths—before I begin. It also helps me to use shamanic drumming tracks (many of which can be found for free on YouTube). Drumming is an age-old and safe technique for bringing us into an altered state of consciousness.

Relaxation: Enter a state of relaxation through deep breathing or meditation to quiet the mind.

Focus: Concentrate on the specific image, symbol, or dream you would like to work with.

Engagement: Allow the image to unfold and move spontaneously in your mind, observing it without judgment. Do not try to control it.

Dialogue: Engage in an inner dialogue with any characters or elements you might encounter, asking questions and exploring their meaning.

Reflection: After the active imagination session, reflect on the insights, emotions, and associations that emerged during the process. You might also want to record your experience in artwork or writing.

ADDENDUM 13: SHAMANIC JOURNEYING

Shamans are healers of body, soul, and spirit who are part of Indigenous cultures around the world. They have existed for millennia, and many scholars believe that we can trace all religions to shamanistic roots. Thus all of us have ancestry rooted in a shared shamanistic heritage.

One useful tool that shamans use in order to move beyond what they call ordinary reality—in Jung's parlance, into the unconscious, or, in Bolte Taylor's, into the right side of the brain—is the shamanic journey. I have found this method exceedingly useful in my own life. Below are some guidelines for how to enter into this state. If you want to go deeper with this, I highly recommend Sandra Ingerman's book *Shamanic Journeying: A Beginner's Guide* (2008). For millennia, drumming has been used as a safe and temporary technique for bringing us into an altered state of consciousness. You can find a variety of shamanic drum tracks or guided shamanic journeys on YouTube. I like to do these journeys supine, on my mat, right after doing yoga and when I'm still in a deeply relaxed state. I suggest revisiting the idea of "sincere pretending" (chapter one, page 7) as you prepare to enter this nonrational, imaginative state. It is also important to note that any information you receive in this way should not be passively accepted; use your judgment to ascertain what feels useful to you.

To Prepare:

- Choose an intention for your journey; this could include seeking guidance on or greater insight into a specific question or concern.
- Create a safe and comfortable space where you won't be disturbed.
- Lie down or sit comfortably. You might even cover your eyes.
- Consider setting this time off as non-ordinary by lighting a candle, burning incense, or some other technique.
- Take a few deep breaths to still your mind and enter intentionally into a meditative state.

Begin the Journey:

- Begin to play your shamanic journey drum track or guided shamanic journey.
- If you are not using a guided journey, follow these instructions: Imagine yourself in a familiar place that makes you feel comfortable and safe. Spend a few moments really feeling yourself in the space. Try to use all your senses; note the feel of the air on your skin and your feet on the ground. Look around and see all there is to see, and listen for any sounds you might hear. Now survey the landscape. We are looking for a way to move to the lower or upper world; these, along with our own middle world, make up the cosmos from a shamanic perspective. Look for either an entryway

into the earth, such as a hole in the ground, a cave, a lake, or a fissure of some sort, or anything that might serve as a means to ascend, such as a tree, a ladder, or a vine. Follow whatever portal you choose, enabling you to go up or down. When you arrive at your next destination, note what it looks like, sounds like, and feels like.

Explore with Openness:

- Go with your imagination, whatever happens. Do not overthink it.
- Allow yourself to experience images, feelings, sounds, or smells spontaneously, without trying to control them.
- Be open to receiving visuals, sensations, and insights without preconceived expectations.

Interact with Figures:

- If you encounter figures or animals during your journey, have questions prepared for them or seek their guidance based on your intention.
- Express gratitude to any figures that appear during the journey before returning the same way you came.
- Write down, or otherwise record, your experience. Reflect on what, if anything, you learned, or any new insights gained.

RESOURCES: FURTHER READING, LISTENING, AND VIEWING

BOOKS CITED AND FURTHER READING

8 Keys to Safe Trauma Recovery, Babette Rothschild (2009).
A Brief History of Hair Art as Seen in Woven Strands: The Art of Human Hair Work at the Mütter Museum, Emily Snedden Yates, Evan Michelson, and John Whitenight (2018).

A Healing Touch: True Stories of Life, Death, and Hospice, edited by Richard Russo (2008).

A Short History of Nearly Everything, Bill Bryson (2003).

A Social History of Dying, Allan Kellehear (2007).

A Year to Live: How to Live This Year as If It Were Your Last, Stephen Levine (1997).

After: A Doctor Explores What Near-Death Experiences Reveal about Life and Beyond, Bruce Greyson (2021).

American Cosmic: UFOs, Religion, Technology, D. W. Pasulka (2019).

Anatomica: The Exquisite and Unsettling Art of Human Anatomy, Joanna Ebenstein (2020).

An Encyclopedia of Shamanism, Christina Pratt (2007).

An Illustrated Dictionary of the Gods and Symbols of Ancient Mexico and the Maya, Mary Miller and Karl Taube (1993).

An Illustrated Encyclopaedia of Traditional Symbols, J. C. Cooper (1987).

Before: Children's Memories of Previous Lives, Jim Tucker (2021).

Being Mortal: Medicine and What Matters in the End, Atul Gawande (2014).

Beyond, Tiffany Hopkins (forthcoming).

Bone: Dying into Life, Marion Woodman (2000).

Braiding Sweetgrass: Indigenous Wisdom, Scientific Knowledge, and the Teachings of Plants, Robin Wall Kimmerer (2013).

Cabarets of Death: Death, Dance and Dining in Early Twentieth-Century Paris, Mel Gordon, edited by Joanna Ebenstein (2024).

Charlotte's Web, E. B. White (1952).

Close to the Bone, Jean Shinoda Bolen (1996).

Consciousness Unbound: Liberating Mind from the Tyranny of Materialism, edited by Edward F. Kelly and Paul Marshall (2023).

Cosmic Serpent: DNA and the Origins of Knowledge, Jeremy Narby (1998).

Cranioklepty: Grave Robbing and the Search for Genius, Colin Dickey (2019).

Dancing in the Flames: The Dark Goddess in the Transformation of Consciousness, Marion Woodman (1996).

Death: A Graveside Companion, edited by Joanna Ebenstein (2017).

Death and the Idea of Mexico, Claudio Lomnitz (2005).

Death as an Altered State of Consciousness: A Scientific Approach, Imants Barušs (2023).

Death Gods: An Encyclopedia of the Rulers, Evil Spirits, and Geographies of the Dead, Ernest L. Abel (2009).

Death in the Dining Room and Other Tales of Victorian Culture, Kenneth L. Ames (1992).

Death: The Final Stage of Growth, Elisabeth Kübler-Ross (1997).

Denial of Death, Ernest Becker (1973).

Design for Death, Barbara Mildred Jones (1967).

Devoted to Death: Santa Muerte, the Skeleton Saint, R. Andrew Chesnut (2011).

Dracula, Bram Stoker (1897).

Feeding Your Demons: Ancient Wisdom for Resolving Inner Conflict, Tsultrim Allione (2008).

Four Thousand Weeks: Time Management for Mortals, Oliver Burkeman (2021).

Frankenstein; or, The Modern Prometheus, Mary Shelley (1818).

From Here to Eternity: Traveling the World to Find the Good Death, Caitlin Doughty (2017).

Ghosts of the Tsunami: Death and Life in Japan's Disaster Zone, Richard Lloyd Parry (2017).

Going into Darkness: Fantastic Coffins from Africa, Thierry Secretan (1995).

Gothic: An Illustrated History, Roger Luckhurst (2021).

Grave, Allison C. Meier (2023).

Healing through the Dark Emotions, Miriam Greenspan (2004).

Heaven and Hell: A History of the Afterlife, Bart D. Ehrman (2020).

Heaven Can Wait: Purgatory in Catholic Devotional and Popular Culture, Diana Walsh Pasulka (2014).

Honoring Your Ancestors: A Guide to Ancestral Veneration, Mallorie Vaudoise (2019).

How God Becomes Real: Kindling the Presence of Invisible Others, Tanya Luhrmann (2020).

How to Meditate: A Guide to Self-Discovery, Lawrence LeShan (1999).

How We Die: Reflections of Life's Final Chapter, Sherwin B. Nuland (1995).

Inner Work: Using Dreams and Active Imagination for Personal Growth, Robert A. Johnson (1986).

Interview with the Vampire, Anne Rice (1976).

It Didn't Start with You: How Inherited Family Trauma Shapes Who We Are and How to End the Cycle, Mark Wolynn (2016).

Japanese Death Poems: Written by Zen Monks and Haiku Poets on the Verge of Death, edited by Yoel Hoffmann (2018).

Jung on Death and Immortality, C. G. Jung, edited by Jenny Yates (2000).

Jung on Synchronicity and the Paranormal, C. G. Jung, edited by Roderick Main (1997).

Jung to Live By, Eugene Pascal (1992).

Land of Desire: Merchants, Power and the Rise of a New American Culture, William Leach (1993).

Life after Life, Raymond Moody (1975).

Life before Life, Dr. Jim B. Tucker (2005).

Luminous Darkness: An Engaged Buddhist Approach to Embracing the Unknown, Deborah Eden Tull (2022).

Making an Exit: From the Magnificent to the Macabre—How We Dignify the Dead, Sarah Murray (2011).

Man and His Symbols, C. G. Jung, Marie-Louise von Franz, Joseph L. Henderson, Aniela Jaffé, and Jolande Jacobi (1964).

Man's Search for Meaning, Viktor Frankl (1946).

Many Lives, Many Masters, Brian Weiss (1988).

Matriarchal Societies: Studies on Indigenous Cultures across the Globe, Heide Göttner-Abendroth (2012).

Medical Miracles: Doctors, Saints, and Healing in the Modern World, Jackie Duffin (2009).

Memories, Dreams, Reflections, C. G. Jung, edited by Aniela Jaffé (1962).

Mexico through the Eyes of José Guadalupe Posada, Alonso Ruiz (2019).

Modern Woman in Search of Soul, June Singer (1998).

My Stroke of Insight: A Brain Scientist's Personal Journey, Jill Bolte Taylor (2008).

On Death and Dying: What the Dying Have to Teach Doctors, Nurses, Clergy and Their Own Families, Elisabeth Kübler-Ross (1969).

On Dreams and Death, Marie-Louise von Franz (1987).

On Grief and Grieving, Elisabeth Kübler-Ross and David Kessler (2005).

On Life after Death, Elisabeth Kübler-Ross (1984).

Otherworld Journeys: Accounts of Near-Death Experience in Medieval and Modern Times, Carol Zaleski (1987).

Psyche and Death: Death-Demons in Folklore, Myths, and Modern Dreams, Edgar Herzog (1983).

Radical Mindfulness: Why Transforming Fear of Death Is Politically Vital, James K. Rowe (2023).

Radical Spirits: Spiritualism and Women's Rights in Nineteenth-Century America, Anne Braude (1989).

Rest in Pieces: The Curious Fates of Famous Corpses, Bess Lovejoy (2013).

Sand Talk: How Indigenous Thinking Can Save the World, Tyson Yunkaporta (2019).

Scream: Chilling Adventures in the Science of Fear, Margee Kerr (2015).

Séance, Shannon Taggart (2019; new edition 2022).

Shamanic Journeying: A Beginner's Guide, Sandra Ingerman (2008).

Staring at the Sun: Overcoming the Terror of Death, Irvin D. Yalom (2008).

Stiff: The Curious Lives of Human Cadavers, Mary Roach (2003).

Strange Case of Dr. Jekyll and Mr. Hyde, Robert Louis Stevenson (1886).

Struwwelpeter: In English Translation, Heinrich Hoffmann (1995).

Synchronicity: Nature and Psyche in an Interconnected Universe, Joseph Cambray (2012).

Talking to the Dead: Kate and Maggie Fox and the Rise of Spiritualism, Barbara Weisberg (2004).

Technologies of the Human Corpse, John Troyer (2020).

The Andean Cosmovision: A Path for Exploring Profound Aspects of Ourselves, Nature, and the Cosmos, Oakley Gordon (2014).

The Artist's Way: A Spiritual Path to Higher Creativity, Julia Cameron (1992).

The Art of Dreaming: Tools for Creative Dream Work, Jill Mellick (2001).

The Body Keeps the Score: Brain, Mind, and Body in the Healing of Trauma, Bessel van der Kolk (2015).

The Book of Symbols: Reflections on Archetypal Images, Archive for Research in Archetypal Symbolism (2010).

The Book of the Dead, translated by E. A. Wallis Budge (1895).

The Death and Resurrection Show: From Shaman to Superstar, Rogan P. Taylor (1985).

The Denial of Death, Ernest Becker (1973).

The Epic of Gilgamesh, translated by Andrew George (2003).

The Essential Edgar Allan Poe Collection: His Best-Loved Tales and His Complete Poems, Edgar Allen Poe (2020).

The Female Thermometer: Eighteenth-Century Culture and the Invention of the Uncanny, Terry Castle (1995).

The Flip: Epiphanies of Mind and the Future of Knowledge, Jeffrey Kripal (2019).

The Gashlycrumb Tinies, Edward Gorey (1963).

The Gentle Art of Swedish Death Cleaning, Margareta Magnusson (2017).

The Grand Guignol: Theatre of Fear and Terror, Mel Gordon (1988).

The Hour of Our Death: The Classic History of Western Attitudes toward Death, Phillipe Ariès (1981).

The Immortality Key: The Secret History of the Religion with No Name, Brian C. Muraresku (2020).

The Labyrinth of Solitude, Octavio Paz (1950).

The Leopard, Giuseppe Tomasi di Lampedusa (1958).

The Master and His Emissary: The Divided Brain and the Making of the Western World, Iain McGilchrist (2009).

The Morbid Anatomy Anthology, edited by Joanna Ebenstein and Colin Dickey (2014).

The Myth of the Goddess: Evolution of an Image, Anne Baring and Jules Cashford (1991).

The Origin of Satan: How Christians Demonized Jews, Pagans, and Heretics, Elaine Pagels (1996).

The Other Side of Sadness: What the New Science of Bereavement Tells Us about Life after Loss, George A. Bonanno (2009).

The Pregnant Virgin: A Process of Psychological Transformation, Marion Woodman (1985)

The Sandman comic series, Neil Gaiman (1989–96).

The Secret Life of Objects, Rebecca Purcell (forthcoming).

The Skeleton at the Feast: The Day of the Dead in Mexico, Elizabeth Carmichael (1992).

The Smell of Rain on Dust: Grief and Praise, Martín Prechtel (2015).

The Tibetan Book of the Dead: First Complete Translation, edited by Graham Coleman and Thupten Jinpa, translated by Gyurme Dorje (2007).

The Top Five Regrets of the Dying: A Life Transformed by the Dearly Departing, Bronnie Ware (2012).

The Uncanny, Sigmund Freud (1919).

The Victorian Celebration of Death, James Stevens Curl (2001).

The Wild Edge of Sorrow: Rituals of Renewal and the Sacred Work of Grief, Francis Weller (2015).

The Wisdom of the Serpent: The Myths of Death, Rebirth, and Resurrection, Joseph L. Henderson and Maud Oakes (1990).

The Worm at the Core: On the Role of Death in Life, Sheldon Solomon, Jeff Greenberg, and Tom Pyszczynski (2015).

The Year of Magical Thinking, Joan Didion (2005).

Theorizing about Myth, Robert A. Segal (1999).

This Party's Dead: Grief, Joy and Spilled Rum at the World's Death Festivals, Erica Buist (2021).

Traveling between the Worlds: Conversations with Contemporary Shamans, Hillary S. Webb (2004).

Will My Cat Eat My Eyeballs? Big Questions from Tiny Mortals about Death, Caitlin Doughty (2019).

Without Sanctuary: Lynching Photography in America, James Allen (2000).

Women Who Run with the Wolves: Myths and Stories of the Wild Woman Archetype, Clarissa Pinkola Estés (1992).

ARTICLES

"A Communion of Little Saints: Nineteenth-Century American Child Hagiographies," Diana Walsh Pasulka, *Journal of Feminist Studies in Religion* (2007).

"A Somber Pedagogy—A History of the Child Death Bed Scene in Early American Children's Religious Literature, 1674–1840," Diana Walsh Pasulka, *Journal of the History of Childhood and Youth* (2009).

"From Alpha to Omega: Ancient Mysteries and the Near-Death Experience," Kenneth Ring, *Anabiosis* (1986).

"Mourning in Japan," Joe Yamamoto, Keigo Okonogi, Tetsuya Iwasaki, and Saburo Yoshimura, *American Journal of Psychiatry* (2006).

"Pandemic Practice: Horror Fans and Morbidly Curious Individuals Are More Psychologically Resilient during the COVID-19 Pandemic," Coltan Scrivner, John A. Johnson, Jens Kjeldgaard-Christiansen, and Mathias Clasen, *Personality and Individual Differences* (2020).

"The Pornography of Death," Geoffrey Gorer, in *Pornographic Art and the Aesthetics of Pornography* (1955).

"Unlocking the Healing Power of You," Erik Vance, with photos by Erika Larsen, *National Geographic* (2016).

"Virtual Mortality and Near-Death Experience after a Prolonged Exposure in a Shared Virtual Reality May Lead to Positive Life-Attitude Changes," Itxaso Barberia, Ramon Oliva, Pierre Bourdin, and Mel Slater, *PLoS One* (2018).

"'You've Got to Find What You Love,' Jobs Says," *Stanford News* (2005).

VIEWING

FILMS THAT DEAL WITH DEATH OR MORTALITY IN
NOTEWORTHY WAYS

All That Jazz (1979)

Apocalypse Now (1979)

Barbie (2023)

Blade Runner (1982)

Charlotte's Web (1973)

Coco (2017)

Dead Poets Society (1989)

Donnie Darko (2001)

Jacob's Ladder (1990)

Orpheus (1950)

Serpent and the Sun: Tales of an Aztec Apprentice (2009)
Solaris (1972)
The Others (2001)
The Seventh Seal (1957)
The Sixth Sense (1999)
The Tree of Life (2011)
Wings of Desire (1987)

TV SHOWS THAT DEAL WITH DEATH OR MORTALITY IN NOTEWORTHY WAYS
American Gods (2017–21)
Six Feet Under (2001–5)
The Good Place (2016–20)
The Leftovers (2014–17)
The Sandman (2022–)
Undone (2019–22)
Wednesday (2022)

HUMOROUS DEATH FILMS
Beetlejuice (1988)
Harold and Maude (1971)
Heathers (1988)
House of Wax (1953)
The Abominable Dr. Phibes (1971)
The Addams Family (1991)
The Loved One (1965)
The Masque of the Red Death (1964)
The Nightmare before Christmas (1993)

CLASSIC SCARY MOVIES
Heavenly Creatures (1994)
Hereditary (2018)
Midsommar (2019)
Poltergeist (1982)
Psycho (1960)
Rosemary's Baby (1968)
Shadow of a Doubt (1943)

Silence of the Lambs (1991)
Strangers on a Train (1951)
The Birds (1963)
The Exorcist (1973)
The Haunting (1963)
The Innocents (1961)
The Night of the Hunter (1955)
The Shining (1980)
The Wicker Man (1973)
The Witch (2015)

DOCUMENTARIES
Flight from Death: The Quest for Immortality, directed by Patrick Shen (2003)
La Santa Muerte (Saint Death), directed by Eva Aridjis Fuentes (2007)
Short films by director Ronni Thomas: three-to-five-minute films by Morbid
    Anatomy filmmaker-in-residence Ronni Thomas, many of which explore death-
    related themes: themidnightarchive.com
We Were Here, directed by David Weissman and Bill Weber (2011)

LISTENING

Authentic New Orleans Jazz Funeral, album by Magnificent Sevenths (2008),
    open.spotify.com/album/4I5nJ5mStgoXUU2BEexLXI?si=JoC8ixY_QZink_n
    -DGC-og
Dreams: Language of the Soul, audiobook by Marion Woodman (2009)
Grief and Praise, recorded lecture by Martín Prechtel (1997)
Sitting by the Well: Bringing the Feminine to Consciousness Through Language, Dreams,
    and Metaphor, audiobook by Marion Woodman (2000)
The Crown of Age, recorded lecture by Marion Woodman (2011)
Theatre of the Imagination, Volume One, audiobook by Clarissa Pinkola Estés (2005)

APPS AND ONLINE RESOURCES

Archive for Research in Archetypal Symbolism (ARAS): https://aras.org (or in per-
    son in New York City at 28 East 39th Street, between Madison Avenue and Park
    Avenue). ARAS is a pictorial and written archive of mythological, ritualistic, and
    symbolic images from all over the world and from all epochs of human history.
    The ARAS archive contains about eighteen thousand art images, each accom-

panied by a scholarly commentary that explores the archetypal content and cultural context of the image. In addition to this image collection, the website offers a rich library of articles on art and symbols and a concordance that allows you to search Carl Jung's *Collected Works* by word or topic.

"Existential Anxiety and the Human Experience": free online class created by the Ernest Becker Foundation on terror management theory; udemy.com/course /existential-anxiety-and-the-human-experience

Free online yoga: Yoga with Adriene, youtube.com/channel/UCFKE7WVJfvaH W5q283SxchA

Meditation app: *Headspace*, headspace.com

University of Virginia School of Medicine Division of Perceptual Studies: podcasts, videos, and other resources about the science of life after death; med.virginia .edu/perceptual-studies

WeCroak memento mori–themed app: wecroak.com

Windbridge Research Center: articles, podcasts, videos, and other resources about the science of life after death; windbridge.org

ACKNOWLEDGMENTS

This book is the culmination of many years of work and life, and there are a great many who have helped along the way, more than I can possibly name.

First off, I would like to express my utmost gratitude to my profoundly supportive husband, Bryan Melillo, who endured months of my obsessive work on this book to the exclusion of nearly everything else in my life, vacations and holidays be damned!

Thanks, as always, are also due to my ancestors: particularly my oma and opa, Dina and Benno Ebenstein, whose non-American wisdom inspired me so deeply, and is so much a part of my being and of this book. Thanks also to the rest of my family, Sandy, Robert, Donna, Laura, and Judy Ebenstein. I am also deeply grateful for the generosity of those who read this book's initial draft, and whose feedback shaped the book very profoundly: namely, Eleanor Crook, Tiffany Hopkins, Patricia Llosa, Diana X. Muñiz, Diana Walsh Pasulka, and Kelley Swindall. Thanks also to the death professionals and members of the Morbid Anatomy community who generously shared their thoughts with me, and empowered me to share them with you: Hannah Haddadi, Kristina Golden, Karen Montgomery, Diana X. Muñiz, and Ann Vidal.

I am also so grateful to my fabulous agent, Kate McKean, for her comments, guidance, and support. Special thanks are also due to the editorial doula of this project: my good friend, and stalwart supporter, Charlie Mounter, who was by my side, lending support and helping me find the right words, from inception to completion. I also thank Anna Sproul-Latimer and Janis Donnaud, who helped shape this project in significant ways in earlier iterations. Thanks to my beloved death community colleagues Colin Dickey, Caitlin Doughty, and John Troyer. And big thanks to some of my favorite humans who helped along the way, with anecdotes, suggestions, inspiration, and support: Ana Patricia Herrera Aguilar, Laetitia Barbier, Oliver Burkeman, Ben Cerveny, Heather Chaplin, Catherine Crawford, Amber Engelmann, Megan Fitzpatrick, Kate Forde, Eva Aridjis Fuentes, Barbara Archer Hand, Peter Hand, Eric Huang, Mary James Ketch, Spencer Lamm, Ross MacFarlane, Cristina Marcelo, Edson Mendes, Evan Michelson, Gerry and Florence Newland, Mark Pilkington, Rebecca Purcell, Hugo Sanchez, Ame Simon, Charlotte Slivka, Amy Slonaker, Frank Szelwach, and Maureen and Ronni Thomas. Immense gratitude to all the inspiring and brilliant students I have worked with over the years, and the Morbid Anatomy community more generally, from whom I have learned—and continue to learn—so, so much. Thanks also to Steven Rand and Julia Knight, who, via their apexart outbound residency, provided me with the space for wisdom to emerge. And thanks to Joshua Foer for sending me their way. And this book would never have happened without David Webber and Thu-Huong Ha, who invited me to give—and coached me so expertly through—

the TEDx Talk that demonstrated to me the larger appeal of this sort of material. Thank you.

I am also deeply grateful to the fabulous editorial team at TarcherPerigee, who helped expertly usher this book from idea to reality: my wonderful editor Lauren Appleton, designer Angie Boutin, and Ashley Alliano.

NOTES

INTRODUCTION

1 John Helliwell et al., eds., *World Happiness Report 2023* (New York: Sustainable Development Solutions Network, 2023), https://happiness -report.s3.amazonaws.com/2023/WHR+23.pdf.

2 Tim Connolly, "Plato: Phaedo," Internet Encyclopedia of Philosophy, https:// iep.utm.edu/phaedo/.

3 Steve Jobs, "'You've Got to Find What You Love,' Jobs Says," *Stanford News*, June 12, 2005, https://news.stanford.edu/2005/06/12/youve-got-find-love -jobs-says/.

4 C. G. Jung and Aniela Jaffé, *Memories, Dreams, Reflections*, rev. ed. (New York: Vintage Books, 1965).

CHAPTER 1. STARTING THE PROCESS: THE DESCENT

1 Carl Jung, *Aion: Researches into the Phenomenology of the Self* (Princeton, NJ: Princeton University Press, 1951).

2 C. G. Jung and Aniela Jaffé, *Memories, Dreams, Reflections*, rev. ed. (New York: Vintage, 1965).

3 O. E. Gordon, "A Therapeutic Relationship Between People and Their Geography in the Andes," *Clio's Psyche* 7, no. 4 (2001).

4 Carl Gustav Jung, *Collected Works*, vol. 14, ed. H. Read et al., trans. R. F. C. Hull (Princeton, NJ: Princeton University Press, 1969).

5 Kira M. Newman, "How Journaling Can Help You in Hard Times," *Greater Good Magazine*, August 18, 2020, https://greatergood.berkeley.edu/article /item/how_journaling_can_help_you_in_hard_times.

CHAPTER 2. WHAT IS DEATH?

1 "United States: Life Expectancy 1860–2020," Statista, accessed January 31, 2024, https://www.statista.com/statistics/1040079/life-expectancy-united-states-all-time/.

2 Max Roser, "Mortality in the Past: Every Second Child Died," Our World in Data, April 11, 2023, https://ourworldindata.org/child-mortality-in-the-past.

3 Stanley B. Burns, *Sleeping Beauty: Memorial Photography in America*, 2nd ed. (Altadena, CA: Twelvetrees Press, 1990).

4 Marion Woodman, *The Pregnant Virgin: A Process of Psychological Transformation* (Toronto: Inner City Books, 1985).

5 Heide Göttner-Abendroth, *Matriarchal Societies: Studies on Indigenous Cultures across the Globe* (New York: Peter Lang, 2012).

6 Carl Gustav Jung, *Collected Works of C. G. Jung*, vol. 13, ed. and trans. Gerhard Adler and R. F. C. Hull (Princeton, NJ: Princeton University Press, 2014), https://doi.org/10.1515/9781400850990.

7 "Top 10 François Jacob Quotes (2024 Update)," Quotefancy, accessed December 28, 2023, https://quotefancy.com/francois-jacob-quotes.

8 C. G. Jung and Aniela Jaffé, *Memories, Dreams, Reflections*, rev. ed. (New York: Vintage Books, 1965).

9 Jung and Jaffé, *Memories, Dreams, Reflections*, rev. ed.

CHAPTER 3. LIFE, DEATH, AND REBIRTH

1 Heide Göttner-Abendroth, *Matriarchal Societies: Studies on Indigenous Cultures across the Globe* (New York: Peter Lang, 2012).

2 Marion Woodman, *Sitting by the Well: Bringing the Feminine to Consciousness Through Language, Dreams, and Metaphor*, read by the author (Louisville, CO: Sounds True, 2000), Audible audio ed., 7 hr., 24 min.

3 Michael Moyer, "Is Space Digital?," *Scientific American* 306, no. 2 (February 2012): 32–37, https://www.jstor.org/stable/26014198.

4 Joseph Campbell, *A Joseph Campbell Companion* (New York: Harper&Row, 1991).

5 Carl Gustav Jung, *The Collected Works of C. G. Jung*, vol. 17, ed. and trans. Gerhard Adler and R. F. C. Hull (Princeton, NJ: Princeton University Press, 1954), para. 331.

6 Marion Woodman, *The Pregnant Virgin: A Process of Psychological Transformation* (Chicago: C.G. Jung Institute of Chicago Bookstore, 1985).

7 Jean Shinoda Bolen, "Crisis as a Turning Point: The Gift of Liminal Time," filmed November 2020 in San Fafael, CA, TED video, 15:23, https://www.ted.com/talks/jean_shinoda_bolen_crisis_as_a_turning_point_the_gift_of_liminal_time.

8 Clarissa Pinkola Estés, PhD, *Women Who Run with the Wolves: Myths and Stories of the Wild Woman Archetype* (New York: Ballantine Books, 1992).

CHAPTER 4. DEATH WITH VALUE: OTHER WAYS OF LOOKING AT DEATH

1 Tim Connolly, "Plato: Phaedo," Internet Encyclopedia of Philosophy, https://iep.utm.edu/phaedo/.

CHAPTER 5. WHAT HAPPENS AFTER YOU DIE?

1 Edward F. Kelly and Paul Marshall, *Consciousness Unbound: Liberating Mind from the Tyranny of Materialism* (Lanham, MD: Rowman & Littlefield, 2021).
2 Marinus van der Sluijs, "Three Ancient Reports of Near-Death Experiences: Bremmer Revisited," *Journal of Near-Death Studies* 27, no. 4 (2009).
3 Carl Jung, *C. G. Jung Letters*, vol. 1, *1906–1950* (Princeton, NJ: Princeton University Press, 1973).
4 C. G. Jung, *Jung on Death and Immortality*, ed. Jenny Yates (Princeton, NJ: Princeton University Press, 1999).
5 Kelly and Marshall, *Consciousness Unbound*.
6 Kelly and Marshall, *Consciousness Unbound*.
7 Kelly and Marshall, *Consciousness Unbound*.
8 Itxaso Barberia et al., "Virtual Mortality and Near-Death Experience after a Prolonged Exposure in a Shared Virtual Reality May Lead to Positive Life-Attitude Changes," *PLoS ONE* 13, no. 11 (2018): e0203358, https://doi.org/10.1371/journal.pone.0203358.
9 Kenneth Ring, "From Alpha to Omega: Ancient Mysteries and the Near-Death Experience," *Anabiosis: The Journal for Near-Death Studies* 5, no. 2 (1985), https://digital.library.unt.edu/ark:/67531/metadc799357/m2/1/high_res_d/vol5-no2-3.pdf.
10 "Division of Perceptual Studies," University of Virginia School of Medicine, https://med.virginia.edu/perceptual-studies/.
11 Imants Barušs, *Death as an Altered State of Consciousness: A Scientific Approach* (Washington, DC: American Psychological Association, 2023).
12 "The Mingling of Faith and Reason: Miracles and the Catholic Church—Catholic Focus," YouTube video, 22:06, posted by Salt + Light Media, February 1, 2012, https://www.youtube.com/watch?v=5N4vlZtMWWo.
13 Erik Vance, "Unlocking the Healing Power of You," *National Geographic*, November 23, 2016.
14 Diana Walsh Pasulka, email message to Joanna Ebenstein, February 20, 2024.
15 C. G. Jung and Roderick Main, *Jung on Synchronicity and the Paranormal* (London: Routledge, 1997).

CHAPTER 6. LOVE AND DEATH: MOURNING THOSE WE'VE LOST

1 "Martín Prechtel: Grief and Praise (1 of 3)," posted by Minnesota Men's Conference, October 26, 2015, YouTube video, 21:43, https://www.youtube.com/watch?v=UUwewfPPSbE.
2 "Unexpressed Emotions Will Never Die," Brighton and Hove Psychotherapy, April 12, 2021, https://www.brightonandhovepsychotherapy.com/blog/unexpressed-emotions-will-never-die/.

3   Hilary Jacobs Hendel, "Ignoring Your Emotions Is Bad for Your Health. Here's What to Do about It," *Time*, February 27, 2018, https://time.com /5163576/ignoring-your-emotions-bad-for-your-health/.

4   Zoe Cormier, "The Truth about Animal Grief," BBC Earth, https://www .bbcearth.com/news/the-truth-about-animal-grief.

5   Joe Moran, "Noli Timere," *Joe Moran's Words* (blog), June 11, 2023, https:// joemoran.net/2023/06/11/noli-timere/.

6   Jessica Pierce, "Do Animals Experience Grief?," *Smithsonian*, August 24, 2018, https://www.smithsonianmag.com/science-nature/do-animals-experience -grief-180970124/.

7   Dahleen Glanton, "Death of Koko, the Signing Gorilla, Reminds Us What It Means to Be an Exceptional Human Being," *Chicago Tribune*, June 26, 2018.

8   Brian Handwerk, "Scientists Discover Oldest Known Human Grave in Africa," *Smithsonian*, May 5, 2021, https://www.smithsonianmag.com/science-nature /scientists-discover-oldest-known-human-grave-africa-180977659/.

9   Brad Milne, "The Complete Guide to Buddhist Burial Practices and Rituals," Better Place Forests, June 16, 2022, https://www.betterplaceforests.com /blog/religion/the-complete-guide-to-buddhist-burial-practices-and-rituals/.

10 Dina Gachman, "How to Connect with Loved Ones after They Die," *Time*, April 11, 2023, https://time.com/6269254/connecting-with-the-dead-excerpt/.

11 Elizabeth Broman, "Treasured Tresses—Hair Jewelry Pattern Books," Cooper Hewitt, May 28, 2014, https://www.cooperhewitt.org/2014/05/28 /treasured-tresses-hair-jewelry-pattern-books/.

12 Toshiyuki Sawaki, "Look-alike Dolls Comfort Bereaved," *Seattle Times*, September 28, 2011, https://www.seattletimes.com/seattle-news/health/look -alike-dolls-comfort-bereaved/.

13 Cathy Resmer, "Memorial Dolls Slideshow," *802 Online* (blog), 7D.Blogs .com, August 8, 2007, https://7d.blogs.com/802online/2007/08/memorial -dolls-.html.

14 Richard Russo, ed., *A Healing Touch: True Stories of Life, Death, and Hospice* (Essex, CT: Down East Books, 2008).

15 Clarissa Pinkola Estés, PhD, *Theatre of the Imagination, Volume One*, read by the author (Louisville, CO: Sounds True, 2005), Audible audio ed., 7 hr., 25 min.

CHAPTER 7. COMMUNING WITH THE DEAD: RITUALS AND CONTACT

1   Misha Gajewski, "Here's Why Some People Say They Hear Dead People," *Forbes*, January 17, 2021, https://www.forbes.com/sites/mishagajewski/2021 /01/17/heres-why-some-people-say-they-hear-dead-people/?sh=48faa 9a6439a.

2   George A. Bonanno, *The Other Side of Sadness: What the New Science of Bereavement Tells Us about Life after Loss* (New York: Basic Books, 2010).

3   Joe Yamamoto et al., "Mourning in Japan," *American Journal of Psychiatry* 125, no. 12 (1969), https://doi.org/10.1176/ajp.125.12.1660.

4   Claudio Lomnitz-Adler, *Death and the Idea of Mexico* (Brooklyn, NY: Zone Books, 2005).

5   Kristin Tablang, "Thomas Edison, B. C. Forbes and the Mystery of the Spirit Phone," *Forbes*, October 25, 2019, https://www.forbes.com/sites/kristintablang/2019/10/25/thomas-edison-bc-forbes-mystery-spirit-phone/?sh=48d1d86429ad.

6   Richard Lloyd Parry, *Ghosts of the Tsunami: Death and Life in Japan's Disaster Zone* (New York: MCD Books, 2017).

7   Mari Saito, "Japan's Tsunami Survivors Call Lost Loves on the Phone of the Wind," Reuters, March 4, 2021, https://www.reuters.com/article/us-japan-fukushima-anniversary-telephone/japans-tsunami-survivors-call-lost-loves-on-the-phone-of-the-wind-idUSKCN2AX03J/.

8   Rose Eveleth, "The History of Trick or Treating Is Weirder Than You Thought," *Smithsonian*, October 18, 2012, https://www.smithsonianmag.com/smart-news/the-history-of-trick-or-treating-is-weirder-than-you-thought-79408373/.

9   Octavio Paz, *The Labyrinth of Solitude; the Other Mexico; Return to the Labyrinth of Solitude; Mexico and the United States; the Philanthropic Ogre*, trans. Lysander Kemp, Yara Milos, and Rachel Phillips Belash (New York: Grove Press, 1985).

CHAPTER 8. FEAR OF DEATH AND THE QUEST FOR IMMORTALITY

1   Dillon Ancheta and Lacy Deniz, "Kilauea's Eruption Comes with a Cultural Connection to Pele: 'This Is Her Land,'" *Hawaii News Now*, May 11, 2018, https://www.hawaiinewsnow.com/story/38151257/pele/.

2   Anne Baring and Jules Cashford, *The Myth of the Goddess: Evolution of an Image* (New York: Viking Arkana, 1991), 168.

3   Baring and Cashford, *Myth of the Goddess*, 168.

4   Ernest Becker, *The Denial of Death* (New York: Free Press, 1973).

5   Jill Bolte Taylor, *My Stroke of Insight: A Brain Scientist's Personal Journey* (New York: Penguin Books, 2009).

6   Marcus Aurelius, *Meditations: The Annotated Edition*, trans. Robin Waterfield (New York: Basic Books, 2021).

7   "14 Stoic Quotes on Death," Daily Stoic, October 11, 2019, https://dailystoic.com/14-stoic-quotes-on-death/.

8   Epicurus, *Letter to Menoeceus* (Scotts Valley, CA: CreateSpace, 2016).

9   Lois Beckett, "Older People Would Rather Die Than Let Covid-19 Harm US Economy—Texas Official," *Guardian*, March 24, 2020, https://www.theguardian.com/world/2020/mar/24/older-people-would-rather-die-than-let-covid-19-lockdown-harm-us-economy-texas-official-dan-patrick.

10 Giuseppe Tomasi di Lampedusa, *The Leopard*, trans. Archibald Colquhoun (New York: Knopf Doubleday, 1961).

11 Sander Gilman, "The Pain Barrier: The Story of Pain, by Joanna Bourke," *Irish Times*, October 18, 2014, https://www.irishtimes.com/culture/books /the-pain-barrier-the-story-of-pain-by-joanna-bourke-1.1966043.

12 Stanton Marlan, *The Black Sun: The Alchemy and Art of Darkness* (College Station: Texas A&M University Press, 2008).

13 Friedrich Nietzsche, *Twilight of the Idols* (Indianapolis: Hackett, 1997).

14 C. G. Jung et al., *Letters of C. G. Jung: Volume I, 1906–1950* (London: Taylor and Francis, 2015), https://public.ebookcentral.proquest.com/choice/public fullrecord.aspx?p=4542776.

15 "Tenzin Gyatso, 14th Dalai Lama Quote," LibQuotes, accessed December 28, 2023, https://libquotes.com/dalai-lama/quote/lbg4k40.

16 Irvin D. Yalom, *Staring at the Sun: Overcoming the Terror of Death* (San Francisco: Jossey-Bass, 2009).

17 "Martin Luther King Jr.: Quotes," Goodreads, accessed January 2, 2024, https://www.goodreads.com/quotes/60289-no-one-really-knows-why-they -are-alive-until-they.

CHAPTER 9. PREPARING FOR YOUR OWN DEATH

1 Edvard Munch, "From my rotting body, flowers shall grow and I am in them and that is eternity," n.d., Quote Catalog, accessed February 17, 2024, https:// quotecatalog.com/quote/edvard-munch-from-my-rotting-baVleN7.

2 Ridwan Karim Dini-Osman, "Ghana's Fantasy Coffins: Fulfilling Burial Dreams One Coffin at a Time," *The World*, February 18, 2022, https://theworld .org/stories/2022-02-18/ghana-s-fantasy-coffins-fulfilling-burial-dreams -one-coffin-time.

3 Dini-Osman, "Ghana's Fantasy Coffins."

4 "Christopher Rivera Amaro, Dead Puerto Rico Boxer, Propped Up and Posed Standing in the Ring at Wake," *HuffPost*, UK ed., February 1, 2014, https:// www.huffingtonpost.co.uk/2014/02/01/christopher-rivera-amaro-murder _n_4707964.html.

5 "Velatorios Famosos (No Tradicionales)," Marin Funeral Home, https:// marinfuneralhomepr.com/velatorios-famosos/.

6 Satsuki Kawano, "Pre-Funerals in Contemporary Japan: The Making of a New Ceremony of Later Life among Aging Japanese," *Ethnology* 43, no. 2 (2004), https://doi.org/10.2307/3773951.

7 Raphael Rashid, "Death from Overwork: Young Koreans Rebel against Culture of Long Hours," *Guardian*, June 18, 2023, https://www.theguardian .com/global-development/2023/jun/18/death-from-overwork-young -koreans-rebel-against-culture-of-long-hours.

8 Daewoung Kim and Youngseo Choi, "Dying for a Better Life: South Koreans Fake Their Funerals for Life Lessons," Reuters, November 6, 2019, https:// www.reuters.com/article/idUSKBN1XG037/.

9 Kristina Golden, personal correspondence with author, July 28, 2023.

10 Yoel Hoffmann, ed., *Japanese Death Poems: Written by Zen Monks and Haiku Poets on the Verge of Death* (Tokyo: Tuttle, 2018).

11 Matt Miller, "Rutger Hauer's 'Tears in the Rain' Speech from *Blade Runner* Is an Iconic, Improvised Moment in Film History," *Esquire*, July 24, 2019, https://www.esquire.com/entertainment/movies/a28496103/rutger-hauers -tears-in-the-rain-blade-runner-roy-batty-death-tribute/.

12 Ridley Scott, dir., *Blade Runner* (Burbank, CA: Warner Bros., 1982).

CHAPTER 10. PLAYING WITH DEATH: DEATH AND POPULAR AMUSEMENT

1 Ronni Thomas, "The Grand Guignol—Mel Gordon," Midnight Archive, accessed January 2, 2024, https://www.themidnightarchive.com/#/the-mid night-archive-1/.

2 Mel Gordon, *Cabarets of Death: Death Dance and Dining in Early Twentieth-Century Paris* (Cambridge, MA: MIT Press, 2023).

3 Marilyn A. Mendoza, "The Healing Power of Laughter in Death and Grief," *Psychology Today*, November 7, 2016, https://www.psychologytoday.com /intl/blog/understanding-grief/201611/the-healing-power-laughter-in-death -and-grief.

4 Jamie Doward, "Black Humour Is Sign of High Intelligence, Study Suggests," *Guardian*, January 28, 2017, https://www.theguardian.com/science/2017 /jan/29/dark-humour-high-intelligence-study.

5 Coltan Scrivner et al., "Pandemic Practice: Horror Fans and Morbidly Curious Individuals Are More Psychologically Resilient during the COVID-19 Pandemic," *Personality and Individual Differences* 168, no. 2 (2021): 110397, https://www.researchgate.net/publication/344342920_Pandemic _practice_Horror_fans_and_morbidly_curious_individuals_are_more _psychologically_resilient_during_the_COVID-19_pandemic.

6 "Victor Hugo: Quotes," Goodreads, accessed January 2, 2024, https://www .goodreads.com/quotes/417184-melancholy-is-the-happiness-of-being-sad.

7 Geoffrey Gorer, "The Pornography of Death," in *Pornographic Art and the Aesthetics of Pornography*, ed. Hans Maes (London: Palgrave Macmillan, 2013).

8 Gorer, "The Pornography of Death."

CHAPTER 11. LIVING YOUR TRUE VALUES

1 Steve Jobs, "'You've Got to Find What You Love,' Jobs Says," *Stanford News*, June 12, 2005, https://news.stanford.edu/2005/06/12/youve-got-find-love -jobs-says/.

2 Lucy Pearson, "I Looked for Happiness in the World's Most Contented Nation—and Learned the Importance of Pessimism," *Guardian*, June 28, 2023, https://www.theguardian.com/commentisfree/2023/jun/28/world-happiest -nation-finland-nature-saunas.

3   "The Strong, Silent Type (4.10)," Sopranos Autopsy, published November 17, 2002, https://sopranosautopsy.com/season-4-2/the-strong-silent-type-4-10/.
4   Malcolm David Eckel, "Buddhism," The Great Courses, 2001, https://www.thegreatcourses.com/courses/buddhism.
5   Eckel, "Buddhism."
6   Robin Wall Kimmerer, *Braiding Sweetgrass: Indigenous Wisdom, Scientific Knowledge, and the Teachings of Plants* (Minneapolis: Milkweed Editions, 2013).
7   "Giving Thanks Can Make You Happier," Harvard Health Publishing, August 14, 2021, https://www.health.harvard.edu/healthbeat/giving-thanks-can-make-you-happier.
8   Emine Saner, "Forget Regret! How to Have a Happy Life—According to the World's Leading Expert," *Guardian*, February 6, 2023, https://www.theguardian.com/lifeandstyle/2023/feb/06/how-to-have-a-happy-life-according-to-the-worlds-leading-expert.
9   Julia Cameron, *The Artist's Way* (New York: TarcherPerigee, 2016).

CHAPTER 12. BRINGING BACK THE TREASURE: YOUR OWN MYTH OR SYMBOL OF DEATH

1   C. G. Jung et al., ed. Aniela Jaffé, *Memories, Dreams, Reflections* (London: Flamingo, 1983).
2   Marie-Louise von Franz, *Creation Myths*, rev. ed. (Boston: Shambhala, 1995).
3   Richard Wilhelm, *The Secret of the Golden Flower* (London: Routledge, 2013).
4   Joanna Ebenstein, "Life, Death and the Pandemic from a Shamanistic Perspective: Interview with Christina Pratt, Author of the Encyclopedia of Shamanism," *Morbid Anatomy Online Journal*, May 7, 2020, https://www.patreon.com/posts/life-death-and-36475418.
5   Marion Woodman, *Bone: Dying into Life* (New York: Penguin Compass, 2001).
6   Ashley Stahl, "Here's How Creativity Actually Improves Your Health," *Forbes*, July 25, 2018, https://www.forbes.com/sites/ashleystahl/2018/07/25/heres-how-creativity-actually-improves-your-health/?sh=184df16513a6.
7   Clarissa Pinkola Estés, PhD, *Theatre of the Imagination, Volume One*, read by the author (Louisville, CO: Sounds True, 2005), Audible audio ed., 7 hr., 25 min.
8   Marie-Louise von Franz, *On Dreams and Death* (Boston: Shambhala, 1987).
9   Carl Gustav Jung, "The Collected Works of C. G. Jung: Structure and Dynamics of the Psyche," in *The Collected Works of C. G. Jung*, vol. 8, ed. H. Read et al., trans. R. F. C. Hull (Princeton, NJ: Princeton University Press, 1981).
10 R. Andrew Chesnut, *Devoted to Death: Santa Muerte, the Skeleton Saint* (New York: Oxford University Press, 2012).

APPENDIX

1   John Troyer, *Technologies of the Human Corpse* (Cambridge, MA: MIT Press, 2020).

ABOUT THE AUTHOR

Joanna Ebenstein is the founder and creative director of Morbid Anatomy. An internationally recognized death expert, she is the author of several books, including *Anatomica: The Exquisite and Unsettling Art of Human Anatomy, Death: A Graveside Companion,* and *The Anatomical Venus: Wax, God, Death and the Ecstatic.* She is also an award-winning curator, photographer, and graphic designer, and the teacher of the many times sold-out class Make Your Own Memento Mori: Befriending Death with Art, History and the Imagination. The descendant of Holocaust survivors, she traces her lineage back to Judah Loew ben Bezalel, credited with creating the Golem in sixteenth-century Prague.